# MODERN LEGAL STUDIES

# REGISTERED LAND

## AUSTRALIA
The Law Book Company Ltd.
Sydney : Melbourne : Brisbane

## CANADA AND U.S.A.
The Carswell Company Ltd.
Agincourt, Ontario

## INDIA
N.M. Tripathi Private Ltd.
Bombay
*and*
Eastern Law House Private Ltd.
Calcutta
M.P.P. House
Bangalore

## ISRAEL
Steimatzky's Agency Ltd.
Jerusalem : Tel Aviv : Haifa

## MALAYSIA : SINGAPORE : BRUNEI
Malayan Law Journal (Pte.) Ltd.
Singapore

## NEW ZEALAND
Sweet and Maxwell (N.Z.) Ltd.
Auckland

## PAKISTAN
Pakistan Law House
Karachi

MODERN LEGAL STUDIES

# REGISTERED LAND

by

DAVID J. HAYTON, LL.D. (Newcastle)

*of the Inner Temple and Lincoln's Inn, Barrister*
*Fellow of Jesus College, Cambridge*

THIRD EDITION

*LONDON*
SWEET & MAXWELL
1981

*First Published - 1973*
*Second Edition - 1977*
*Third Edition - 1981*

*Published in 1981 by*
*Sweet & Maxwell Limited of*
*11 New Fetter Lane, London*
*Printed in Great Britain*
*by Thomson Litho Limited*
*East Kilbride, Scotland*

**British Library Cataloguing in Publication Data**
Hayton, David John
  Registered land.—3rd ed.—(Modern legal studies).
  1. Land titles—Registration and transfer—Great Britain
  2. Conveyancing—Great Britain
  I. Title     II. Series
  346'.42'0438      KD979

ISBN 0-421-28160-X
ISBN 0-421-28170-7 Pbk.

# OTHER BOOKS IN THE SERIES

*Human Rights and Europe* (Second Edition), by R. Beddard
*Economic Torts* (Second Edition), by J. D. Heydon
*Administrative Procedures*, by G. Ganz
*Mortgages* (Second Edition), by P. B. Fairest
*Anatomy of International Law* (Second Edition), by J. G. Merrills
*Small Businesses*, by Michael Chesterman
*Immigration Law*, by J. M. Evans
*The Court of Justice of the European Communities*, by L. Neville Brown and Francis G. Jacobs
*Exclusion Clauses in Contracts*, by David Yates
*Constructive Trusts*, by A. J. Oakley
*Council Housing*, by David Hoath
*Natural Justice* (Second Edition), by Paul Jackson
*Development Control*, by John Alder
*Remedies for Breach of Contract*, by Hugh Beale
*The Protection of Privacy*, by Raymond Wacks
*Drugs and Intoxication*, by David Farrier
*Squatting*, by A. M. Prichard
*Taxation and Trusts*, by Geraint Thomas

# PREFACE

This book deals with the relatively recent system of registration of title to land which already applies to three-quarters of conveyancing transactions, and will eventually cover all conveyancing in England and Wales. This system is superimposed upon the traditional principles of land law and it will be assumed that readers will be conversant with these basic principles so that they will only be discussed by way of explanation of the registration of title position or by way of comparison.

The object of the book is not to provide a fully comprehensive guide to the details of registered conveyancing so as to rival the standard work, *Registered Conveyancing* by Ruoff and Roper, or lesser useful works such as Ruoff, *Concise Land Registration Practice*, Wontner, *Guide to Land Registry Practice* or Lewis and Holland, *Principles of Registered Land Conveyancing*. This book is nowhere near so full of practical mechanical detail (though it does afford some practical assistance especially in Chapters 5, 6, 7 and 8) nor so much of a merely descriptive exposition of the law and practice of land registration.

Instead, the book is calculated to develop and enhance a real understanding of the fundamentally new principles underlying the system whilst stimulating fresh constructive thinking on particular aspects of the system. It is intended to guide readers through the voluminous mass of legislation, whilst preventing them from becoming mere technicians, who have been said to be men who understand everything about their job except its ultimate purpose and its place in the order of the universe. It is hoped that the book will show not just what the law is but what the law is for.

As Ruoff, the former Chief Land Registrar, has written in *An Englishman Looks at the Torrens System*, page 59, "In matters of land transfer the customer is always right . . . [His] requirements should receive consideration first, last and all the time. This proposition means there must be a business-like system, used in a business-like way by the lawyers, and administered as a business-like undertaking by the public officials who have the privilege and responsibility of serving the man in the street who seeks registration." Customers, however, may have conflicting interests. The system of registration has always to balance as harmoniously as possible the interests of purchasers, who want life made as simple as possible for them by the register of title recording as much as possible, unregistered matters being void against them, and the interests of occupiers and incumbrancers who would be prejudiced by a requirement that their interests must be recorded on the register to be valid, especially if they could not reasonably be expected to know the need to record their interests or to have had professional legal advice. The greatest strength of the system in one view may be its greatest weakness in another view. In examining the existing law and any proposed reforms it is vital to take these factors into account.

To assist readers develop a full understanding of registered conveyancing and the necessary skills of analysis and synthesis so that the efficiency of the system may properly be measured with a view to improvement, the book begins by examining the system in general and then proceeds to deal with a few select vital topics in more depth than will be found elsewhere. These topics are selected according to their practical significance and the treatment of them is intended to broaden readers' perspectives, to develop their analytical and synthetical faculties, and to stimulate them to think critically and constructively for themselves. It will be seen that despite the fundamental merit of the system it is, as yet, by no means worthy of the indiscriminate praise lavished upon it by most authors. Some of the weaknesses, however, merely highlight defects in ordinary land law principles and thus suggest reform of the substantive law itself.

It is felt that the quality of a system of land transfer, like the quality of politics, improves or deteriorates in direct relation to the quality of public debate about it, which, in its turn, varies directly with the quality of information and understanding displayed by its interlocutors. This quality is very poor indeed if the debates leading to the Land Registration Act 1966 are anything to go by: one fundamental consequence of the 1966 Act had to be reversed by the 1971 Land Registration and Land Charges Act. It remains to be seen to what extent section 24(*a*) of the Administration of Justice Act 1977 requires benevolent interpretation by the courts or further legislation to prevent it from accidentally removing the protection from rectification hitherto accorded to a registered proprietor in possession. It is hoped this book will do something towards improving the present quality of information and understanding displayed by persons in registered conveyancing matters.

More specifically, the book is intended for students of land law or conveyancing as part of a university or professional course. It is hoped it will also be useful for anyone who needs to familiarise himself with the principles of, and some of the social problems raised by, registered conveyancing, and that the treatment of select topics will provide some assistance even for experienced practitioners.

I have taken advantage of the opportunity afforded by this third edition to do more than merely update the book to take into account, *inter alia*, sections 24-26 of the Administration of Justice Act 1977 and *Williams & Glyn's Bank* v. *Boland*. New material appears in Chapters 6, 8 and 9 to cope with problems that are likely to crop up in practice in the near future. In particular, emphasis is placed upon the crucially privileged "Registrar's darling," a purchaser under a registered disposition for value without there being any entry on the register, the registered land equivalent of "Equity's darling," the bona fide purchaser of a legal estate without notice of any equitable interest.

An enormous debt of gratitude is owed to Professor Patrick McAuslan, the General Editor of the series in which this book appears, for instigating the series and this book.

The law is stated from sources available on September 21, 1980.

David Hayton

Stone Buildings,
Lincoln's Inn.

# ADDENDUM

*The following case was reported too late for inclusion in Appendix I where it should appear on page 208.*

*Spectrum Investment Co.* v. *Holmes* [1981] 1 All E.R.6.

Mrs. D was registered proprietor of a lease of 24/12/02 for 99 years under Title LN 66166. Since Miss H obtained title to lease by adverse possession the Registry closed LN 66166 and registered Miss H as first registered proprietor with possessing title of the lease under Title NGL 65073.

Spectrum ("S") had been registered as freehold proprietor with possory title in 1957 and was registered with title absolute in 1975 but subject to lease NGL 65073. To defeat Miss H's claim, Mrs. D in May 1975 executed in S's favour a surrender of the lease under Title LN 66166. S claimed this merged the lease in S's freehold interest so entitling S to evict Miss H: *Fairweather* v. *St. Marylebone Property Co.* [1963] A.C. 510.

*Held:* I bound by by Miss H's lease NGL 65073. Under L.R.A., s. 11 Miss H subject to adverse right of S but these only arose on expiry of lease which dit not occur on surrender on May 1975 by Mrs. D, since surrender invalid since Mrs. D not then registered proprietor of lease and in any event an effective surrender requires to be entered on register: sections 69(4), 21, 22.

Mrs. D not entitled to rectification reinstating her as lease proprietor, and enabling her to execute registered surrender, since Miss H properly registered under mandatory requirements of section 75(3). Thus, once squatter rightly registered under s. 75(3) the freeholder cannot, unlike unregistered land position, defeat the squatter's rights by a surrender from the ousted lessee.

# CONTENTS

*Preface* ............................................................ vii

*Table of Cases* ................................................ xiv

*Table of Statutes* ............................................ xvii

*Table of Rules* ................................................ xxii

*Abbreviations* ................................................ xxiii

1. Introduction ................................................ 1
2. General Principles of Registration of Title ................ 8
3. Leases ...................................................... 43
4. Getting onto the Register .................................. 50
5. The System in Operation .................................... 60
6. Overriding Interests ....................................... 76
7. Mortgages .................................................. 118
8. Priorities ................................................. 131
9. Rectification and Indemnity: The Insurance Principle

                                           163

*Appendix:* Cases ............................................. 191

            Compulsory Registration Areas ................. 214

*Index* ....................................................... 219

# TABLE OF CASES

ABIGAIL v. Lapin 159, 147, 148, 191
Arsenal Football Club v. Smith 93
Assets Co. v. Mere Roihi.......... 169
Att.-Gen. v. Odell............. 166, 185
—— v. Parsons..................... 3, 142

BAILEY v. Barnes.............. 102, 159
Baker and Selmon's Contract,
  Re ........................................ 58
Bannister v. Bannister.............. 184
Barclay v. Barclay................ 98, 99
Barclays Bank v. Taylor 122, 131,
  141, 143, 144, 153, 191
Beaney, Re.................. 96, 177, 192
Binions v. Evans........ 101, 116, 184
Birmingham Canal Co. v.
  Cartwright............................ 112
Boyle's Claim, Re ....... 81, 104, 128,
  136, 192
Breskvar v. Wall...................... 159
Briant Colour Printing Co., Re 90
Bridges v. Mees........... 84, 96, 112,
  178, 192
Brikom v.Carr ...................... 94, 97
Brine and.Davies' Contract, Re 38
British Maritime Trust v.
  Upsons Ltd.............. 54, 56, 193
Brown v. Bush...................... 89, 90
—— v. Rolls Royce Ltd. .......... 106
Buckland v. Duke Cohan &
  Co........................................ 107
Buckley v. Lane Herdman &
  Co........................................ 107
Bull v. Bull.................. 98, 99, 212
Butler v. Broadhead ................ 68
—— v. Fairclough..... 148, 150, 193

CALGARY & EDMONTON LAND
  CO. LTD. v. Discount Bank ... 27
Cato v. Thompson.................... 69
Cator v. Newton.......... 67, 159, 193
Caunce v. Caunce.............. 17, 200
Cavanagh v. Ulster Weaving
  Co........................................ 106
Chivers & Sons Ltd. v. Air
  Ministry............................... 67

Chowood v. Lyall...... 166, 176, 194
—— v. —— (No. 2).......... 166, 174
Chowood's Registered Land, Re 69,
  77, 174, 179, 185, 187, 194
Church of England B.S. v.
  Piskor ............................ 125, 213
City Permanent Building
  Society v. Miller.............. 45, 194
Clark v. Barrick........................ 159
Clearbrook Property Holdings
  Ltd. v. Verrier ...................... 210
Clements v. Ellis...................... 119
Courtenay v. Austin ................ 159
Coventry Permanent Economic
  B.S. v. Jones ................. 112, 133
Crabb v. Arun D.C. ..... 17, 20, 156

D.H.N. FOOD DISTRIBUTORS
  v. London Borough of Tower
  Hamlets................................ 101
Dances Way, Re ............... 4, 80, 81
David v. Sabin.......................... 68
De Lusignan v. Johnson .... 19, 126,
  132, 134, 135, 169, 181,
  195, 206, 207
Dearle v. Hall........................... 131
Dennis v. Malcolm .................. 38
Dovto Properties Ltd. v. Astell 95,
  195
Duke v. Robson ....................... 138

EASTWOOD v. Ashton.... 67, 68, 174
Efstratiou v. Glantschnig.......... 169
Elias v. Mitchell .......... 28, 153, 196
Ellis v. Rogers ......................... 69
Epps v. Esso Petroleum..... 58, 171,
  175, 176, 178, 183, 196
Errington v. Errington.............. 101
Evans' Contract, Re............ 21, 197

FAIRWEATHER v. St. Maryle-
  bone Property Co. .......... 93, 116
Faruqi v. English Real Estate
  Ltd. .................................. 1, 197
Fay v. Miller, Wilkins & Co..... 68
Forsey and Hollebone's Con-
  tract, Re ............................... 11

Foster v. Robinson.................... 116
Franzom v. Registrar of Titles    170
Frazer v. Walker......    20, 168
Freer v. Unwins Ltd......   4, 45, 132,
    136, 137, 144, 168, 173, 176, 179,
        180, 182, 183, 186, 197, 199

GEORGE WIMPEY v. I.R.C. .......  143
—— v. Sohn.........................  68, 70
Goody v. Baring...............  102, 106
Grace Rymer Investments Ltd.
    v. Waite ...  96, 104, 121, 126, 198
Great Western Rly. Co. v. Fisher  68
Greene v. Church Commis-
    sioners ............................  16, 133
Groom v. Crocker.....................  106
Gross v. Hillman ......................  94

HAIGH'S CASE........................ 3, 142
Halsall v. Brizell.......................    20
Heron.......................................    90
High St. (No. 139) Deptford,
    Re ..........  171, 174, 176, 177, 199
Hissett v. Reading Roof Co.    70, 71
Hodges v. Jones.........  132, 176, 199
Hodgson v. Marks...  22, 74, 78, 89,
    91, 97, 98, 102, 127, 137, 139, 179,
    180, 184, 185, 188, 200, 203, 205
Hollington Brothers Ltd. v.
    Rhodes..........  16, 29, 36, 55, 112,
        133, 181
Hopgood v. Brown ..................    20
Hughes v. Waite...............  126, 200
Hunt v. Luck........................  86, 87

I.A.C. FINANCE PTY. v.
    Courtenay..............................  142
Inwards v. Baker......................  178
Ives Investment Ltd. v. High ....  17,
        20, 156, 171, 178

JONES v. Lipman ........  19, 20, 132,
        135, 168, 201, 206, 207

KING v. David Allen.................  101
King's Settlement, Re..............    74
Kitney v. M.E.P.C. Ltd.....  55, 140,
        141, 181, 201

L. & S.W. RLY. CO. v. Gomm    112
Lake v. Bayliss .........................  139
—— v. Busby ...........................  107

Laundon v. Hartlepool B.C......    90
Laurence v. Lexcourt Holdings
    Ltd. .....................................  171
Lee v. Barrey........................  6, 202
Lee-Parker v. Izzet ...........  96, 112,
        115, 202
—— v. —— (No. 2)............  95, 203
Leighton's Conveyance, Re .....  169,
        179, 203
Lester v. Burgess    27, 28, 167, 204
Lever Finance Ltd. v. Needle-
    man's Trustees .....................  121
Lloyd's Bank v. Savory.............  106
London & Cheshire Insurance
    Co. v. Laplagrene ......  74, 78, 81,
        82, 96, 103, 112, 128, 136,
            137, 174, 203, 204

M.E.P.C. LTD. v. Christian-
    Edwards .............................    38
McCarthy & Stone Ltd. v.
    Hodge Ltd..............  17, 143, 159
Magee v. Pennine Insurance
    Co....................................  171
Marks v. Attallah ........  93, 139, 205
May v. Platt .........................  68, 70
Midland Bank Trust Co. v.
    Hett....................................  106
Miles v. Bull (No. 2)    132, 133, 181
Miller v. Minister of Mines.....    28
Monolithic Building Co. Ltd.,
    Re ...........................  113, 135, 169
Montgomery v. Continental
    Bags (No. 2) Ltd. .................    71
Morelle v. Wakeling ............  3, 159
Morgan's Lease, Re..................    24
Mornington P.B.S. v. Kenway    126
Morrisons Holdings Ltd. v.
    Manders ..............................    90
Murray v. Two Strokes Ltd......  205

NATIONAL PROVINCIAL BANK
    v. Ainsworth ......  85, 94, 100, 205
—— v. Hastings Car Mart
    Ltd. ..........................  76, 96, 196

ORAKPO v. Manson Invest-
    ments Limited ......................  168

PAGE v. Midland Rly...............    68
Panorama Developments
    (Guildford) Ltd. v. Fidelis
    Furnishing Fabrics Ltd.........  102

Parkash v. Irani Finance Ltd...... 27, 132, 142, 150, 169, 206
Parker v. Judkin......................... 68
Payne v. Adnams ................. 83, 206
Peffer v. Rigg    20, 134, 169, 206, 207
Perpetual Executors' Association of Australia Ltd. v. Hosken .................................. 38
Pilkington v. Wood............... 68, 107
Piper v. Daybell, Court-Cooper   107
Poster v. Slough Estates........ 17, 156
Price Bros. Ltd. v. Kelly Homes Ltd........................ 28, 204
Pritchard v. Briggs ............. 112, 205
Property & Bloodstock Ltd. v. Emerton .............................. 49
Property & Reversionary Co. Ltd. v. Secretary of State for the Environment ................... 74

R. v. Tao.................................... 90
Randeo Mahabir v. Payne........ 82
Rawlplug v. Kamvale Properties Ltd. ................ 27, 28, 204
Ray, Re ................................... 68
Robertson's Application, Re...... 68
Ross v. Caunters ....................... 106

SAUNDERS v. Vantier ........... 55, 58, 178, 179
Schwab & Co. v. McCarthy....... 92, 121, 128, 138
Sea View Gardens, Re ....... 171, 174, 177, 207
Security Trust Co v. Royal Bank of Canada..................... 126
Sharkey v. Wernher.................. 167
Sharp v. Coates ........................ 133
Sharpe, Re ................. 96, 100, 101, 104, 116, 146
Sheridan v. Dickson ................. 92
Shiloh Spinners Ltd. v. Harding   17
Shropshire Union Rly. Co. v. R. ......................................... 159
Simmons v. Pennington............. 106
Smith v. Jones ........................... 95

Smith v. Morrison ....... 60, 135, 151, 206, 207
Solomon, Re............................. 101
Spiro v. Lintern........................ 146
Stait v. Fenner.......................... 68
Stone and Saville's Contract, Re ..................................... 1, 208
Stoney v. Eastbourne R.D.C...... 67
Strand Securities Ltd. v. Caswell......... 4, 5, 29, 43, 51, 52, 82, 85, 86, 89, 91, 92, 101, 119, 122, 132, 142, 169, 208, 209
Suarez (No. 2), Re.................... 58
Sykes v. Midland Bank............. 107

TADDER v. Catalano ................. 149
Taylor v. London Banking Co.    159
Timmins v. Moreland Street Property Co. Ltd.................... 69
Tiverton Estates Ltd. v. Wearwell ................... 26, 28, 210

WAIMIHA SAWMILLING CO. v. Watone Timber Co. ........... 169
Watts v. Waller........ 25, 26, 29, 140, 146, 148, 150, 153, 167, 210
Webb v. Pollmount ......... 22, 78, 84, 96, 112, 211
Weston v. Henshaw.................... 24
White v. Bijou Mansions Ltd...... 30, 32, 36, 37
White Rose Cottage, Re..... 119, 121, 123, 124, 136, 138, 141, 142, 211
Wicks v. Bennett ....................... 169
Wilkes v. Spooner................. 54, 181
Wille v. St. John ...................... 159
Williams & Glyn's Bank v. Boland............. 22, 24, 78, 87, 88, 91, 95, 98, 112, 134, 212
Wilson v. Bloomfield ................. 108
Woolwich Equitable B.S. v. Marshall........... 96, 112, 126, 212
Wright v. Dean ......................... 112
Wroth v. Tyler ............. 26, 146, 149

YANDLE & SONS LTD. v. Sutton   107

# TABLE OF STATUTES

1832 Prescription Act (2 & 3
Will. 4, c. 71) ......... 1
1862 Land Registry Act (25
& 26 Vict. c. 53) 13, 14,
163, 166
1875 Land Transfer Act (38
& 39 Vict. c. 87) 14, 83
s. 18(7) ...................... 47
s. 95 ........................... 166
s. 96 ........................... 166
1891 Stamp Act (54 & 55
Vict. c. 39) ............. 50
1897 Land Transfer Act (60
& 61 Vict. c. 65) ...... 14,
18, 164
s. 7(2) ...................... 166
s. 16(3) ...................... 69
1914 Bankruptcy Act (4 & 5
Geo. 5, c. 59)—
s. 2 ............................. 173
1922 Law of Property Act
(12 & 13 Geo. 5, c.
16) .............. 16, 18, 101
s. 33 ..................... 16, 112
Sched. 16, para. 5 ...... 47
1924 Law of Property
(Amendment) Act
(15 & 16 Geo. 5,
c. 5) .............. 16, 18, 101
Sched. 8, para. 16 ...... 170
1925 Settled Land Act (15 &
16 Geo. 5, c. 18) 14, 24,
25, 111, 112, 140
s. 4(1) ...................... 184
s. 36(4) ...................... 212
Trustee Act (15 & 16
Geo. 5, c. 19) ......... 14
Trustee Act (15 & 16
Geo. 5, c. 19)—
s. 14 ............ 100, 105, 212
Law of Property Act (15
& 16 Geo. 5, c. 20) 14,
25, 124, 134
s. 2 ..................... 100, 138
s. 14 ....................... 16, 92
s. 25 ........................... 188
(9) ...................... 188

1925 Law of Property Act—
cont.
s. 27 ............ 100, 105, 138
s. 29 ........................... 172
s. 30 .............. 99, 100, 129
s. 39 ........................... 170
s. 40 ........................... 210
s. 44 .... 11, 32, 35, 51, 123
(5) ...................... 36
s. 45(2) ...................... 35
(3) ...................... 35
s. 49(2) ...................... 197
s. 54(2) ...................... 46
s. 59 ........................... 211
s. 60(1) ...................... 68
s. 62 ..................... 34, 84
s. 68(1) ...................... 204
s. 76(1) ................. 67, 68
(6) ...................... 174
s. 85 ........................... 118
(2) ...................... 170
s. 86 ........................... 118
(2) ...................... 170
s. 87 ........................... 118
s. 94(2) .............. 129, 158
s. 101 ........................ 211
s. 115(10) ................... 129
s. 137 ........................ 131
s. 186 ........................ 115
s. 198 .............. 11, 16, 36
s. 199 ........................ 36
(1) (ii) .......... 66, 70
s. 205(1) (xix) ............ 92
Sched. 1 ...................... 170
Sched. 2, Pt. I ........ 66, 68
1925 Land Registration Act
(15 & 16 Geo. 5,
c. 21) .............. 2, 3, 15,
18, 19, 30, 38, 66,
131, 134, 140, 141, 168,
174, 185, 194, 198, 199,
201, 207
s. 1(1) ......................... 48
s. 2 .................... 820, 121
(1) ..... 43, 44, 136, 140
(iii) .................. 124
s. 3(v) ......................... 134

1925  Land  Registration  Act
         s. 3—*cont.*
         (x) ......................... 195
         (xii) ...................... 22
         (xv) ... 97, 98, 112, 131,
                        136, 196
         (xvi)   21, 22, 23, 78, 80
         (xviii) ........ 20, 92, 171
         (xxi) .......... 133, 207
         (xxii) ................... 135
         (xxiv).............. 84, 197
         (xxvii)................. 47
     s. 4 ............................ 164
     s. 5 .......... 2, 35, 53, 57, 58,
              69, 70, 81, 84, 131,
              133, 134, 140, 164, 168,
              174, 178, 185, 201
         (b) ................ 192, 194
     s. 6 ............................ 38
     s. 7 ............................ 38
     s. 8(1)..................... 35, 43
         (a) .......... 43, 44, 47
         (b) ................... 44
         (2) .............. 43, 44, 49
     s. 9 .......... 2, 35, 53, 57, 69,
              81, 84, 131, 133, 134,
              168, 174, 178, 185
     s. 10 :.......................... 37
     s. 11 ........................... 38
     s. 12 ........................... 38
     s. 13(c) ................. 38, 164
     s. 18 ......................... 135
         (3)...... 43, 45, 49, 122,
              127, 136, 137, 141,
                                   153
         (4)... 22, 121, 124, 127
         (5)......... 124, 131, 135
     s. 19 ............. 2, 55, 56, 72,
                        127, 213
         (1)....................... 71
         (2)........ 43, 44, 45, 51,
              78, 83, 122, 136, 137,
              153, 172, 180, 198
         (a) ............. 45, 172
         (3)...................... 84
     s. 20 ........ 69, 81, 127, 142,
              146, 149, 153, 156
         (1)    58, 70, 84, 93,
              122, 124, 133, 134,
              137, 140, 143, 152,
                                   181
         (4).................. 36, 132

1925  Land  Registration  Act
         —*cont.*
     s. 21 .......................... 135
         (3)............. 43, 45, 49,
                        122, 138
         (4)................. 22, 124
         (5)............... 124, 131
     s. 22 ..................... 2, 55, 56
         (2)........ 43, 44, 45, 51,
              78, 83, 136, 137, 193
         (a) ................. 45
         (3)...................... 84
     s. 23 .......... 2, 3, 19, 37, 38,
              69, 81, 131, 142, 146,
              149, 156, 168, 174,
                                   185
         (1).... 58, 84, 122, 124,
              133, 134, 137, 152
         (a) ................. 35
         (b) ................. 37
         (2)...................... 37
         (5)...................... 36
     ss. 25-36 ................... 121
     s. 25(3) (i) ................ 120
     s. 26 ............. 118, 119, 121
         (1)...................... 121
     s. 27 ....... 21, 119, 121, 143
         (3)........ 124, 143, 144,
                        145, 198
     s. 29 ............. 129, 131, 145
     s. 30 ..................... 103, 158
     s. 33 ............................ 3
     s. 34 ..................... 121, 123
         (4) ............. 125, 131
     s. 35 ......................... 130
     s. 38(2)....................... 68
     s. 39 ......................... 2, 60
     s. 40 ............. 136, 143, 144,
                        145, 146
         (1)...................... 143
         (3)...................... 143
     s. 48 ............. 45, 143, 144,
                        145, 172
         (1)................. 83, 182
     s. 49 ............. 122, 136, 182
         (1)....................... 12
         (c) ........ 25, 83, 119
         (d) ................. 156
         (f) ............. 20, 119
         (g) ................. 26
         (2) ................. 25, 156
     s. 50 ..................... 30, 136

1925 Land Registration Act
  s. 50—*cont.*
    (2)   37, 144, 181, 182
  s. 52 ............. 25, 140, 141,
               143, 175, 201
    (1) ...................... 179
  s. 53 ......... 26, 53, 110, 140
  s. 54 ........ 26, 72, 122, 136,
                156, 196
  s. 55(1) ...................... 78
  s. 56(2) ............... 141, 145
    (3) .................. 26, 210
  s. 58 ........................... 136
    (2) ...................... 24
  s. 59 ........................... 201
    (1) ...................... 84
    (2) .............. 12, 83, 84
    (3) ...................... 32
    (6) ......... 19, 122, 131,
      133, 134, 151, 153,
      168, 181, 206, 207
  s. 61(3) ...................... 28
    (6) ............... 133, 207
  s. 61(10) ...................... 32
  s. 64 ...........................
    (1) (*a*) ........... 208, 209
    (*b*) .................. 122
    (*c*)   12, 23, 25, 51,
            122, 140
  s. 65 ....... 31, 119, 120, 140
  s. 66 .... 123, 136, 143, 144,
      145, 146, 153, 192
  s. 69 ..... 3, 53, 81, 142, 198
    (1) ...................... 57
  s. 70 ............ 80, 81, 84, 94,
             137, 174
    (1) ......... 79, 101, 115
    (*a*) ... 67, 78, 82, 83,
        138, 199, 206
    (*c*) .................. 67
    (*f*)  67, 85, 109, 156,
      179, 187, 192, 194
    (*g*)   23, 24, 43, 44,
    47, 55, 58, 71, 78,
    85, 86, 87, 92, 93,
    94, 95, 96, 98, 100,
    101, 102, 103, 106,
    108, 111, 112, 114,
    115, 125, 126, 127,
    128, 129, 138, 139,
    140, 179, 180, 184,
    185, 192, 193, 196,

1925 Land Registration Act
  s. 70(*g*)—*cont.*
    199, 200, 201, 202,
    203, 204, 205, 206,
    209, 210, 211, 212,
                213
    (*k*) .... 44, 45, 47, 49,
    109, 126, 127, 128,
    129, 138, 153, 194,
    195, 199, 201, 211
    (2) ......... 4, 22, 31, 80
    (3) ............. 22, 31, 80
  s. 74 ........ 19, 88, 131, 133,
           134, 164, 168
  s. 75 ........................... 85
    (4) ............... 187, 189
  s. 76 ........................... 202
  s. 77 ........................... 39
    (2) ...................... 39
    (*b*) .................. 39
  s. 79(1) ...................... 152
    (4) ...................... 151
  s. 82 .............. 39, 144, 192
    (1) ......... 95, 171, 173,
            177, 192
    (*a*)-(*h*) .............. 167
    (*a*) .... 58, 166, 168,
    178, 185, 194, 204,
                210
    (*b*) .... 28, 166, 168,
    170, 204, 210
    (*c*)-(*h*) .............. 167
    (*d*) .................. 169
    (*f*) .................. 170
    (*g*) .... 95, 169, 190,
                194
    (*h*) ... 168, 170, 171,
          194, 204
    (2) ...................... 166
    (3) ....... 171, 172, 173,
    175, 177, 186, 192,
      194, 196, 207
    (*a*)   174, 175, 177,
         194, 199
    (*b*) .................. 177
    (*c*) ... 176, 182, 197,
              199
    (4) ............... 171, 172
  s. 83 ........................... 182
    (2) ...................... 39
    (3) ...................... 152
    (4) ...................... 185

1925  Land Registration Act
        s. 83—*cont.*
          (5) (*a*) .......... 39, 163,
                              184, 187
              (*b*) ................. 184
              (*c*)................. 184
          (6) ..................... 183
              (*b*) ................. 197
          (7) ..................... 183
          (10)................... 182
          (11)....... 183, 184, 197
        s. 86(1)...................... 184
          (2)........... 97, 98, 112,
                          140, 185
        s. 87(3)...................... 184
        s. 97 ......................... 129
        s. 101.......... 23, 55, 61, 143
          (1) .................... 124
          (2)........... 23, 45, 84
          (3) ....... 45, 124, 140
        s. 102......................... 145
          (2) .................... 131
        s. 104(1) .................. 124
        s. 106.... 119, 121, 122, 143
          (1) .................... 123
          (2) ....... 97, 122, 191
          (3) ............. 122, 157
          (4) .................... 192
        s. 107.......... 143, 144, 145,
                          146, 155
          (1) .................... 143
        s. 109..................... 61, 143
        s. 110  32, 51, 52, 110, 157
          (5) ............. 124, 197
        s. 112....................... 31
          A....................... 32
        s. 123.... 43, 50, 55, 56,
                    61, 193, 213
          (1) .................... 53
          (3) .................... 55
        s. 127....................... 5
        s. 129....................... 32
        s. 144.............. 18, 154
        s. 205 (xxvii).............. 48
1925  Land Charges Act (15
        & 16 Geo. 5, c. 22)
        14, 15, 18, 25, 36, 56,
        94, 111, 140, 145, 180
        s. 10 .................. 115, 201
        s. 13 ......................... 201
          (2)...... 16, 17, 54, 112,
                      133, 143

1925  Land Charges Act—
        *cont.*
          s. 15(8)...................... 12
          s. 19(1)...................... 133
          s. 20(8)...................... 133
1925  Administration of
        Estates Act (15 &
        16 Geo. 5, c. 23)        15
        s. 41 .......................... 50
1936  Land Registration Act
        (26 Geo. 5 & 1
        Edw. 8, c. 26)..........  18
        s. 3(2)......................... 189
1936  Tithe Act (26 Geo. 5
        & 1 Edw. 8, c. 43)—
        s. 13(11) .................... 80
1938  Coal Act (1 & 2 Geo.
        6, c. 52)—
        s. 41 .......................... 80
1939  Limitation Act (2 & 3
        Geo. 6, c. 21)...... 22, 109
1945  Law Reform (Contribu-
        tory Negligence)
        Act (8 & 9 Geo. 6,
        c. 28) ...................... 187
1946  Coal Industry Nationali-
        sation Act (9 & 10
        Geo. 6, c. 59)—
        s. 5 ........................... 80
1948  Companies Act (11 &
        12 Geo. 6, c. 38)—
        s. 437(1) ................... 102
1954  Landlord and Tenant
        Act (2 & 3 Eliz. 2,
        c. 56) ...................... 113
        Pt. II.......................... 48
1961  Housing Act (9 & 10
        Eliz. 2, c. 65)—
        s. 32 .......................... 46
        s. 33 .......................... 46
1962  Building Societies Act
        (10 & 11 Eliz. 2,
        c. 37)—
        s. 37(1)...................... 130
1964  Perpetuities and Accu-
        mulations Act (c.
        55)—
        s. 9(2)........................ 117
1964  Law of Property
        (Joint Tenants) Act
        (c. 63)..................... 97

1966 Land Registration Act
    (c. 39)................ 6, 18,
                40, 44, 173
1966 Yorkshire Registries
    Amendment Act
    (c. 26)—
    s. 8 ............................ 33
1967 Misrepresentation Act
    (c. 7)...................... 71
1967 Matrimonial Homes Act
    (c. 75)..................... 156
    s. 2(1)......................... 146
    (7) ........................ 97
1975 Leasehold Reform Act
    (c. 88)—
    s. 5(5)......................... 97
1969 Law of Property Act
    (c. 59)...................... 33
    s. 24 ........................ 11
    (3)........................ 11
    s. 25 ........................ 11
    (9)........................ 11
    (10) ..................... 11
1970 Land Registration
    Act (Northern Ire-
    land) (c. 18)—
    s. 40 ......................... 141
1971 Land Registration and
    Land Charges Act
    (c. 54)................ 18, 187
    s. 1 ............................ 164
    s. 2 ............................ 183
    (2) ....................... 184
    s. 3 ............................ 6, 39

1971 Land Registration and
    Land Charges Act
    s. 3—*cont.*
    (1) ......................... 173
    s. 4 ............................ 40
    s. 9 ............................ 56
1972 Land Charges Act (c.
    61).......... 36, 48, 56, 115
    s. 2(4) (iv) ................. 115
    s. 4 .............. 16, 17, 36, 54,
                112, 133
    (6) ........................ 143
    s. 14(3)....................... 56
1975 Finance Act (c. 7)
    Sched. 12, para.
    5(5) ......................... 25
1977 Rentcharges Act (c. 30)    20
1977 Administration of Jus-
    tice Act (c. 38)—
    ss. 24-26 ..................... 18
    s. 24 ............. 173, 174, 177
    (*a*)....................... 6
    s. 26 ............... 2, 119, 157
1979 Land Registration (Scot-
    land) Act (c. 33)—
    s. 6 ............................ 30
    s. 7 ............................ 141
    s. 13(4)....................... 187
1979 Charging Orders Act
    (c. 53)—
    s. 3(3)......................... 26
1980 Limitation Act (c. 58)..... 1
1980 Housing Act (c. 51) .... 40, 44

# TABLE OF RULES

1925 Land Registration Rules
(No. 1093)—

| | |
|---|---|
| r.3 | 30 |
| (2) | 32 |
| r. 6 | 31 |
| r. 7 | 31 |
| r. 10 | 33 |
| r. 13 | 167 |
| r. 14 | 167 |
| r. 17 | 72 |
| r. 25 | 103 |
| r. 29 | 164 |
| r. 41 | 80 |
| r. 42 | 53, 110 |
| r. 45 | 30 |
| r. 46 | 103 |
| r. 48(2) | 103 |
| rr. 50-54 | 20 |
| r. 71 | 110 |
| r. 73 | 53, 56, 110 |
| (2) | 54 |
| r. 74 | 5, 60 |
| r. 75 | 5 |
| r. 76 | 68 |
| r. 77 | 68, 69 |
| (1) | 70 |
| (b) | 69 |
| r. 78 | 60 |
| r. 83 | 136, 179 |
| (2) | 81, 104 |
| r. 90 | 83 |
| r. 96 | 61 |
| r. 131 | 167 |
| r. 154(2) | 120 |
| r. 170(5) | 164 |
| r. 197 | 80, 81 |
| r. 198 | 103 |
| r. 199 | 45 |
| r. 211 | 167 |
| r. 215(2) | 39 |
| r. 218 | 103 |
| r. 219 | 141 |

1925 Land Registration Rules—
cont.

| | |
|---|---|
| r. 220 | 5, 141 |
| rr. 239-242 | 122 |
| r. 239 | 120, 123, 136 |
| (2) | 142 |
| (4) | 74, 122, 142 |
| r. 240 | 123 |
| r. 242(1) | 122 |
| r. 245(b) | 120 |
| (c) | 120 |
| r. 247 | 204 |
| r. 248 | 167 |
| rr. 251-258 | 84 |
| r. 253 | 103 |
| r. 258 | 80 |
| r. 267 | 130 |
| r. 269 | 51 |
| rr. 276-277 | 167 |
| r. 276 | 103 |
| r. 278 | 30 |
| r. 284 | 202 |
| r. 286 | 33 |
| r. 288 | 32 |
| r. 292 | 32 |
| r. 295 | 32 |
| r. 296 | 32 |
| r. 298 | 5 |
| r. 300 | 103 |
| rr. 311-314 | 103 |
| r. 317 | 60 |
| r. 322 | 208 |

1969 Land Registration (Official
Searches) Rules (No.
1179)—

| | |
|---|---|
| r. 5 | 152 |

1978 Land Registration (Official
Searches) Rules (No.
0000)—

28, 32, 110, 119, 135, 150

| | |
|---|---|
| r. 5 | 29, 60, 208 |

# ABBREVIATIONS

| | |
|---|---|
| The Act | Land Registration Act 1925 |
| Brickdale & Stewart-Wallace | The Land Registration Act 1925 (4th ed.) by them |
| Curtis & Ruoff | Registered Conveyancing (1st ed.) by them |
| Emmet | Notes on Persuing Titles and on Practical Conveyancing (16th ed.) |
| Equity's darling | bona fide purchaser of a legal estate for value without notice |
| Farrand | Contract and Conveyance by J. T. Farrand (3rd ed.) |
| Key & Elphinstone | Precedents in Conveyancing (15th ed.) Vol. 3 |
| L.C.A. | Land Charges Act 1972 |
| L.P.A. | Law of Property Act 1925 |
| Practice Notes | Registered Land Practice Notes of the Joint Advisory Committee of the Law Society and H.M. Land Registry |
| Purchaser | a purchaser for value, including a lessee or mortgagee |
| Registered land | land, the title to which has been registered at the Land Registry |
| Registrar's darling | a purchaser under a registered disposition for value without there being any entry on the register |
| Ruoff & Roper | Registered Conveyancing (4th ed.) by them |
| Unregistered land | land, the title to which has not been registered |

# Chapter 1

# INTRODUCTION

THE idea of land registration or, more strictly, title registration is a good one. Each legal title to land is inserted in a register which, on its face, reveals the position as if a conveyancer had carried out the traditional investigatory process of abstract, perusal, requisition, reply and verification and so is a substitute for the documentary title. It is still necessary, though, to make on the spot inspections and inquiries for those interests which are relatively so ascertainable by such means that they often do not appear on the documentary title (*e.g.* rights of persons in actual occupation), or cannot by nature be documented (*e.g.* rights being acquired under the Prescription Act 1832 or the Limitation Act 1980).

The idea is that the transfer of land will be simpler, safer, quicker and cheaper (after first registration) in view of the fact that (1) the register acts as a mirror reflecting accurately, completely and irrefutably the current facts material to the title except for overriding interests and interests released off the register[1], (2) all trusts are kept off the title, (3) the state guarantees a title, once it has been registered, so that a registered proprietor is completely safe except for fairly rare circumstances where a full indemnity will be paid him out of moneys provided by Parliament if the register is rectified against him. A "prospectus" produced by H.M. Land Registry and entitled "Registration of Title to Land" paints a nice rosy picture of the situation but makes exaggerated claims for the system.

Eventually registration of title will cover the whole of England and Wales. Over 75 per cent. of the total population now resides in compulsory registration of title areas and the number of registered titles exceeds seven million.[2] About three-quarters of conveyancing transactions concern the system of registration of title. Unfortunately, the system giving effect to the idea of registration of title is by no means as good as the idea. Moreover, as any draftsman (or tennis or squash player) knows, it is the execution of ideas that is in reality the essence of them.

The most striking thing about the system is the sheer volume of the statutory sections and rules with the force of statute which number over 500, together with the official forms numbering over 100 that have to be used. It is enough to give any student of the system analysis paralysis. In such a mass of legislation there ought to be some clearly spelled out principles supplying the essential framework, so that the system can work out to be as simple as possible and as free as possible from anomalies and requirements producing inconvenience and injustice. The procedural requirements essential to any system of registered conveyancing should, especially, be clear and simple since they have to be observed in everyday practice if persons' interests are to be properly protected *e.g.*in respect of registration of leases where for some time there was much doubt and confusion (see F.R.R Burford's instructive article in (1936) 1 Conv.(N.S) 344) and in respect of protection of mortgages until the position was improved by Administration of Justice Act 1977, s.26.

However, in scrutinising this mass of legislation it is difficult to put one's finger on exactly what the general principles are, since the legislation nowhere sets out any guiding framework. As a result of the failure to spell out the fundamental notions of registered conveyancing there is a particular danger in being misled by the treatment of individual sections and rules apart from the total framework. Any isolated point may involve a wide sweep that is particularly difficult to explain coherently except by constant reaffirmation of certain principles that do underpin the structure of the Act *e.g.* the vital notion that no legal interest passes under any disposition by any documents executed by any owner: the legal interest only passes when the disposition is completed by the statutory magic of registration and/or entry of a notice on the burdened land (ss. 5, 9, 19, 20, 22, 23, 39), so a purchaser only acquires the legal interest after he has registered his interest and/or noted it. There is also the Registrar's darling principle (corresponding to the Equity's darling principle) protecting a purchaser for value without there being any minor interest protected on the register. The fact of registration may make even void dispositions voidable as a purchaser obtains a valid title (*Morelle* v. *Wakeling* [1955] 2 Q.B 379, 411 *Att.-Gen.* v. *Parsons* [1956] A.C 421, 441, *Haigh's Case,* p. 185 below, ss. 20, 23, 33, 69). In the absence of registration, however, interests may still have independent force as overriding interests. Further difficulties arise, which have been well canvassed by Professor Jackson in (1972) 88 L.Q.R 93 and in (1978) 94 L.Q.R 239, from the fact that the relationship between the registered land principles, hidden in the Act, and general unregistered land law principles is left most uncertain by the Act.

By and large, the legislation, though badly drafted with much confusing nomenclature, in contrast to the other property statutes of 1925, has been made to work rather well by the efforts of Land Registry officials (*e.g.* the "title shown" procedure in the case of building estates, a testimony to the Registrar's view[3] that until the legislature moves on any particular subject it is the plain duty of the Registry to improvise the machinery necessary to ensure that the wishes of the man in the street are effectually carried out) and of conveyancing solicitors, coupled with a pragmatic native ability to muddle through somehow. However, now that registration of title has expanded so much, and more anomalous situations are being found to arise, and one or two cases are even going beyond the Registrar to the courts, it has become apparent that the flabby legislation needs to be knocked into a radically fitter form. To this end the Law Commission have been engaged most constructively in examining the whole registered land system in Published Working Papers Nos. 32, 27, 45 and 67 between the summers of 1970 and 1976. The last Working Paper[4] is particularly noteworthy for the Law Commission getting away from unregistered land law principles and the idea that registered land is mere conveyancing machinery, changing unregistered substantive land law as little as possible, and favouring the idea of registered land as a self-contained self-consistent system of substantive land law in its own right.

Hopefully, the courts, too, will become more registration
minded. This must surely be where the future lies, even before
all land in England and Wales is registered land. Perhaps, even
those baffling terms "legal" and "equitable" might be
dispensed with in favour of absolute ownership and specified
interests protectable by notices, restrictions, cautions, inhibitions
or as overriding interests![5]

The Commission's work has certainly helped to expose many
of the deficiencies of the system to some of which a Nelsonian
blind eye has been turned for too long. In this respect it would
be most helpful if a series of Registered Land Reports
(including practice rulings covering more matters than
currently dealt with in the Practice Notes jointly promulgated
by the Registry and the Law Society) could be produced
showing exactly how the enormous discretionary power of the
Registrar is exercised, *e.g.* in respect of caution hearings and
rectification and indemnity cases, for as Professor Ryder has
pointed out, often "no-one knows where the shoe pinches
except those practitioners who are actually involved in cases of
difficulty."[6] If such a series of reports is not commercially
viable, as seems probable, then it should be subsidised out of
the registration fees as being a valuable service carried on for
the benefit of "customers" of the Registry. Furthermore, it
really is high time that legal aid was made available for
persons engaged in hearings before the Registrar, especially
when a person's house is normally his most important
possession and when the mass of legislation is so difficult even
for experienced lawyers to understand.

A classic instance of this was *Strand Securities Ltd.* v.
*Caswell* [1965] Ch. 958 where the Court of Appeal held that
the settled practice of the Registry was wrong and by way of
riposte the Registrar was able to show in (1965) 62 L.S Gaz.
507 that the court of Appeal had no proper understanding of
the "day list" procedure of the Registry. The Court of Appeal,
however were already "one up"by reason of *Re Dances Way*
[1962] Ch. 490 where Diplock L.J. (as he then was) had
pointed out that the provisions of section 70 (2) concerning the
noting of easements were obligatory and excluded the
Registrar's discretion. Seriously though, it would be rather
sensible if in all cases where points of registered land law and

procedure arose the Registrar was specifically invited to appear in person or by counsel as *amicus curiae*, as in Queensland.

Talking of the settled practice of the Land Registry it had been suggested that that practice, just like the practice of conveyancers, ought to make law.[7] This was quite rightly rejected by the Court of Appeal[8] for Registry practice can hardly be equated with the practice of conveyancers evolved over centuries in a sphere where there has been no attempt to provide a fully comprehensive set of legislative rules, especially in view of the last Registrar's own admission that the views of himself and his predecessors "may well be coloured by the many complex exigencies of administration."[9] Not that this is to belittle those views which only very rarely have been found to be incorrect in respect of dealings in the Registry.

The Registrar, himself, is in a unique position to influence the way in which the system of land registration functions and develops. By section 127 it is he alone who conducts the whole business of registration under the Act, and frames and causes to be printed and circulated, or otherwise promulgated, such forms and directions as he may deem requisite or expedient for facilitating proceedings under the Act. Moreover, these forms have to be used for all dealings, though they may be adapted of course (rr. 74, 75). He also has vast discretionary powers (*e.g.* as to class of title, upgrading title, the wording of restrictions) as well as wide judicial functions set out in rules 220 and 298. These rules concern *inter alia* the warning off of cautions, the ascertaining of priorities, the mode in which any entry should be made or dealt with in the register. The Registrar has wide powers to rectify the register and may by agreement resolve claims to an indemnity against loss resulting from rectification or non-rectification. Finally, much assistance is rendered by the writings of the Registrar and senior officials at the Registry.

The last five Registrars have all written leading works on land registration: Brickdale, Stewart-Wallace, Curtis, Ruoff and Roper. The current leading work is Ruoff and Roper, *The Law and Practice of Registered Conveyancing* (4th ed.), which is more balanced and realistic than its previous editions which were rather complacent when compared with its predecessor, Brickdale and Stewart-Wallace on the *Land Registration Act 1925,* particularly in respect of the category of overriding interests and the curative aspect of first registration (especially in view of *Lee* v. *Barrey*[1957] Ch.255 where the "Brand X" plan prevailed over the plan on the Land Certificate[10] and the fact that as 12 per cent. of plans submitted to the Registry are known to be defective[11] some more, statistically speaking, must slip through the net). Inadequate Registry plans continue to cause problems[12].

Many other useful books produced by Registry officials tend to be too complacent and uncritical (*e.g.* Ruoff's *Concise Land Registration Practice,* Wontner's *Guide to Land Registry Practice*, and the sections in Halsbury's *Laws of England*, Vol. 23 and the *Encyclopaedia of Forms and Precedents*, Vol. 17) as is Lewis and Holland's *Principles of Registered Land Conveyancing* which has been said to be "Curtis and Ruoff guaranteed."[13] Of course, such close involvement ensures that the practical advice is very sound indeed from the point of view of Registry practice but it is sometimes true that such close involvement can make it difficult to be completely objective and to have sufficient breadth of vision.

On the other hand, outsiders can be a little too alarmist and despondent, *e.g.*Robinson in a series of articles in *The Conveyancer*[14] and Potter, who rendered invaluable service in his exposition and examination of registered conveyancing (*Principles of Registered Land* and Key and Elphinstone's *Precedents*, Vol. III (14th ed)—the 15th ed. is by a Registry official).

A more balanced picture, provoking fresh thinking rather than preserving complacency, emerges in Farrand's *Contract and Conveyance* (especially the 2nd edition which is fuller than the 3rd) and in the Law Commission's Published Working Papers Nos 32, 37, 45 and 67. Happily, the most alarming deficiency has been remedied by the Land Registration and Land Charges Act 1971, s. 3 of which was passed in response to a penetrating article by Cretney and Dworkin in (1968) 84 L.Q.R 528, entitled "Rectification and Indemnity: Illusion and Reality," which revealed how the Land Registration Act 1966 had, unnoticed by the Legislature, taken away rights of compensation for innocent persons against whom the register had been rectified. Unfortunately, the Administration of Justice Act 1977, s. 24 (a) inadvertently may well have removed the protection from rectification accorded to a proprietor in possession: see p. 173, *infra*.

There are, however, still many old deficiencies remaining. We will now proceed to obtain a general understanding of the framework of the system before progressing to examine some specific areas of practical significance. The purpose is to develop and enhance our understanding of the system and to stimulate constructive thought about improving the system. It remains to be seen how many hostages to fortune may have been given.

## Notes

[1] There is plenty of scope still for requisitions on these matters and on adverse entries: Farrand, p.148, *Re Stone & Saville's Contract* [1963] 1 W.L.R. 163, *Faruqi* v. *English Real Estate Ltd.* [1979] 1 W.L.R. 963.

[2] Registrar's Report 1979–80, paras. 1,20.

[3] *An Englishman Looks at the Torrens System*, p. 64.

[4] See summary, p. 155.

[5] See Kenya Registered Land Act 1963, Israel Land Law 1969 (especially s. 161), Simpson's *Land Law and Registration*, Chaps. 21, 22.

[6] (1966) 19 C.L.P. 26,28. For an interesting indemnity case see Ruoff & Roper, p. 794, note 93 where it emerges without any reason being given, that Mr. Freer, of *Freer* v. *Unwins Ltd.* [1976] Ch. 288 fame, obtained an indemnity despite the court's view that such was probably not payable: see p. 183 *infra* and [1980] Camb. L.J. 381

[7] *Strand Securities Ltd.* v. *Caswell* [1965] Ch. 373, 386.

[8] *Strand Securities Ltd.* v. *Caswell* [1965] Ch. 958.

[9] (1965) 62 L.S. Gaz.507 (T.B.F.Ruoff).

[10] But see Practice Note 27.

[11] (1968) 84 L.Q.R. 528, 534; (1969) 32 M.L.R. 121, 127 (T.B.F. Ruoff).

[12] [1979] Conv. 317–319, 399.

[13] (1967) 83 L.Q.R. 614 (Paul Jackson) referring to Ruoff and Roper's predecessor.

[14] (1971) 34 Conv. (n.s.) 21,100,168.

CHAPTER 2

# GENERAL PRINCIPLES OF REGISTRATION OF TITLE

## *The Background*

FOR centuries people have been busy trying to simplify the business of transferring land. After all, why should the purchase of land be more complex than, say, the purchase of a diamond, a horse, a barrel of beer, a ship, a car or stocks and shares? Well, land is much more fundamentally useful for satisfying human needs than anything else. And, as human needs have increased in more complex ways so have legal concepts in land increased. Moreover, land as the most unique of the three fundamental factors of production—land, labour and capital—is bound to cause special problems.

There is an economic need for land to be freely alienable, for whole absolute ownership to be freely transmissible, but this has to be reconciled with the human desire for fragmentation of ownership and for keeping property within the family.[1] Economic and commercial needs are satisfied by ensuring that the whole capital interest in land (*i.e.* the fee simple absolute) is always alienable subject to legal leases and mortgages that have to be permanently binding, whilst private human needs are satisfied behind a trust of the whole capital interest which divides up individual rights to income and ultimately, to capital with the utmost freedom subject only to the Rule against Perpetuities. This rule has outgrown its historical origins and now prevents contingent rights to income from being tied up for too long. However, since such rights can only exist behind a trust, the rule ensures that every so often every trust must come to any end, the trust capital thereupon becoming risk capital

8

and helping to create a dynamic relationship between the amount of trust capital (which is safe capital *par excellence*) and risk capital circulating in the economy.[2]

Further special problems arise from the uniqueness of land. It is uniquely immovable so that it is easy to enforce all sorts of rights against it such as the rights of persons with the benefit of easements, profits, restrictive covenants, rentcharges or mortgages. It is uniquely attached to other land giving rise to mutual rights and obligations such as rights of support. Indeed, each piece of land is considered to be so unique that rights of enjoyment of land are specifically enforceable in equity by a court action so making equitable interests of such rights. These rights of enjoyment are very varied and arise from the virtual indestructibility of land which allows for all sorts of successive interests existing in or over it for years and years giving rise to the doctrine of estates, the doctrine of waste, the Rule against Perpetuities, and settlements whether under the Settled Land Act or a trust for sale. Land is also specifically apt for satisfying concurrent needs giving rise to concepts such as joint tenancy and tenancy in common. Land is particularly divisible vertically (*e.g.* semi-detached houses), or horizontally (*e.g* maisonettes and flats), so giving rise to many problems as to mutual rights and obligations. Finally, the unique inelasticity of supply of land has specially singled it out for governmental control whether central or local.

At least when you buy a car you do not find that you and purchasers from you must always carry Mrs A in the back seat whenever she desires to go to Reading, that you have a right to be carried in Mr. A's lorry into St. Albans whenever he goes there, that you cannot carry groceries in the car, that you must never drive the car into Bristol, that you must allow Mr. B to siphon off petrol from your car whenever he wants, that you must always give a lift to hitch-hikers you pass, and that you are not allowed to fit a sun roof to your car! You do not find that as a car owner you will be liable for road charges if the road on which it stands is made up by the local authority, nor is it likely to be demolished for want of planning permission or compulsorily purchased. You do not find that the boundaries of the car are uncertain or that the car is subject to a tenancy and sub-tenancies with various repairing obligations. If all the above were the case then the purchase of a car would not be such a simple matter!

## Registration of Deeds

One method for simplifying the purchase of land, though only very slightly, is the system of registration of deeds which was first put forward in a draft Bill submitted to Parliament in 1529. The idea originated in records accumulated by royal officials in the centuries after the Norman Conquest and the proposals had as many political and administrative advantages as they had private advantages for parties desiring greater security for their conveyancing transactions. The system is a simple one as it makes no change in the method of conveyancing since all it does is to set out on a register a copy or "memorial" of all deeds dealing with the property which have been seen by the registrar. A purchaser is entitled to disregard all dealings with the land which do not appear on the register and so is protected against the danger of concealed and secret documents, though not forged documents. It is still up to the purchaser to investigate title in the traditional complex way.

However, despite numerous Bills submitted to Parliament, *e.g.* in 1653, 1664, 1670, 1685, 1693, 1694, 1697, 1698, 1699, 1734, 1758, 1831, and 1833 no *national* deeds registry was ever set up, though *local* deeds registries were set up in 1703, 1707, 1708 and 1735 to cover the West Riding of Yorkshire, the East Riding, Middlesex and the North Riding respectively. This system applied until registration of title became compulsory in Middlesex in 1936 and Yorkshire in 1972. The deeds registries are now all closed.

## Registration of Charges

Another method of simplifying the transfer of land is to provide for the registration in one national registry of those charges or incumbrances of such an unusual nature that a purchaser may fail to discover them in an ordinary investigation of title. *e.g* where such incumbrances may well not appear on the title deeds. Thus annuities for life charged on land were made registrable in 1777 whilst judgments affecting land and pending actions over land were made registrable in 1839. If such incumbrances had not been registered then a purchaser was unaffected by them.

The great advantage of such a system is that on inspecting the register a purchaser knows exactly where he stands in relation to registrable incumbrances. Nevertheless, in all other respects investigation of title continues in the traditional complex way. The system was greatly extended by the 1925 Property Legislation, as we shall shortly see, but it has one major defect: registration is effected against the name of the owner of the burdened land at the time of registration.

So long as prospective purchasers of the land can ascertain the names of former owners so as to enable a search of the register to take place there are no problems. However, in the course of time the names of early owners of the land will increasingly become unascertainable as their periods of ownership increasingly fall before the period necessary for showing a good root of title. The danger, since registration of a charge is deemed to give everyone actual notice of it (Law of Property Act 1925, s. 198), is thus that a purchaser, unless all the old search certificates have been preserved with the title deeds, as may be the case, may find himself bound by a charge whose existence he could not possibly have discovered.

Under section 44 of the L.P.A 1925, 30 years was the necessary period for showing a good root of title so no problems could arise until 1956. Accordingly, the Roxburgh Committee on Land Charges (1956 Cmd. 9825) considered the problems but reported that no satisfactory short-term solution could be found: salvation only lay in the rapid extension of registration of title throughout the country whereby the problems would solve themselves as charges affecting registered titles are registered against the land, not the name of the landowner.

In 1969 another Law of Property Act reduced the 30 year period to 15 years, thereby increasing the problems of purchasers of unregistered land.[3] However, section 25 of this 1969 Act produced a palliative by providing for compensation to be paid to any purchaser who suffers loss through being bound by a charge of which he was ignorant, due to it being hidden behind the root of title.[4] The real solution will only come with the extension of registration of title to the whole country.

## Registration of Local Land Charges

Local land charges registers present none of the problems of the national Land Charges Registry kept at Plymouth as local land charges are registered against the land itself. The need for these local registers arose out of the increasing powers of local government to control the use of land, to acquire land, and to carry out public works that also benefited private individuals. Generally speaking, the registers only contain charges or matters of a local or public nature that affect land, *e.g.* prohibitions or restrictions on the use of land under planning law, certain proceedings for compulsory purchase, charges for making up a road imposed on land fronting the road and the like. The registers are kept by each county council and each district or borough council.

## Relationship of Different Types of Registration

It is *vital* to realise that (1) registration of deeds, (2) registration of charges within the traditional conveyancing system and (3) registration of title are mutually exclusive systems of conveyancing, and that the system of registration of local land charges operates in the same manner whichever of the three conveyancing systems is applicable (L.C.A. 1925, s. 15 (8)). Exceptionally, where the registration of title system prevails a local land charge to secure money must be registered at the Land Registry as a registered charge before it can be enforced (s. 59 (2) proviso of the Act). This can create practical difficulties for the local authority because the land certificate, if outstanding, must be lodged at the Registry before the charge can be registered (s. 64 (1) (*c*)). It is also possible, though very rare indeed, to enter notice of a local land charge on the register of title (s. 49 (1)) though, again, the land certificate needs to be lodged at the Registry for this. Almost invariably local land charges take effect as "overriding interests" (for which see below).

## *Registration of Title*

As we have seen, registration of deeds and registration of charges left the traditional system of private conveyancing very much unaffected so that the transfer of land remained a complex matter. How much better it would be if, as a London solicitor[5] suggested to the Real Property Commissioners of 1830, to whom the question of reform of the land law had been referred, there were set up a register containing full particulars of the title to property which should, in itself, be evidence not of a deed or deeds but of the *title* and thus accomplish facility and cheapness of transfer as well as security of title. A system of registration of title could obviate the necessity for the repetitive investigation of title deeds on sale by presenting a prospective purchaser with the net result of former dealings with the property unlike the system of registration of deeds, which merely places the dealings before him and leaves him to investigate the dealings himself. In the first case he finds the sum worked out for him: in the latter case he has the figures given him and he has to work out the sum himself.

However, in 1830 the substantive land law was in such a tortuous and ungodly jumble that, in essence, no system of registration of title could work properly since the only available figures were Roman numerals: it was not until the 1925 Property Legislation that the necessary Arabic numerals came to hand. As Holdsworth pointed out:

> "It was impossible to make title secure and to get cheap conveyancing so long as the law permitted a large series of estates present and future, legal and equitable; so long as it continued to have two sets of rules for succession on intestacy, and two sets of representation on death; so long as conveyances were needlessly lengthy; so long as the system of strict settlement admitted of the creation of all sorts of charges upon land; so long as estates in common were admitted; and so long as the system of mortgaging land remained unreformed."

Nevertheless, in 1859 a Royal Commission produced a report proposing the creation of a system of registration of title which led to the passing of the Land Registry Act 1862. Most significantly, as Stewart-Wallace pointed out in *Principles of Land Registration* (1937), p.33:

> "The commissioners called on to make practical
> recommendations for the introduction of land registration
> into England had to consider what was financially feasible
> and what would produce least opposition on introduction.
> They decided . . . that the Act introducing registration
> should be confined to making changes in the machinery of
> conveyancing merely. The alternative of introducing
> substantive changes applicable to registered land only, so
> that the substantive law affecting registered land would
> differ from that affecting unregistered land, was rejected."

However, the Act was impractical and a complete failure, only 507 titles being registered up to 1868. As a result of another Royal Commission appointed in 1868 there was passed the Land Transfer Act 1875 which practically repealed the 1862 Act and established the Land Registry of today with an entirely different system of registration of title. In particular, the Registrar was given discretion to accept titles that were less than impeccable but were substantially good holding titles, there was introduced what is now known as the general boundaries rule under which the exact line of legal ownership is left undetermined, and registration was confined to the full legal ownership of persons who were absolute owners or who had power to sell the land.

However, since registration was purely voluntary, the higher conveyancing costs of registering under the system coupled with the conservatism of the legal profession ensured that little use was made of the system under the 1875 Act.[6] Accordingly, in 1897, the Land Transfer Act applied the principle of compulsion and compulsory registration was introduced from 1898 onwards on the occurrence of any sale of land in London. No further extension of the compulsory system was made until after the 1925 Property Legislation.

## The 1925 Property Legislation

This legislation (in particular the Settled Land Act, the Trustee Act, the Law of Property Act, the Land Charges Act and the Administration of Estates Act) resolved the difficulties emphasised by Holdsworth in the passage quoted earlier. At this stage, it will be helpful to outline the general framework of land law principles so that a comparison may be drawn with the fundamentally new framework provided by the system of registration of title enshrined in the Land Registration Act 1925.

### Legal and Equitable Interests

The basic division in land law used to lie between legal and equitable interests. Legal interest were rights *in rem* and so were good against the whole world. They could be enforced against anyone who interfered with them, whether or not he knew of them, and could only be lost under various Limitation Acts by various periods of adverse possession. Equitable interests were rights *in personam* and were not good against the whole world. They could not be enforced against a bona fide purchaser of a legal estate for value without notice (actual, constructive or imputed) or his successors in title. This special person, privileged under what is known as the equitable doctrine of notice, will be called "Equity's darling."

There used to be a very large number of legal estates and interests with a complementary number of equitable estates and interests since "Equity follows the Law" so that, on the one hand, a purchaser's position was perilous since there were all sorts of legal estates and interests which might exist and bind him even though he had no notice of them, whilst, on the other hand, the position of a person holding an equitable estate or interest was also perilous since equity's darling might acquire the land.

### 1925

In 1925 the position of these two classes of person was vastly improved. Where a purchaser was concerned, the number of legal estates was reduced to two, the fee simple absolute in possession and the term of years absolute, and the number of possible legal interests was substantially reduced so as to include only easements, profits, rentcharges and rights of entry enduring for a period corresponding to the two legal estates, and, also charges by way of legal mortgage and charges on land not created by any instrument but imposed by law. Legal mortgages have to be treated as *sui generis* as they take effect directly or indirectly as legal estates in the nature of leases or sub-leases and can give rise to a legal power to dispose of the whole mortgaged fee simple or term of years. At any rate, all other estates, interests and charges in or over land henceforth can only take effect as equitable interests.

This meant there were many more persons holding equitable interests so it became more necessary than ever to do something to protect them from the clutches of Equity's darling. To this end most equitable interests were made either overreachable or registrable in a register of charges.

If the equitable interest is overreachable then, irrespective of notice to a purchaser, on a sale of the land in which beneficiaries have equitable interests, the beneficiaries' interests are detached from the land and attached to the proceeds of the sale if the proper overreaching machinery is used, *e.g.*payment to two trustees. If the equitable interest is registrable then, if it is registered under the Land Charges Act 1925, everyone is deemed to have actual notice of it so that no one can possibly claim to be equity's darling.[7] If it is not registered then it is void as against purchasers, irrespective of whether or not such purchasers may have actual notice or whether or not the person with the equitable interest (*e.g.* an agreement for a lease) is in actual occupation.[8] Actual occupation was intended to be an alternative method of protecting a registrable equitable interest (see L.P.A 1922, s.33 which was in Part 1 which contained the land charge provisions in s.14). However, when consolidated in the 1925 property legislation, L.P.A 1922, s. 33 became L.P.A 1925, s. 14 only, and inadvertently was omitted from the Land Charges Act 1925, all the 1925 property legislation passing through both Commons and Lords on the nod, their joint committee having (erroneously) certified that the consolidation of the Law of Property Act 1922 and the Law of Property (Amendment) Act 1924 into the various 1925 Acts made no change in the law.

What determines whether an equitable interest is overreachable or registrable is whether the interest is generally of a "family" nature entitling its owner to enjoy the fruits of land ownership, when the interest is fully suited to becoming an interest in money instead of land (*e.g.* life or co-ownership interests), or whether the interest is generally of a "commercial" nature, giving its owner limited rights over land enjoyed and possessed by another, when the interest is only valuable because of the specific land to which it relates (*e.g.* restrictive covenants, estate contracts, equitable easements).

Certain commercial interests that are normally easily discoverable were not made registrable (*e.g.* equitable mortgages protected by deposit of title deeds and restrictive covenants in leases) whilst restrictive covenants entered into before 1926 were not made registrable as to have done so would have affected already existing rights in a retrospective and detrimental manner.

Those equitable interests not precisely covered by the registration of land charges provisions or by the overreaching provisions remain subject to the old equitable doctrine of notice, which may be said to have a "long-stop" function, *e.g.* equitable mortgages protected by deposit of title deeds; restrictive covenants in leases; pre-1926 restrictive covenants; unregistered registrable land charges not specifically made void by section 13 (2), L.C.A 1925, or section 4, L.C.A 1972 (*e.g.* in the case of a purchaser for value as opposed to money or money's worth *cf. McCarthy & Stone Ltd.* v. *Hodge* [1971] 1 W.L.R 1547, [1976] *Current Legal Problems* 26): overreachable interests not overreached by the proper machinery as in *Caunce* v. *Caunce* [1969] 1 W.L.R 286; equitable rights of re-entry as in *Shiloh Spinners Ltd* v. *Harding* [1973] A.C 691; equitable proprietary estoppel interests as in *Ives Investments Ltd.* v. *High* [1967] 2 Q.B 379 and *Crabb* v. *Arun D.C.* [1976] Ch. 179; probably the equitable right of the owner of a hired fixture to remove it if the hirer breaks his contract: *Poster* v. *Slough Estates* [1969] 1 Ch. 495.

## Classification of Interests in Unregistered Land

The classification of interests in land that emerges is thus sixfold: (1) legal estates (2) legal mortgages (3) legal interests

(4) equitable interests capable of being overreached irrespective of notice to a purchaser (5) equitable interests capable of being protected by entry on a register of charges under the Land Charges Act 1925 which, when so protected, bind a purchaser irrespective of notice and which, if unprotected, do not bind a purchaser irrespective of notice and (6) equitable interests that are precisely covered neither by the overreaching nor by the registration provisions but which remain fully subject to the equitable doctrine of notice.

Conveyancing is carried on in the traditional manner but this classification of interests brought about by the 1925 property legislation greatly simplifies the task.

## THE LAND REGISTRATION ACT 1925

The Land Registration Act 1925 (hereafter called "the Act") as slightly amended by the 1936, 1966 and 1971 Land Registration Acts and the Administration of Justice Act 1977, ss.24-26 and the rules made under section 144 of the Act now contain the law relating to the system of registration of title. The Act, though it repealed the 1897 Land Transfer Act, was based largely on the 1897 Act but it did contain some important changes which had been recommended by a Royal Commission in 1908 and a Committee in 1919 and had been inserted in the Law of Property Act 1922 and the Law of Property (Amendment) Act 1924. In particular, the emphasis moved away from merely simplifying and facilitating conveyancing towards providing state-guaranteed titles to land through the means of an insurance fund.

This insurance principle of a state-guaranteed title and consequent indemnity to persons suffering loss if any mistakes are made is one of three principles that underlie the system of registration. There is also the mirror principle that the register acts as a mirror reflecting accurately, completely and irrefutably the current facts material to a title (except for certain types of interests that necessarily have to be "overriding interests") and the general curtain principle, enshrined also in the other 1925 property legislation, that trusts must be kept off the title at all costs so as to simplify the transfer of the legal estate.

## Classification of Interests in Registered Land

The provisions of the Act also reveal more clearly than before the superficial resemblance between the classification of interests in registered land and the classification of interests in unregistered land. However, as we are about to see, it is vital to appreciate that the types of interests falling into each class by no means correspond completely and that, most remarkably of all, interests in registered land by no means fall exclusively into one class. The classification of interests in registered land that emerges is as follows: (1) registrable interests (2) registered charges (3) overriding interests (4) minor interests capable of being overreached even when protected by an entry on the register, *e.g.* beneficiaries under a trust for sale or a settlement protected by a restriction (5) minor interests capable of being protected by an entry on the register, which are secure when so protected but which, if unprotected, do not bind a purchaser irrespective of notice.

Strictly speaking, in a system of registration of title there is no scope for a sixth class of interests in registered land dependent upon the new registered proprietor having actual or constructive notice of such interest. He takes the legal estate subject to entries on the register and to overriding interests but otherwise free from all other interests whatsoever: sections 20, 23, 59 (6) and 74 and *De Lusignan* v. *Johnson* (1973) 230 E.G 499 where a person taking a registered charge with actual knowledge of an earlier unprotected minor interest (an estate contract) was held not to be bound by the minor interest. Thus, the new registered proprietor is not bound by unprotected minor interests of which he has notice *qua* successor in title to the former proprietor. However, if equitable fraud is present then the new registered proprietor is directly bound in right of his own conscience by the unprotected minor interest, *e.g.* if he deliberately led the minor interest holder to leave the interest unprotected, or if the new registered proprietor is the A Co. Ltd. having taken a transfer from A to attempt to defeat P's earlier unprotected contract to purchase A's land (see *Jones* v.

*Lipman* [1962] 1 W.L.R 832; *Peffer* v. *Rigg*,[9] [1977] 1 W.L.R
285 *Frazer* v. *Walker* [1967] 1 A.C. 569, 585).It may thus be
said that outside the system of registration of title there may lie
an *in personam* action wherever equitable fraud can be proved.
Where equitable proprietary interests arising from acquiescence
are concerned (like the informal right of way in *Ives* v. *High*
[1967] 2 Q.B. 379 or *Crabb* v. *Arun D.C.* [1976] Ch. 179) that
are not protected by a caution against dealings or a notice
under section 49 (1) *(f)* or as overriding interests it would
seem that the new proprietor's conscience ought not to be
directly bound in the absence of special circumstances.
However, the equitable estoppel rights arising from the
principle that a person cannot enjoy the benefits of an
arrangement without giving effect to the burden imposed on
such benefits would seem to found an *in personam* action
against the new proprietor: see *Ives* v. *High* (above); *Halsall* v.
*Brizell* [1957] Ch. 169; *Hopgood* v. *Brown* [1955] 1 All E.R.
550.

(1) *Registrable interests*

Fundamental to the whole system are "registrable
interests" which roughly correspond to legal estates. For
present purposes it suffices to say that they comprise fees
simple absolute in possession and terms of years absolute with
at least 21 years unexpired in land (*e.g.* houses, flats, tunnels,
mines and minerals severed from the land), and also
rentcharges.[10] These interests can be registered independently
with separate titles and separate land certificates.

It is the *title* of an estate owner to a legal interest in land
that is registered and not the land itself despite the fact that the
Act and common use refer to "land" as registered. However,
for the sake of simplicity and uniformity we will refer to land,
the title to which is registered, as "registered land". We will
also refer to the process of registration of an interest in land,
whereupon the proprietor of the interest is issued with a land
certificate, as "substantive registration."

Whilst title to registered land derives from the fact of
registration at the Land Registry, so the land certificate is
merely evidence (usually out of date) of the state of the register,
the land certificate is to a large extent treated as replacing the

title deeds, except that in the case of leasehold land the lease itself (or its counterpart) remains an essential title deed revealing the exact details a purchaser needs to know, for the register only replaces the subsequent chain of title. The certificate must usually be produced to the Registry when any dealing with the land takes place, when the certificate will be brought up to date to reflect the position on the register itself. Cautions, however, can be entered at the Registry without production of the land certificate.

Substantive registration of registrable interests must be clearly distinguished from the noting of such interests. This is a process whereby a note of a subordinate registrable and registered interest is entered on the register of the superior title. For example, the fee simple and a term of years exceeding 21 years in the same land may be registered, when they will comprise separate titles with separate land certificates, but the term of years will also be noted on the register of title to the fee simple.

The benefit of an easement or profit that is capable of subsisting as a legal interest and appurtenant to registered land is usually entered on the property register of the registered land as part of the description of the land. The effect of such entry is to confer an absolute, good leasehold, qualified or possessory title (see below) to the easement or profit according to the nature of the title to the land. Essentially, the easement or profit is treated as itself part of the registered land: section 3 (xxiv), *Re Evans' Contract* [1970] 1 W.L.R. 583.

### (2) Registered charges

The classic way of mortgaging registered land is by registered charge which, unless made or taking effect by demise or sub-demise, takes effect as a charge by way of legal mortgage (s.27). Although a charge is said to be registered when an entry showing the charge and the name of the proprietor has been made in the register of title to the land affected it is not a registrable interest in our sense since it is not capable of substantive registration. Moreover, such a charge cannot be an overriding interest (see below) since an overriding interest is defined by section 3 (xvi) as an interest "not entered on the register" nor can it be a minor interest (see below) since it is created by and can be disposed of by a registered disposition (ss. 3 (xxii), 18 (4) and 21 (4) and a minor interest is defined in section 3 (xv) as an interest " not capable of being disposed of or created by registered dispositions."

The proprietor of the charge is issued with a *charge* certificate with the original charge annexed, and so long as the charge is subsisting, the *land* certificate is retained in the Registry, so safeguarding the interests of the proprietor of the charge.

## (3) Overriding interests

Overridding interests, like legal interests, bind the land affecting purchasers irrespective of notice. They comprise those interests, whether legal or equitable, that are *not* mentioned at all on the register (s. 3 (xvi) and which fall within a category set out primarily in section 70 but also in the rules and in later statutes. This category includes easements and profits not being equitable easements required to be protected by notice on the register, rights acquired or in the course of acquisition under the Limitation Act 1939, rights of occupiers, local land charges and leases for terms of 21 years or less granted at a rent without taking a fine, so that, by way of contrast with the traditional unregistered system, equitable profits and the equitable rights of occupiers as overriding interests now bind the whole world (including equity's darling) irrespective of notice.[11]

The characteristic feature of the interests is that they are often neither shown in title deeds nor mentioned in abstracts of title in unregistered conveyancing, and they are usually easily discoverable by the inspections and inquiries which are already carried out in traditional unregistered conveyancing. Unfortunately, the task is made more difficult in registered conveyancing for, as we shall see in Chapter 6, the category of overriding interests is so broad and uncertain that really intensive and extensive inspections and inquiries need to be conducted before a purchaser can fully appreciate the burdens to which the land is likely to be subject. It is also a little confusing that interests within the category (*e.g.* easements noted under section 70 (2) or overriding interests noted under section 70 (3)) may appear on the register in which case they are not overriding interests but minor interests (s. 3 (xvi), overriding interests being defined as interests *not* entered on the register.

## (4) and (5)  *Minor interests*

Minor interests are a residual category embracing all interests in registered land other than registrable interests, registered charges and overriding interests. They need to be protected by one of the four types of entry which are possible in the register—and protection by *entry* on the register must be clearly distinguished from actual registration. They comprise interests that in unregistered land may be legal or equitable, and their capacity to bind registered land turns on whether or not they are protected by an entry in the register. The extent of the protection will depend upon whether the entry is a notice, a caution, a restriction or an inhibition.

Which method of protection is used turns, in practice, upon whether or not the minor interest falls (1) into a class which corresponds roughly with overreachable equitable interests in unregistered conveyancing or (2) a class which roughly corresponds with charges registrable under the Land Charges Act in unregistered conveyancing or (3) within section 101 as a disposition or dealing made by a registered proprietor as if his land were not registered, *e.g.* sales and mortgages not completed by registration. Under section 101 (2) these last interests take effect onlyin equity but they may be protected by an appropriate entry, otherwise they will be completely overridden by any registered disposition for valuable consideration unless ranking as overriding interests, *e.g.* under section 70 (1) *(g)* since what would otherwise be minor interests can become overriding interests if supported by actual occupation or receipt of rents. Of course, the purpose of section 101 is to deal with those cases where the proprietor fails to take advantage of the proper statutory provisions.

It is most significant that only a caution may be entered if the land certificate is not deposited at the Registry to enable a notice or restriction to be entered: section 64 (1) *(c)*.

*Protection by restriction.* In the first case of overreachable interests (*e.g.* beneficial interests under a trust for sale or a

Settled Land Act settlement) protection is usually afforded by the entry of a restriction which does not reveal what the beneficial interests are (since they remain "behind the curtain" as in unregistered conveyancing) but which prevents any dealing with the land except in compliance with the terms of the restriction, *e.g.* terms ensuring that capital moneys are paid to two trustees or a trust corporation and that only authorised dispositions under the Settled Land Act take place. Once the restriction is complied with the beneficial interests are overreached. If no restriction (or other entry) were entered then in the case of settled land a purchaser would take a perfectly valid title from the registered proprietor[12] subject only to possible problems of rectification and indemnity (see Chapter 9). An interest under a trust for sale, however, may be protected by virtue of being an overriding interest within section 70 (1) (*g*) as in *Williams & Glyn's Bank* v. *Boland* [1980] 3 W.L.R. 138.

Restrictions can also be very useful in recording other legal restraints on a registered proprietor's powers of disposition, *e.g.* a company's land cannot be charged unless certain of its officials certify that the charge does not contravene the company's memorandum or articles, and certain charity lands cannot be dealt with except with the consent of the Charity Commissioners.

Whereas in the case of settled land there is a duty imposed upon the tenant for life or the trustees to apply for the appropriate restrictons, in the other instances there is a duty imposed upon the registrar to enter restrictions. However, subject to the concurrence of the registered proprietor, who has to produce his land certificate, or if the land certificate is already at the Registry (*e.g.* owing to a registered charge) subject to no valid objection from the proprietor, any restriction may be placed on the register subject to the Registrar's discretion to refuse to do so where he deems such a restriction unreasonable or calculated to cause inconvenience (s. 58 (2)). This flexibility is a special advantage of registered conveyancing enabling persons to ensure that certain bounds cannot be transgressed either absolutely or without the consent of certain persons, *e.g.* by such means positive covenants can indirectly be made to bind land where consent to a disposition can be refused unless the disponee agrees to be bound by the positive covenant.[13]

*Protection by notice.* In the case of those interests roughly corresponding with charges registrable under the Land Charges Act in unregistered conveyancing complete protection is afforded by the entry of a notice,[14] which reveals the exact nature of the interest protected and which ensures that thereafter all dealings take effect subject to the interest protected so far as it is valid and is not capable of being overreached under other Acts (*e.g.* L.P.A. and S.L.A. 1925): section 52. By section 49 (2) a notice cannot be entered to protect interests under S.L.A. settlements or trusts for sale (except pending appointment of trustees).

This protection, however, is only available with the assistance of the registered proprietor of the land affected if the land certificate is not in the Registry as it is only if his land certificate is produced that the Registrar will enter a notice, except for creditors' notices, notices of a lease and notices of an Inland Revenue charge for capital transfer tax: section 64 (1) (*c*) and Finance Act 1975, Sched. 12, para. 5 (5). If the land certificate is already in the Registry (*e.g.* owing to a registered charge) a notice will not normally be entered without the proprietor being afforded an opportunity to make a valid objection unless the notice relates to a Class F charge of a spouse: *Watts* v. *Waller*[1973] 1 Q.B. 153, Law Commission Working Paper No. 67, para. 25, Ruoff & Roper, pp. 319, 747. The exception is to protect a spouse against an angry husband, though his angry violence may be all the greater when he finds out!

The device of entering a notice is also used, as we have seen, to note subordinate registrable and registered interests, such as certain leases and rentcharges, on the register of the superior freehold title. It is also used to note the burden of a legal easement or profit. Finally, entry of a notice must not be confused with a notice of deposit of a land or charge certificate (in the case of mortgages and sub-mortgages) which confusingly takes effect as a caution (see Chap. 7).

*Protection by caution.* Protection by a caution is in the nature of a temporary "holding" device and is very common as it is the only device available where it is not possible to use the land certificate for the entry of a restriction or a notice. Entry of a caution is thus a hostile act while entry of a restriction or notice is often a friendly act except where Class F rights or charging orders are protected by a notice: *Watts* v. *Waller* [1973] 1 Q.B. 153; *Wroth* v. *Tyler* [1974] Ch. 30; Charging Orders Act 1979, s. 3 (3), L.R.A. s. 49 (1) *(g)*. A cautioner has to make a statutory declaration in support of his claim and there are penalties for false declarations. Moreover, if anybody lodges a caution without reasonable cause he is liable to compensate any person who thereby sustains damage: section 56 (3). Since it is unclear what is "reasonable cause" the court in interlocutory proceedings for vacation of a caution may tell the cautioner, "You may keep the caution on the register if you undertake to pay the landowner any damages caused by its presence if it is afterwards held that it was wrongly entered. But if you are not ready to give such an undertaking, then the caution must be vacated" (*Tiverton Estates Ltd.* v. *Wearwell Ltd.* [1974] Ch. 146). No doubt in a special case the court might act similarly in respect of a notice.

There are two types of caution: a caution against first registration (s. 53) and a caution against dealings (s. 54.) The first type of caution is used to ensure that the person who lodged the caution (known as the cautioner) has an opportunity to learn about any application for first registration of the unregistered land in which he is interested in some way, and to oppose it if he wishes. The Registrar has to notify the cautioner of any application for registration and if the cautioner does not object within the prescribed time limit (14 days) then registration is effected. If the cautioner enters an appearance within the limit and goes on to make a valid objection the registration will either not be proceeded with or will be effected only subject to the cautioner's interest in some way. If the prospective cautioner is specifically entitled to be registered as proprietor of the land in any way and desires to oust any rival applications in respect of the land that may be made within a fortnight or so, then the temporary device of a priority notice against first registration should be used (for which see rule 71 and Ruoff and Roper, pp. 250-251).

A caution against dealings in registered land similarly

entitles the cautioner to be notified of any proposed dealing and to oppose it if he wishes. He will also be notified where the proprietor has applied to have the caution removed as where a prospective purchaser quite naturally and rightfully requires the vendor to clear up the position.[15] The onus is on the cautioner to take action for if he does not object within the prescribed time limit (14 days after notification or such other period not being less than 7 days, that the Registrar may specify) then the caution is cancelled and his interest ignored: the caution is said to have been "warned off." The cautioner may state his case orally or in writing and the Registrar has a very broad discretion, after hearing both sides and subject to appeal to the Chancery Division of the High Court, to do what he thinks appropriate, *e.g.* cancel the caution, refuse to allow the proposed dealing to go through, allow the dealing to go through but subject in some way to the cautioner's interest as by entry of a notice to protect a cautioner against a dealing by way of registered charge (Ruoff & Roper, p. 736), or allow the dealing to go through free from the cautioner's interest unless within a fixed period the cautioner institutes some legal proceedings when the caution will remain to protect the pending action. At any stage the Registrar may refer any question directly to the Chancery Division: rule 220 (4).

Unfortunately, it is difficult to ascertain the exact principles upon which the Registrar exercises his discretion as such cases are, a little suprisingly, considered so unimportant by the Registrar as not to warrant mention amongst the few cases that former Registrars sometimes reported in *The Conveyancer.* The key to the Registrar's approach, however, lies in the two similar statements of the last Registrar: "Cautions are not intended to enable hostile claims to be indefinitely prolonged but merely to allow reasonable time for claimants to take definite action" [16], "the function of cautions is to afford temporary and even ephemeral protection to a claim, not permanent protection of an established right." [17] Thus, whenever there is any real matter of substance in dispute (*e.g.* as to the existence of a contract) then the Registrar will warn off the caution unless the cautioner smartly institutes legal proceedings to determine the dispute so that there is a pending action to be protected by the caution, which may ultimately lead to recognition on the register of an established right, whether by actual registration or by entry of a notice or a restriction.

These two statements usefully serve to emphasise that a cautioner must have as a cautionable interest an estate or interest capable of being registered or noted, or a right to have a document conferring an estate or interest executed and then registered or noted, or an interest specifically authorised to be protected by the lodging of a caution: see Robinson (1971) 35 Conv. 21, *Miller* v. *Minister of Mines* [1963] A.C. 484, 497; *Elias* v. *Mitchell* [1972] Ch. 652.

In urgent cases where a caution has been entered to protect a non-existent or unenforceable contract or to protect a *lis pendens* which is frivolous, vexatious or an abuse of process the court may grant speedy interlocutory relief on motion so that the caution is vacated: *Price Bros Ltd.* v. *Kelly Homes Ltd.* [1975] 1 W.L.R. 1512; *Rawplug Co. Ltd.* v. *Kamvale Properties Ltd.* (1968) 20 P. & C.R. 32; *Tiverton Estates Ltd.* v. *Wearwell* [1974] 1 Ch. 146. The court proceeds under its general jurisdiction or under section 82 (1) *(b)*: *Lester* v. *Burgess* [1973] 26 P. & C.R. 536.

*Protection by inhibition.* Protection by an inhibition is very rare indeed. It has the effect of preventing all dispositions of the land for a specified period or until further order and can only be entered on the register by order of the Registrar or of the Court. The only instances seem to be where a proprietor's land certificate has been stolen [18] or where section 61 (3) applies in the case of receiving orders in bankruptcy when an entry is made on the register, "No disposition or transmission is to be registered until a trustee in bankruptcy is registered".

*Protection by official search certificate.* It is standard conveyancing practice to take advantage of the protection afforded by the official search certificates now obtainable under the Land Registration (Official Searches) Rules 1978. Any bona fide purchaser for value intent upon aquiring a registrable interest or a registered charge may make an official search whereupon he acquires a 20 working day priority period. During this period the register is, in effect, frozen so that entries made in the period are postponed to a subsequent application to register the instrument effecting the purchase and, if the purchase is dependent upon a prior dealing, to a subsequent application to register the instrument effecting that prior dealing. It is vital, however, that this subsequent application[19] is delivered *within* the priority period (which may be extended for a further 15 working days in certain circumstances) for otherwise the official search certificate affords no protection against intervening minor interests: *Watts* v. *Waller* [1973] 1 Q.B. 153.

An example will serve to illustrate this. Let us say V contracts to sell his interest in land to $P_1$ who, expecting the sale to go through in a reasonable time, conforms to standard conveyancing practice and does not enter a caution (or a notice). V then contracts two months later to sell the land to $P_2$ who, in the course of negotiations, conforms to standard conveyancing practice by searching the Register and, of course, finds no reference to any interest of $P_1$. The search certificate only gives him 20 working days priority. Six weeks later as $P_2$ expects to complete the purchase within a week he searches the register again. Much to his horror he finds that $P_1$, a little suspicious of V's prevarications had entered a caution a week ago to protect his contract.

In such a case if $P_2$ completes the purchase he will take subject to whatever are $P_1$'s rights under the contract.[20] The position would be the same in unregistered conveyancing if $P_2$ had obtained official search certificates from the Land Charges Registry at Plymouth and $P_1$ had registered an estate contract.[21]

## The "Register"

Unfortunately, the term "register" is used in the Act in several senses so that it can be a source of confusion *e.g.* in *Strand Securities Ltd.* v. *Caswell* [1965] Ch. 373. It is used to cover the whole Register kept by the Land Registry on the card index system at the 13 District Land Registries throughout England and Wales. It is used to cover the register of each individual title. It is used to cover the names given to the three subdivisions of the register of each indvidual title: the Property Register, the Proprietorship Register and the Charges Register- this seems a relic of the days when separate register books were kept for these items. It is used where there is a leasehold title and a superior freehold title, and a purchaser of the leasehold takes subject to incumbrances on the register, to cover the register of the superior freehold title: *White* v. *Bijou Mansions Ltd.* [1937] Ch. 610 (concerned with "register" in sections 20 and 50).

To avoid the confusion generated by these various meanings the Henry Committee on Registration of Title To Land in Scotland (1969 Cmnd. 4137) suggested that in Scotland the register of each individual title should be called "Title Sheets", as now in the Land Registration (Scotland) Act 1979, s. 6, and the sub-divisions called "Sections." It would certainly assist if such simple terminological changes were introduced in England and Wales.

For the present, to ascertain the correct meaning of "register" it is necessary to pay careful regard to the context in which it is used. We will use the "Land Register" to denote the whole register, the "register" to denote the record of each individual title whilst the Property Register, Proprietorship Register and Charges Register will be called such.

### The subdivisions of the register

The first subdivision is the *Property Register* (the "credit" side of the register) which describes the property and the estate for which it is held and refers normally to a filed plan but sometimes to the Land Registry's general map based on the ordnance survey. The boundaries will be general boundaries, the exact line being left undetermined (under r. 278), unless the boundaries are noted as being "fixed." There will be notes so far as the *benefit* of any easements, rights or privileges are concerned and also as to claims to restrictive covenants and mines and minerals where express application has been made in that behalf (r. 3).

If the title is leasehold, then, brief particulars of the lease are shown including its date, term, and the rent payable under it. Moreover, if the lease contains some prohibition against alienation without licence, all estates, rights, interests, powers and remedies under the lease, arising upon, or by reason of, any alienation without licence, are expressly excepted from the effect of registration (r. 45). This is to save the Registrar the excessively onerous task of confirming that the person giving the licence was in fact the owner of the reversion for the time being. A purchaser thus has to satisfy himself as to the licence, as in the case of unregistered land where he is normally content with a licence from the person in receipt of the rent without inquiring into his title.

If the title is to a rentcharge, then, brief particulars of the document under which it was created will be set out together with the amount of the rent, the dates on which it is payable, and the property on which it is charged.

The second subdivision is the *Proprietorship Register* which states the class of the title (*i.e.* absolute, good leasehold, qualified or possessory), the name and address and description of the registered proprietor, and the details of any *cautions, restrictions* or *inhibitions* affecting his powers of disposition (r. 6). Since November 1976 the price paid for, or value of, the land is only entered on the register where the proprietor makes a specific request: S.I. 1976/1332.

The third subdivision is the *Charges Register* (the "debit" side of the register) which, as its name indicates, contains entries and *notices* of charges or incumbrances *adversely* affecting the title, *e.g.* restrictive covenants, easements, rentcharges, registered charges, registered leases (r. 7, ss. 70 (2), 70 (3).

These three subdivisions are correlated on to the one index card and a copy of this and of the filed plan or general map delineating the land, called the land certificate, is given to each registered proprietor as some evidence of title, since all instruments of transfer and charge are filed at the Registry. However, the land certificate will be retained by the Registry if a charge on the land is registered (s. 65). It is vital, however, to realise that it is not the land certificate that is the proprietor's proof of title but the register itself, especially as the land certificate may be out of date if entries, such as cautions or notes of sub-leases or creditors' notices, have been made in the register since the land certificate was last in the Registry.

*Inspection of the register*

As the register is the registered proprietor's proof of title and as the register is not open to public inspection (s. 112) the authority of the proprietor is necessary to enable any purchaser to inspect the register. Accordingly by section 110 once a prospective purchaser (but not a lessee or chargee) has agreed to buy a registered property the vendor *must* supply him with an authority to inspect the register and a copy of the entries and documents noted in the register and of the filed plan affecting that property. This corresponds to the vendor's obligation to provide an abstract of title in unregistered conveyancing.

This authority to inspect the register must contain the title number of the property and a short description of the property (form 80 in the Schedule to the Rules) and not only entitles the holder to inspect the register but also entitles him under rule 292 to make an official search, with the protection afforded by the 1978 Official Searches Rules and rule 295, and to obtain office copies of all entries and documents which he is entitled to see (r. 296).

Exceptionally, certain person or bodies may inspect parts of the register without any authority from the proprietor (r. 288, ss. 112A, 129, 59 (3), 61 (10) and r. 3 (2) of the 1967 Rules). These instances where there is any interference with the privacy of the register are fairly rare. However, is there any real justification for such an intense concern with privacy, especially when lessees are deemed to be affected with notice of incumbrances (such as restrictive covenants and mortgages) noted on the register of the reversionary title or titles although they cannot inspect these titles,[22] as at present, without the authority of the proprietors, which may not be forthcoming? After all, most financial matters (*e.g.* price paid for, or value of, the land; the amount of a registered charge) are not ascertainable from the register and if a price is specified in a notice protecting a contract little difficulty would arise in masking out this detail where the applicant for an official search had no authority from the proprietor. Personal searches should be impossible without the proprietor's authority since the register itself could not be masked out. Moreover, there should be no right to obtain office copies of filed documents without the authority of the proprietor. It is significant that as from November 1976 the price paid for, or the value of, the land has only been entered on the register if requested by the registered proprietor. In a few years' time when inflation will have obscured the significance of pre-November 1976 prices and value it will be easier to adopt the above proposals for public inspection of the register.

If these proposals were adopted, then, much time and expense would be saved by tenants, local authority organisations, statutory undertakers, property developers and others with legitimate reasons for wishing to communicate with the owner of a property, whilst prospective lessees would be in a position fully to appreciate the existence of all incumbrances affecting the property in question. Moreover, these proposals, which are canvassed with others in greater detail by the Law Commission in their Published Working Paper No. 32, ought not to meet with very much opposition since registers in other countries, including Scotland and Northern Ireland, are "open" and no outcry was raised when section 8 of the Yorkshire Registries Amendment Act 1966 (now repealed by the L.P.A. 1969) proposed registration of deeds by microfilm recording each entire document and open to public inspection. Indeed, memorials, which do not record the price paid for a property or the amounts of mortgages, have always been open to public inspection in the Yorkshire Registries.

*The index map and the parcels*

Although, at present, the register itself is not open to public inspection, that part of the Land Register that contains the Index Map and Parcels Index and a special list (the "pending list") of pending applications for first registration (dealing under rule 10 with the hiatus between receipt of such applications and their indexing on the map) is open to public inspection.

As a result, anyone can ascertain whether a particular property is registered or is about to be registered or is subject to cautions against first registration and, if it is registered, what its title number is. It is not possible to discover the name and address of the proprietor or any other information unless, of course, the written authority of the proprietor is obtained, if he can be discovered by some means.

It is standard practice when searching the Indices to make an official search under rule 286 in form 96. Although rule 286

(2) requires that applications for an official search should
describe the land to which it relates by means of a copy of or
extract from the Ordnance Map on the largest scale published,
the helpful practice of the Land Registry, as set out in Practice
Note 16 and Ruoff and Roper, p. 51, is for the Registry to act
on any written description sufficient to identify the property
(*e.g.* the ordinary street address) where the property is in a
compulsory registration area.

Even when solicitors are dealing with property which
appears to be unregistered from the fact that investigation of
title is based on perusal of an abstract of title instead of a
photographic office copy of the register, they ought to search
the Indices. It is always just possible that the land may have
been voluntarily registered at some time and then subsequently
dealt with as if it were still unregistered so leaving the legal
estate vested in the original registered proprietor. In practice,
however, few solicitors do make such a search when dealing
with what appears to be unregistered land. The 20th edition of
Gibson's *Conveyancing,* p. 250, however, ought to make future
generations of solicitors aware of the problem.

CLASSES OF TITLE

An applicant for registration may be registered with one of four
classes of title with varying degrees of conclusiveness since all
claims, other than those subject to which the registration takes
effect by law, are barred by the conclusiveness of the
registration, subject only to possible rectification and indemnity
in special cases (see below).

*Absolute Title*

Absolute title is the best class of title and is granted in 99 per
cent. of freehold applications. It vests in the applicant the legal
estate[23] together with all appurtenant rights (corresponding to
those passing under section 62 of the L.P.A. 1925 in
unregistered conveyancing) whether mentioned on the register
or not but subject to (1) entries on the register, (2) overriding
interests, unless the register states the land is free from them,

(3) minor interests of which the applicant has notice where he is a trustee (so that trustee-proprietors hold the land subject to the claims of their beneficiaries), and where the land is leasehold, (4) the express and implied covenants and obligations and liabilities incident to the land (ss. 5, 9). It is thus vital where the land is leasehold to discover whether there have been any breaches of covenant and any liability to forfeiture—and this is so where the land has already been registered (s. 23 (1) *(a)*). This involves exactly the same evidence by way of last receipts and the same consequences as in unregistered conveyancing.[24]

Absolute titles to leaseholds are not found as often as one might expect since such a title cannot be registered unless the Registrar can guarantee that the lease was validly granted. He can only do this if he knows and approves the title to any superior leaseholds and the freehold (s. 8 (1) proviso). Due to section 44 of the L.P.A. 1925, which restricts the title a lessee can call for in the absence of express agreement it is market forces, determining who has greater bargaining power, that determine whether a lessee is not able to discover the position relating to unregistered superior titles so the Registrar cannot register him with absolute title.

However, where the superior titles are already registered internal examination of them by the Registrar enables him to register the subordinate leaseholds with absolute title. The Registrar will also enter on the Charges Register of the lessee's title all the restrictive covenants and other incumbrances binding the leasehold, which appear on the Charges Registers of the superior titles. The applicant may well then learn for the first time of incumbrances affecting his leasehold: if so, he has to consider himself a sacrificial victim of a conveyancing situation based on the then existing superior bargaining strength of lessors in a lessor's market. Subsequent purchasers, at least, will know the position as to the burdens affecting the land.

In this respect, registered conveyancing is superior to unregistered conveyancing because a purchaser of an unregistered leasehold, though (without the consent of the superior owners) being unable to investigate the title to all superior interests and so discover the names of the superior owners and the existence of incumbrances, is bound by these undiscoverable incumbrances if they are registered against the superior owners' names under the Land Charges Act 1925 or 1972, since registration is deemed to constitute actual notice to all persons for all purposes by section 198 of the L.P.A. 1925 which overrides section 44 (5) of the L.P.A.:*White* v. *Bijou Mansions Ltd.* [1937] Ch. 610. For a purchaser of a registered leasehold with absolute title the incumbrances are set out on the register as plain as can be. The extensions of registration of title bringing with it registration of more titles to superior leaseholds and freeholds will enable more leasehold titles to be absolute and so confer greater security in leasehold conveyancing.

The effect of a transfer by a proprietor registered with absolute title is, when completed by registration, to vest the registered legal estate in the transferee for value subject to (1) entries on the register (2) overriding interests unless the register states the land is free from them and, where the land is leasehold (3) the express and implied covenants and obligations and liabilities incident to the estate transferred. It should be noticed that this list differs from the list concerned with the effect of first registration in only one respect. For a transferee for value takes free from all minor interests, except those which bind him as being protected by an entry on the register. If they are not so protected he takes free from them even if he has actual knowledge of them[25] just as in unregistered conveyancing a purchaser for value (or sometimes just for money or money's worth)[26] takes free from unregistered registrable land charges (L.P.A. 1925, s. 199; L.C.A. 1925, s. 13 (2); L.C.A. 1972, s. 4 and *Hollington Bros. Ltd.* v.*Rhodes* [1951] 2 T.L.R. 591). However, if the transfer is made without valuable consideration then by section 20 (4) and section 23 (5) the transferee takes subject to any minor interests that affect the transferor. In all other respects the transfer has the same effect as if it had been for value.

## Good Leasehold Title

Where a lessee cannot obtain absolute title (since the superior title cannot be investigated) then, he will apply for good leasehold title which has the same effect as an absolute title *except* that the registered proprietor and a purchaser from him will further take subject to any estate right or interest affecting or in derogation of the title of the lessor interest affecting or in derogation of the title of the lessor to grant the lease, since the Registrar cannot know about such matters and thus cannot guarantee that the lease has been validly granted (ss. 10,23).

It must also be remembered that, like an applicant for first registration of a leasehold with absolute title, an applicant for first registration with good leasehold title also takes subject to any incumbrances protected by entry in the Charges Register of a superior title, which he may have no authority to inspect (or, if the superior title is unregistered, subject to any incumbrances entered in the Land Charges Registry) *e.g.* restrictive covenants protected by a notice (*White* v. *Bijou Mansions Ltd.* [1937] Ch. 610; ss. 23 (1) *(b)*, 23 (2), 50 (2)).

Unlike the absolute title position, once registration with good leasehold title take place it still affords no protection to a subsequent purchaser since the Registrar cannot enter in the register all the restrictive covenants and other incumbrances affecting the superior titles (and therefore the subordinate leasehold) as the Registrar will not have seen the superior titles. Subsequent purchasers may thus find themselves bound by undiscoverable incumbrances. The problem, however, will solve itself as registration of title spreads and all superior titles come to be registered, so enabling subordinate leases to be registered with absolute title.

## Possessory Title

If an applicant finds that he cannot establish his title in the normal way by title deeds and other documentary evidence, then, he may apply for possessory title which, as the name implies, is based on actual possession of the land or constructive possession where the applicant is in receipt of the rents and profits yielded by the land. However, if the Registrar is in fact satisfied with the title he may register it as absolute or good leasehold despite the fact that the application was only for possessory title.

Registration of the applicant's title as possessory has the

same effect as an absolute title *except* that the proprietor and a purchaser from him are also subject to all adverse interests existing at the date of the first registration (ss. 6, 11, 20 and 23). Thus, no guarantee is given as to the title prior to first registration and so it must be investigated in the traditional unregistered manner with the usual inquiries and inspections. Because of this, failure to disclose to a purchaser that a title is merely possessory will enable him to rescind the contract: *Re Brine and Davies' Contract* [1935] Ch. 388. The title is, however, guaranteed as to all matters subsequent to the date of registration.

## Qualified Title

Very occasionally (perhaps once in 100,000 cases) the Registrar will feel unable to grant any of the above classes of title. In such a case, with the applicant's consent, the Registrar may register the applicant with a qualified title: an applicant cannot apply for such a title initially. Registration with qualified title has the same effect as an absolute title *except* that the proprietor and a purchaser from him are also subject to the estates rights and interests arising either before a specified date or under a specified instrument (ss. 7, 12, 20 and 23).

## The Registrar's Discretion

Finally, it is important to realise the Registrar does not require impeccable titles to be adduced to him before registering property with even an absolute title. It is a fundamental feature of the system that the Registrar has complete discretion (which he exercises liberally)[27] to accept what he considers to be a good holding title and grant absolute title in such a case (s. 13 *(c)*): *M.E.P.C. Ltd.* v. *Christian-Edwards* [1979] 3 W.L.R. 713, 720-21 (H.L.). However, if the Registrar finds that a title is, in his opinion, not fit for registration as absolute no appeal lies from his refusal to register it as absolute, though his action or inaction may well be controlled by mandamus proceedings: see *Dennis* v. *Malcolm* [1934] Ch. 244 and *Perpetual Executors' Association of Australia Ltd.* v. *Hosken* (1912) 14 C.L.R. 286.

Rectification proceedings under section 82 may be invoked if someone is aggrieved by an entry made by the Registrar.

## Upgrading the Class Title

Here again the Registrar's discretion plays an important part since by section 77 (2) on any transfer for value the Registrar may at his discretion upgrade the class of title *e.g.* from possessory to absolute or from good leasehold to absolute. A registered proprietor may apply under section 77 for upgrading if his land has been registered with possessory title for 15 years, if freehold, or 10 years, if leasehold, when the Registrar *must,* on being satisfied that the proprietor is in possession and certain precribed notices have been given, upgrade the title to absolute or good leasehold title, as the case may be. If the proprietor's title has been registered with good leasehold title for 10 years then, on his application the Registrar *may* upgrade the title to absolute.

## Cautions against Conversion

Since upgrading or conversion to a better class of title may possibly affect the rights of persons with an adverse claim to land merely registered with a possessory or qualified or good leasehold title, such persons may enter in the register what is called a caution against conversion (r. 215 (2)). The Registrar cannot then convert the title until notice has been served on the cautioner affording him the opportunity to present his case to the Registrar or otherwise being "warned off". An appeal may lie to the Chancery Division of the High Court.

If any person other than the proprietor suffers loss by reason of the conversion of title he is entitled to be indemnified under section 77 (6) and 83 (2) as if a mistake had been made in the register. However, if such a person caused or contributed to this "mistake" by his fraud or lack of proper care (which may be wide enough to cover the conduct of a person who was not under any disability and yet failed to enter a caution) then no compensation will be payable (s. 83 (5) *(a)* as substituted by Land Charges and Land Registration Act 1971, s. 3).

### Compulsory and Voluntary Registration

Until 1966 any holder of a registrable interest in England or Wales could apply to have his title registered. As a result of the Land Registration Act 1966 registration is now only possible and, most vitally, is obligatory (see Chap. 4) except for small plots of souvenir land exempted by Land Charges and Land Registration Act 1971, s. 4, in those areas which, over the years of extension of the system of registration, have been designated compulsory areas. Exceptionally, registration in a non-compulsory area is possible in limited circumstances, *e.g.* where title deeds have been lost or destroyed or where there are complex building estates, or where council houses are sold to tenants under the Housing Act 1980.

### Rectification and Indemnity

This subject is dealt with at length in Chapter 9. For present purposes it suffices to say that no title is ever really absolute, all titles being relative (though less relative than in unregistered conveyancing), since it is always possible that the register may be rectified if it turns out to be incorrect for some reason. Registration with title absolute thus never confers the complete safety and positive security of an unimpeachable title which was for many years proclaimed as a main advantage over unregistered conveyancing.[28] Only in certain special, but fairly broad cases, however, will the register be rectified against a registered proprietor in possession.

Almost but not quite complementary to the rectification provisions are provisions providing for indemnity to be payable to those persons who suffer loss by reason of the rectification or non-rectification of the register and who have not been fraudulent or negligent. These provisions are fundamental to the basic concept of a state-guaranteed title that underlies the system of registration of title.

### Notes

[1] F. H. Lawson, *Introduction to the Law of Property* (Oxford 1958), pp. 80 *et seq.*

[2] *Ibid.* p. 144.

[3] L.P.A. 1969, s. 24, however, assists purchasers by providing that in determining any question as to a purchaser's knowledge of a registered land charge *at the time of entering into a contract* for the disposition of an interest in unregistered land the question shall be determined by reference to his actual knowledge without regard to L.P.A. 1925, s. 198 (so overriding dicta in *Re Forsey and Hollebone's Contract* [1927] 2 Ch. 379, except that local land charges fall outside the scope of L.P.A. 1969, s. 24 (3)).

[4] Unfortunately, a purchaser who is a lessee or sub-lessee does not obtain the benefit of s. 25: see s. 25 (9) and s. 25 (10) defining "registered land charge".

[5] T.G. Fonnerau, *Appendix to 2nd Report Real Property Commissioners* (1830), p. 97.

[6] Only 48 applications were made up to 1879: Holdsworth's *History of English Law,* Vol. XV, p. 188.

[7] L.P.A. 1925, s. 198.

[8] L.C.A. 1925, s. 13 (2); *Hollington Bros. Ltd.* v. *Rhodes* [1951] 2 T.L.R. 691; L.C.A. 1972, s. 4; *Greene* v. *Church Commissioners* [1974] Ch. 467.

[9] See also p. 133 below.

[10] See 2, 3 (viii), rr. 50-54. Few rentcharges can be created after the Rentcharges Act 1977 so this book ignores them.

[11] *Webb* v. *Pollmount* [1966] Ch. 584; *Hodgson* v. *Marks* [1971] Ch. 892; *Williams & Glyn's Bank* v. *Boland* [1980] 3 W.L.R. 138.

[12] See, *e.g.* I. Leeming (1971) 35 Conv. (N.S.) 255, 258-259. This is more straightforward than the unregistered land position: *cf. Weston* v. *Henshaw* [1950] Ch. 510, *Re Morgan's Lease* [1972] Ch. 1, the problem posed by Megarry and Wade, pp. 307-308, and p. 184 below.

[14] s. 49 (1) *(c)* provides for notices in respect of "land charges until the land charge is registered as a registered charge". It seems the clause, "if it is a charge to secure money" should be inserted if the para. is to make sense: see 1st ed. hereof., pp. 60-62.

[15] *Parkash* v. *Irani Finance Ltd.* [1970] Ch. 101, 109; *Calgary & Edmonton Land Co. Ltd.* v. *Discount Bank* [1971] 1 W.L.R. 81: *Rawlplug Co. Ltd.* v. *Kamvale Properties Ltd.* (1968) 20 P. & C.R. 32, *Lester* v. *Burgess,* 26 P. & C.R. 536.

[16] Ruoff and Roper, p. 737.

[17] *An Englishman Looks at the Torrens System,* p. 80.

[18] Ruoff and Roper, p. 759

[19] Under Land Registration (Official Searches) Rules 1978, rule 5 an application for registration lodged pursuant to an official search does not lose its protection if it is not "in order" so that requisitions are raised thereon by the Registry, so long as it is eventually completed by registration.

[20] See Chap. 8, p. 145; D. J. Hayton [1976] *Current Legal Problems* 26.

[21] See *per* Harman J. in *Hollington Bros. Ltd.* v. *Rhodes* [1951] 2 T.L.R. 691, at foot of p. 696 and see p. 161 below, note 29.

[22] *White* v. *Bijou Mansions Ltd.* [1937] Ch. 610; L.P.A. 1925, s. 44.

[23] See Chap. 4, p. 57 indicating that the equitable estate must also pass.

[24] L.P.A. 1925, s. 45 (2) (3); Farrand, pp. 135-137.

[25] See Chap. 8, pp. 131-135.

[26] It is anomalous that in unregistered conveyancing unregistered contracts, restrictive covenants and equitable easements are void against purchasers for money or money'sworth whilst in registered conveyancing if unprotected they are void against transferees for value, *i.e.* including marriage consideration.

[27] For the view that he is too liberal, see C. T. Emery (1976) 40 Conv. 122.

[28] Ruoff and Roper (3rd ed.), p. 10.

CHAPTER 3

LEASES

THIS is a confused area so confused that it merits special
treatment. The relevant law is to be found in fragmentary
fashion in section 2 (1), 8 (1), 8 (2), 18 (3), 19 (2), 21 (3), 22
(2), 70 (1) *(g)* *(k)*, and 123 and is so difficult to piece together
in a coherent, integrated form that writers in legal periodicals
had a field day in the early days of the system.[1] The provisions
have also caused some confusion in practice and they contain
traps for unwary solicitors: a remarkable situation for a system
that is supposed to facilitate and simplify the transfer of
interests in land and dealings with them! The present situation
is as follows where it will be seen that leasehold tenants may
have a registrable interest or an overriding interest or a minor
interest.

*As Registrable Interests*

(1) Where the reversionary title is *registered* when the lease is
granted then, *whether or not* the land is in a compulsory area,
the lease if granted for more than 21 years, *must* be registered
as constituting a disposition by a registered proprietor (ss. 19 (2)
and 22 (2). A separate land certificate is issued in respect of the
lease and a notice (a debit entry) will be entered against the
superior title. To this end the lessor's land certificate will
usually be lodged at the Registry but this is not essential:
*Strand Securities Ltd.* v. *Caswell* [1965] Ch. 958.

(2) Where the reversionary title is *not so registered* then if
the land is in a *compulsory area.*

(a) a lease granted for *40* or more years *must* be
registered, as also *must* a lease when it is assigned on sale
when it has *not less than 40 years* to run (s. 123) whilst

(b) a lease granted for more than 21 but less than 40 years *may* be registered, as also *may* a lease when it is assigned on sale when it has less than 40 but more than 21 years to run (s. 8 (1) *(a)*).

*(3) Where the reversionary title is not registered* and the land is *not* in a compulsory area then no leases can be registered unless they fall within the exceptions under the Land Registration Act 1966 allowing voluntary registration where deeds have been lost or destroyed in the war or where there are building estates or under the Housing Act 1980 on the grant of a long lease to a council house tenant.

(4) The following interests are incapable of substantive registration: an agreement for a lease (ss. 2 (1), 8 (1) *(b)*); a lease which contains an absolute prohibition against alienation *inter vivos* (s. 8 (2)); a lease granted for 21 years or less (ss. 19 (2), 22 (2)). Where a lease has been granted out of registered land for more than 21 years but at the time of the application to register it (as required by section 19 (2) or section 22 (2)) there are less than 21 years to run, the Registrar will, in his discretion, normally register it despite section 8 (1) *(a)* which provides that tenants may apply to register their leases where there are more than 21 years to run and which, apart from sections 19 (2) and 22 (2), might lead one to suppose that leases with not more than 21 years to run are not registrable. The strong wording of sections 19 (2) and 22 (2) must be taken to prevail over the weaker wording of section 8 (1)*(a)*: see Ruoff and Roper, p. 449 and Key and Elphinstone (15th ed.), p. 115.

## As Overriding Interests

If a lease has not been substantively registered, or a lease or an agreement for a lease is incapable of substantive registration, then, so long as it is not protected by some entry such as a notice on the register of the superior title, it may rank as an overriding interest if it falls within section 70 (1) *(g)*, "The rights of every person in actual occupation of the land or in receipt of the rents and profits thereof..." or section 70 (1) *(k)* "Leases for any term or interest not exceeding 21 years granted

at a rent without taking a fine." Paragraph *(k)* does not cover
agreements for leases *(City Permanent Building Society* v.
*Miller* [1952] Ch. 840) nor leases granted at a premium or for
no rent but it does cover terms commencing in the future, *e.g.* a
term of seven years to commence on the next quarter day.
Legal leases for a term not exceeding 21 years taking effect in
possession or within one year from the date thereof granted at a
rent without taking a fine, take effect as registered dispositions
immediately upon being granted: sections 18 (3), 19 (2), 21 (3),
22 (2). They take effect subject to minor interests then
protected on the register and to overriding interests then
subsisting: *Freer* v. *Unwins Ltd.* [1976].Ch.288.


## As Minor Interests

If a lease has not been substantively registered, or a lease or an
agreement for a lease is incapable of substantive registration,
then, it will be a minor interest capable of protection by entry
of a notice or a caution (s. 101 (2) (3)). However, it is only
where the term granted is not an overriding interest that
application may be made for entry of a notice under section 48
and, indeed, the Registrar can refuse to enter a notice on the
footing that the lease is of an obvious character: rule 199,
sections 19 (2) *(a)*, 22 (2)*(a)*. Thus, in practice, section 70 (1)
*(k)* leases are not protected by any entry on the register.
Essentially, it is only leases not exceeding 21 years where a fine
is taken or no rent is reserved and leases exceeding 21 years
where there is an absolute prohibition against *inter vivos*
dealings that are protected by notice as minor interests.


## Reform[2]

At present much unnecessary confusion is caused by the use of
"may" and "must" and by the differing periods of 21 and 40
years which, according to the circumstances, determine the
registrability of a lease: confusion is the worse confounded by
reference in some cases to terms "exceeding" 21 years and in
other cases to terms "not less than" 40 years. There seems no
reason why the period should not be the same in all cases and
why registration should not be compulsory in all such cases, the

dividing line between compulsorily registrable and
unregistrable leases being drawn at terms or unexpired terms
exceeding 21 years. The 21 year period was chosen, probably,
because of the old unregistered conveyancing practice of not
normally entering on the abstract of title leases of up to 21
years, but nowadays is 21 years not too lengthy a term? Would
14 or seven or three[3] years be better? After all, leases for terms
exceeding three years have to be created by deed under section
54 (2) of the Law of Property Act 1925 and the more the Land
Register accurately records the legal position the better.

However, the information on the Land Register needs to be
accurate and reliable and short leases are often varied or
terminated in an informal manner, in circumstances where it
would be unlikely that the Registrar would be informed. The
register would then be unreliable, necessitating further
enquiries by prospective purchasers, so that it would hardly be
worth the time, trouble and expense to record short leases.
More importantly, it is where there are short leases that it is
most likely that tenants will be without legal assistance and
will not know how to go about protecting their position—short
leases should thus always be capable of being overriding
interests.

In this respect, it should be borne in mind that another
reform should be to prevent interests that are capable of
substantive registration from having omnipotent effect as
overriding interests (see p. 109 infra). Accordingly, it would be
bad social policy to provide for substantive registration of all
terms exceeding three years. It might just be feasible to cover
all terms exceeding seven years though, here again it may be
that since such terms just escape sections 32 and 33 of the
Housing Act 1961 (which imposes repairing obligations upon
landlords who let dwellinghouses for terms of less than seven
years) there may be too many such terms entered into by
lessees without proper advice and also varied or terminated
informally. A social research project could be instituted and it
might well find that, where dwellinghouses are concerned, there
are many seven year terms but very few terms exceeding seven
years where the lessees have not been legally represented, so
that terms exceeding seven years could be made registrable. At
present it seems safest to suggest that the arbitrary line be

drawn at terms of 14 (or, perhaps, even 10) years. Leases granted for less than 14 (or 10) years would then rank as overriding interests within s. 70 (1) *(g)* or *(k)* so that there would be two classes of leases: registrable leases (those granted for 14 (or 10) years or more) and overriding interests (those granted for less than 14 (or 10) years).

Further reform of paragraph *(k)* could be suggested since, at present, it only covers leases for terms not exceeding 21 years "granted at a rent without taking a fine." It seems anomalous that leases granted at a premium are not included (even though they are rarely found due to inflation and taxation considerations) as neither are leases granted for no rent. Accordingly, the words "granted at a rent without taking a fine" could be repealed to advantage.

Paragraph *(k)* further covers leases, though not agreements for leases, that take effect either imediately or in in the future (see "term of years absolute" in s. 8 (1) *(a)* as defined by s. 3 (xxvii) to include reversionary leases) and even though the tenant is not in actual occupation. Significantly, section 18 (7) of the Land Transfer Act 1875 covered "leases and agreements for leases and other tenancies for any term not exceeding 21 years or for any less estate in cases where there is an occupation under such tenancies." The change caused by the Law of Property Act 1922, Sched. 16, para. 5 seems remarkable because it means that a purchaser will be bound by a tenant's interest even though the tenancy was neither entered on the register nor discoverable by inspection of the property. However, the position must also be considered from the tenant's point of view. Would not a tenant, who had informally entered into a monthly or yearly or three year tenancy, without any legal assistance, but who had not yet moved in, find it hard if his landlord had meanwhile sold the reversion so that a purchaser took free from the tenant's interest? Laws are made for ordinary people not people for laws and it would be ludicrous to expect such tenants to protect their interests by entering a notice on the register. Accordingly, it is necessary to incline the balance between tenants and purchasers in favour of tenants in this instance. This echoes the unregistered land position where tenants have legal interests that bind the whole world except where they are entitled only under an agreement for a lease (an equitable estate contract registrable under the Land Charges Act 1972) but, even then, if they are in occupation and paying rent they will have a legal periodic tenancy often protected under the Rent Acts or the Landlord and Tenant Act 1954, Pt. II.

Nevertheless, it still seems remarkable that, for example, a lease for 10 years or even 21 years, at present, to commence in five years' time can be an overriding interest within paragraph *(k)*. A purchaser is hardly likely to discover it from an inspection of the property! However, if the land were unregistered he would be bound by it as future or reversionary leases are legal interests (ss. 1 (1) and 205 (xxvii)). The social justification becomes apparent on considering a simple example. Someone could, without any formalities or legal assistance, easily take up a three year lease of a dwellinghouse for himself and his family to commence on the next quarter day (perhaps, meanwhile entering under a licence). If this did not constitute a legal lease then he could be evicted by a purchaser of the fee simple from the landlord before the term commenced, since, if his interest were merely equitable it would have been very unlikely that he would have taken the appropriate steps to protect his interest under the Land Charges Act.

However, what social justification is there where a company, well-stocked with legal advisers, decides to take over some shop or office or factory premises and negotiates a 10 year, or, at present, even at 21 year lease to commence in five or even 10 years' time.

There is thus a case for distinguishing the two situations and amending the principles affecting registered and unregistered land correspondingly. The difficulty lies in fixing upon some distinguishing factor. Should leases that are to commence in *over* one year's time not rank as overriding interests or legal interests[4] (*vis-à-vis* registered and unregistered land respectively) since it is unlikely that informal "family" leases would be created to take effect so much *in futuro?* Should leases of premises, other than dwellinghouses, that are to commence *in futuro* not rank as overriding interests or as legal interests? Some such distinction ought to be made as it is not fair to purchasers to tilt the balance in favour of tenants in those cases where tenants can reasonably be expected to look after their own interests by protecting them by a simple entry on a register. As between a purchaser who has done all that can reasonably be required of him and a "commercial" tenant who has done none of the things that can reasonably be required of him, surely the rights of the purchaser should prevail?

Finally, there seems no point in the provision in section 8(2) which makes inalienable leases incapable of substantive registration. Leases containing absolute prohibitions against alienation can always be alienated if the landlord waives the prohibition and will, without such waiver, be alienable if such prohibitions become to be construed as covenants against assignment without the landlord's consent, which could not be unreasonably withheld, as recommended by the Jenkins Committee on leaseholds.[5] Nothing would be lost if this exceptional provision in section 8 (2) were abolished so allowing inalienable leases to be registered.

## Notes

[1] F.R.R. Burford (1936) 1 Conv. (N.S.) 344.

[2] See generally Law Com. Published Working Paper No. 32.

[3] G. Dworkin (1961) 24 M.L.R. 135.

[4] It is significant that powers of disposition of a proprietor expressly include the power to grant "a lease [or underlease] for a term not exceeding 21 years to take effect *in possession or within one year from the date thereof* at a rent without taking a fine": ss. 18 (3), 21 (3). Unfortunately there is nothing to require such a qualification to be read into s. 70 (1) *(k)*.

[5] (1950) Cmd. 7982, paras. 309-311; Law Com. Published Working Paper No. 25, pp. 12-33; and see *Property & Bloodstock Ltd.* v. *Emerton* [1968] Ch. 94, 119-120 *per* Danckwerts L.J.

# CHAPTER 4

# GETTING ONTO THE REGISTER

ASSUMING we have a registrable interest in a compulsory area how do we register it and what happens if we fail to register it?

Well, we are not going to concern ourselves with the details of the matter as they can straightforwardly be obtained from Ruoff and Roper or from the smaller practice manuals[1] which set out the relevant application forms and the lists of supporting documents. It is important to take care to fill these forms in correctly because sloppy form filling may well lead the Registrar to doubt the reliability of the application cover and the statement that there are no doubts arising on the title and so to raise requisitions that complicate and prolong the application.

## *"On Sale"*

It should be noted that other than grants of terms of 40 years or more (or 21 years or more where the reversion is registered) it is only conveyances or assignments of registrable interests *on sale* that need to be registered though by section 123 (3) an exchange where equality money is paid is covered by this expression though not a bare exchange. The justification for these provisions is that it is only when land is sold for money or money's worth that a thorough investigation of title will take place. Thus a voluntary conveyance and a conveyance made in consideration of marriage are not covered. It is doubtful whether a conveyance in exchange for shares is a "conveyance on sale" in the ordinary sense of the Land Registration Act for though covered by special provisions in the 1891 Stamp Act there are no such special provisions in the Land Registration Act.[2]

In such a case it will be advisable to apply for registration *ex abundante cautela* and obtain a ruling: it is likely that registration will be granted as Ruoff and Roper makes clear at page 174 so that courts will probably never be afforded any opportunity for deciding the matter. Other problems arise on the meaning of "on sale" (*e.g.* where there are appropriations by personal representatives under section 41 of the Administration of Estates Act 1925) and, whilst the safest course is always to apply for registration when in doubt, it would be much better if the Act were amended to include a definition of "on sale."[3]

## Noting Subordinate Interests on Superior Title

If the registrable interest has been granted out of a superior registered title, as where a lease or rentcharge is granted out of a freehold or superior leasehold, then it is necessary to obtain not only substantive registration of the lease or rentcharge but also to have the subordinate interest noted on the Charges Register of the superior title if the lessee or chargee is to obtain a legal interest (ss. 19 (2) and 22 (2)). This is automatically done by the Registrar on receiving a duly made out application for registration.

At one time the Registrar insisted that the superior land certificate had to be lodged with the Registry for the application to be duly made, the laudable idea being that the land certificate could then be brought up to date so as accurately to reflect the true state of the superior title. This created difficulties in the case of leaseholds because, in the absence of express agreement a lessee has no right to call for his lessor's title and likewise has no right to call for his lessor's land certificate.[4] However, in *Strand Securities Ltd.* v. *Caswell* [1965] Ch. 958 the Court of Appeal held that the Registrar could not insist on production of the land certificate and that an application for first registration was complete without it. The Registrar's practice was based on a wide interpretation of section 64 construing register as the Land Register and not the individual register and the Court held, "We cannot allow the registrar by his practice to make bad law and it is bad law to insist on the lessee producing his landlord's land certificate—to which he has no right."[5]

Unfortunately, the decision can be explained on the narrow ground of the wording of section 64 (1) (*c*) which exempts lessees from producing the superior land certificate in the case of "the entry of a notice of a lease at a rent without taking a fine." Accordingly, following the strict letter of the decision, it remains the Registrar's practice (see Ruoff & Roper, p. 451) to demand production of the land certificate if the lease is at a premium instead of at a rent even though the lessee is still, in the absence of express agreement, not entitled to call for his landlord's land certificate.[6] However, if the landlord's land certificate ever happens to be lodged with the Land Registry then, unless the certificate has been lodged with written directions under rule 269 that it is to be held for a specified purpose only, the lodging can be used to make the lessee's application duly complete.[7] Thus in the case of registrable leases at a premium, which are far, far more common than registrable rack rent leases, the prospective lessee ought to have the lessor bound by contract to deposit his land certificate at the Registry for the specified purpose of enabling the lease to be completed by being noted on the superior title.

The position is, indeed, curious. The Act should be amended to make it clear that where a lessee has no right to call for his landlord's certificate and the landlord has, in fact, refused or failed to reply within one month to a written request of the lessee, sent by the recorded delivery service, for the land certificate to be lodged with the Registry, then, the Registrar must treat the application for registration as duly complete, having protected it by a caution as from its receipt: the onus on the lessee to try to obtain production of the certificate is to accord with the aim of having the certificate reflect the position as accurately as possible. The problem, however, solves itself if the proposals for public inspection of the Register are accepted as proposed in Chapter 2 so that a lessee may take the benefit of section 110.[8]

### Date of Registration

Since the legal estate is not transferred absolutely validly by the instrument of transfer but only by the statutory magic of registration (ss. 5, 9, 69) and an average interval of 64 working days (according to paragraph 25 of the Registrar's Report for 1979–80) elapses between the date of application for registration and the actual date of registration a transferee must be protected from any intermediate dealings with the land. Accordingly, rule 42 provides for registration (including noting of subordinate interests) to take effect as of the date of the delivery of the application to register, whilst rule 73 deals with another problem by providing that any dealings with the land which take place between the date of the conveyance, grant or assignment necessitating registration and the date of the application to register shall take effect as if they had taken place after the date of the application subject to section 123 (1) *infra.* Before being in a position to apply for first registration a contracting purchaser may protect himself by entry of a Class C (iv) land charge in the Land Charges Registry or by a caution against first registration at the Land Registry.

## *Section* 123 (1): *Effect of Failure to Register in Time*[9]

Section 123 provides that in compulsory areas "every conveyance on sale of freehold land and every grant of a term of years absolute not being less than 40 years . . . and every assignment on sale of leasehold land held for a term of years absolute having not less than 40 years to run . . . shall (save as hereinafter provided) on the expiration of two months from the date thereof or of any authorised extension of that period, *become void so far as regards the grant or conveyance of the legal estate* in the freehold or leasehold land . . . unless the grantee or his successor in title or assign has in the meantime applied to be registered as proprietor of such land." The saving clause in parentheses refers to provisions enabling the Registrar, on application showing sufficient cause, to extend the above period and providing for an appeal to the High Court in case of refusal by the Registrar. So far there have been no appeals because the Registrar "is always willing to make an order if some quite ordinary but reasonable excuse for the delay is put forward by the applicant's solicitors and the proper fee is paid."[10]

Since failure to register can affect derivative interests such as

charges or mortgages, rule 73 (2) authorises chargees or
mortgagees to lodge an application on behalf of the proper
applicant for the first registration of the estate. After all
chargees or mortgagees will have the applicant's title deeds and,
obviously for fear of losing priority, will not want to part with
the title deeds to allow an application by the borrower. Holders
of other derivative interests such as lessees who, as shown by
*British Maritime Trust Ltd.* v. *Upsons Ltd.* [1931] W.N. 7, can
be affected just as much are not so authorised because they
have no right in the absence of express agreement to call for
the proper applicant's title and, more importantly, have no
right to obtain the applicant's title deeds. In practice their safe
course is only to complete after the freehold or superior
leasehold has been registered. This course is not open to
chargees or mortgagees as their money is needed straight away
in order to effect the purchase of the registrable freehold or
leasehold in the first place and so rule 73 (2) is vitally
necessary in their case.

    Where there is failure to register the interest, then, the grant
or conveyance only becomes void so far as regards the grant or
conveyance of the *legal estate* so that it remains fully operative
for all other purposes. The avoidance of the legal estate is not
retrospective but only takes effect upon the expiration of the
two-month period: *British Maritime Trust Ltd.* v. *Upsons Ltd.*
[1931] W.N. 7. Surprisingly enough, the Act does not say what
is to happen to the legal estate after the purchaser has been
divested of it but it seems it must revest in the vendor who will
hold the legal estate as a bare trustee for the purchaser.
However, since the purchaser was for two months a purchaser
of a legal estate this suffices for making incumbrances not
registered under the Land Charges Act void against him as a
purchaser of a legal estate under section 13 (2) of the 1925 Act
or section 4 of the 1972 Act despite the contrary view in Ruoff
and Roper, p. 177. The reasoning is that incumbrances once
destroyed by the land falling into the hands of equity's darling
(a bona fide purchaser of a legal estate for value without
notice) are not revived when the land passes into the hands of
someone who is not equity's darling but for example a person
who has notice or is not a purchaser: *Wilkes* v. *Spooner* [1911]
2 K.B. 473. By analogy, incumbrances once destroyed for want

f registration are not revived unless some statute specifically so
provides (*cf. Hollington Brothers Ltd.* v. *Rhodes* [1951] 2 All
E.R. 578, 580, *Kitney* v. *M.E.P.C.* [1977] 1 W.L.R. 981). No
such provision is to be found in the Act or the Rules or
elsewhere.

Where a purchaser has been divested of the legal estate
under section 123 then he can always obtain the legal estate
from his vendor-trustee under the rule in *Saunders* v. *Vautier*
(1841) 4 Beav. 115 as being *sui juris* and solely entitled to the
whole beneficial interest in the property. A deed so vesting the
legal estate in the purchaser would itself fall within section 123
since subsection (3) thereof defines the expression "conveyance
on sale" as "an instrument made on sale by virtue whereof
there is conferred or completed a title under which an
application for registration may be made."

*Overlapping Relationship between* (1) *Section* 123 *and* (2)
*Sections* 19 *or* 22

Where the event which requires first registration is a lease
granted out of *registered* land then this is a registered
disposition within sections 19 and 22 which requires to be
completed by registration and noting on the superior registered
title in order for the legal estate to pass. There is no prescribed
time limit but the lessee only has a minor interest merely
taking effect in equity under section 101 until he registers his
title. However, where he is in actual occupation or in receipt of
rents, then he will have the complete protection of an
overriding interest within section 70 (1) (*g*). If the lease had
been granted out of *unregistered* land in a compulsory area
then section 123 would apply and the lessee would have his full
legal lease until the expiry of the statutory period after which
time, if he failed to register his title, he would have an
equitable lease ranking as an overriding interest within section
70 (1) (*g*) if he were in actual occupation or in receipt of rent,
or otherwise capable of protection under section 53 by a
caution against first registration.

Where the lease is granted out of registered land in a
compulsory area for a term of 40 years or more then it falls
within both section 123 and section 19 (if the registered land be

freehold) or section 22 (if the registered land be leasehold).
Which provisions apply, as differing results ensue as we have
seen above? Nothing can be found that specifically resolves the
conflict and an amendment to the Act is called for to do just
that. At present it seems the provisions in sections 19 or 22
should prevail (despite the contrary assumption in *British
Maritime Trust* v. *Upsons Ltd.* [1931] W.N. 7) since the grant
seems more appropriately treated as a registered disposition
(Key and Elphinstone (15th ed.), p. 115).[11] After all, where the
superior title has already been registed, making matters easier
for the grantee of the subordinate interest, there is not the
justification for affording the grantee the protection provided by
rule 73 to transactions within section 123 where there are
dealings with the land between the date of the grant and the
date of the application to register it.

*Land Charges Created in Instruments Requiring First
Registration*

Do land charges, such as restrictive covenants, created in
conveyances leading to first registration and affecting the estate
conveyed, need to be protected under the Land Charges Act,
since such land, prior to registration, is unregistered land and
protection by notice on the register of title, which will
ultimately occur, does not validate an otherwise void claim, as
where a land charge has become void against subsequent
purchasers for want of registration under the L.C.A. 1925 or
1972?

The answer for areas where registration is *compulsory* and
where the registrable instrument is executed on or after July
27, 1971, is now a categorical "No," owing to section 14 (3) of
the Land Charges Act 1972 (replacing s. 9 of the Land
Registration and Land Charges Act 1971). This is a very
useful reform saving solicitors the tedious exercise of registering
land charges for the short period before the title to the affected
land is registered.[12]

However, in *non-compulsory* areas, particularly in the case
of building estates for which voluntary registration of title is
still unrestricted, it is still necessary to register land charges
under the Land Charges Act to cover the period prior to

registration of the title to the affected land and thus obtain
validity for the land charge when it is protected by entry of a
notice on the register of title. To have provided otherwise for
non-compulsory areas would have been totally impractical and
inexpedient since there is obviously no guarantee that land in
such areas will be registered, and any proviso covering such
land if registered within x months of the creation of the land
charge would merely create more problems for purchasers and
also incumbrancers who, in any event, would register their
charges in case registration of the title to the land affected did
not occur within the prescribed period.

## The Effect of First Registration

The effect of first registration with absolute title of a freehold is
to vest in the proprietor "an estate in fee simple in possession"
(together with all appurtenant rights) subject to charges and
minor interests protected on the register and subject to
overriding interests, though if the proprietor is a trustee
nothing is to relieve him from his obligations in respect of his
beneficiaries' minor interests: otherwise, the proprietor's estate
is "free from all other estates and interests whatsoever" (s. 5).[13]
Section 69 (1), a general provision headed, "The effect of
registration on the legal estate," provides that the registered
proprietor is to "be deemed to have vested in him the legal
estate in fee simple in possession."

It is odd that nowhere is the obvious expressly stated *viz.*
that the equitable estate is also vested in the registered
proprietor, though the "everything but" approach of section 5
suggests that the legal and equitable estate in fee simple is
meant to be vested in the proprietor.[14]

Normally, of course, the conveyance on sale leading to first
registration will, indeed, pass the legal and equitable estate to
the purchaser, so that on registering himself as proprietor there
will be no need for any statutory provision to shift it to him.
But what if the conveyance were void for forgery or the vendor
had no title at all to the land, having already conveyed the land
to someone previously before the area was one of compulsory
registration?

Unless section 5 implicitly shifts the equitable estate as well as the legal estate to the purchaser the equitable estate remains in the victim, "V," of the forgery or of the double conveyancing. V will then not merely have a statutory claim to rectification but will have a full equitable interest entitling him to have the proprietor transfer the legal estate to him under the rule in *Saunders* v. *Vautier* (1841) Cr. & Ph. 240 and thereby preventing the proprietor claiming any indemnity, the proprietor's loss arising from his own act in having to comply with V's request rather than from any rectification of the register. It may, however, be that if the proprietor refuses to comply with the request so that he is taken to court then the court might have power of its own motion to order rectification of the register under section 82 (1) (*a*) so as to preserve the proprietor's claim to an indemnity: see p. 178, *infra*. If the equitable estate remains in V then it may be an overriding interest within section 70 (1) (*g*) and as such a very powerful ground for rectification not only against a first registered proprietor but even against subsequent registered proprietors in possession. If the proprietor contracts to sell the land in which V's equitable estate remains together with the adjacent land of the proprietor then V may be able to compel the proprietor as his trustee to go ahead and complete the sale, even if for special reasons personal to the proprietor the proprietor wishes lawfully or unlawfully to resile from the contract.[15]

All in all, the arguments in favour of section 5 carrying the legal and equitable estate, illuminated by the disadvantages of a contrary conclusion indicate that the legal and equitable estate must be vested in the first registered proprietor by section 5. Unfortunately, there are judicial dicta to the contrary, Templeman J. in *Epps* v. *Esso Petroleum Ltd.* [1973] 1 W.L.R. 1071 indicating at pp. 1075 and 1078, without giving any reasons, that he assumed that section 5 only passed the legal estate, the victim of the forgery or double conveyancing retaining the equitable interest. He had not the benefit of *Re Suarez (No. 2)* [1924] Ch. 19 being cited to him. Romer J. there held that the first registered proprietor was *beneficially* entitled to the property free from the Crown's interest, under the doctrine of escheat, arising upon the death intestate without heirs of the registered proprietor's predecessor in title.

## Notes

[1] *e.g.* Ruoff's *Concise Land Registration Practice* and Wontner's *Land Registry Practice.*

[2] Farrand, p. 14.

[3] As indicated by Emmet, p. 638.

[4] Law of Property Act 1925, s. 44 and s. 110 of the Act.

[5] [1965] Ch. 958, 977.*Cf.* sub-lessees of unregistered land who are entitled to see the lease out of which the sub-lease is derived.

[6] (1965) 62 L.S.Gaz. 507; [1965] Ch. 958, 991 reporting a Land Registry letter read out before the Appellate Committee of the House of Lords.

[7] *Strand Securities Ltd.* v. *Caswell* [1965] Ch. 958.

[8] Further see Law Com. Working Paper No. 67, paras. 89–97 and p. 157, *infra.*

[9] See generally D. G. Barnsley (1968) 32 Conv.(N.S.) 391, though parts are too alarmist: see previous ed., pp. 83–84, Farrand, p. 140.

[10] Ruoff and Roper, p. 179. Query whether progressively increasing penalties should be provided for as in Kenya Registered Land Act, s. 40.

[11] Also Practice Note 24, Ruoff and Roper, p. 448.

[12] (1971) 12 N.L.J. 215; (1971) 35 Conv.(N.S.) 398. S. 14 (3) only applies where an instrument conveys, grants or assigns an estate in land *and* creates a land charge affecting that estate. Thus, estate contracts require protection by a Class C (iv) land charge entry or a caution against first registration.

[13] S. 9 is the corresponding provision for leaseholds.

[14] See S. Palk (1974) 38 Conv.(N.S.) 236. For subsequent transfers of registered land ss. 20 (1) and 23 (1) make it clear that the transfer operates as if the transferor or grantor were entitled to the registered land for his own benefit.

[15] Presumably, if the proprietor contracts to sell the land, in respect of which V has either an equitable interest or merely a claim to rectification, the purchaser on discovering the position will not be able successfully to object to the title *if* the proprietor can show that he has V's concurrence which he can compel as where V requests the sale: *cf. Re Baker and Selmon's Contract* [1907] 1 Ch. 238.

CHAPTER 5

## THE SYSTEM IN OPERATION

FORM-FILLING is the most obvious characteristic of the system in
operation. Rule 74 requires that the forms scheduled to the
rules have to be used in all matters to which they refer or are
capable of being applied or adapted with such alterations and
additions, if any, as are necessary or desired and the Registrar
allows. Where no form is prescribed or a form cannot
conveniently be adapted then the instrument has to be in such
form as the Registrar directs or allows. By analogy with the
official models the instrument, in fact, will need to be short
and, normally, must not refer to trusts or to extraneous
documents. Helpful precedents are to be found in Ruoff's *Land
Registration Forms*, Hallett's *Conveyancing Precedents*, Key
and Elphinstone's *Precedents*, Vol. III and the *Encyclopedia of
Forms and Precedents*, Vols. 17 and 19. Unfortunately leases
and sub-leases are as long and complicated as in unregistered
conveyancing.

It is vital to ensure that all instruments are proper in form
and substance for otherwise the Registrar has power by rules
78 and 317 to reject the instrument though he has broad
discretionary powers to accept applications that are
substantially in order: *Smith* v. *Morrison* [1974] 1 W.L.R. 659.
Under the Land Registration (Official Searches) Rules 1978, r.
5 there is no longer the danger of losing the priority afforded
by an official search certificate if the application is not delivered
in order within the priority period, so long as the application is
eventually completed by registration, having been delivered not
in order but within the priority period.

The function of all this form-filling, of course, is to carry out
transactions on the register whenever that is possible as this is
fundamental to the whole system. In this respect section 39

provides that where any transaction relating exclusively to
registered land or to a registered charge is capable of being
effected and is effected by a registered disposition then, subject
to prescribed exceptions (r. 96), any deed or instrument, other
than the registered disposition, which is executed by the
proprietor for the purpose of giving effect to the transaction
shall be void, but only so far as the transaction is carried out by
the registered disposition. Moreover, section 109 provides that
dispositions authorised by the Act "shall be effected under and
in the manner required . . . and when so required shall be
registered or protected as provided by this Act or the Rules."
Sanctions, however, lie elsewhere in the Act *e.g.* ss. 101, 123
(see F. W. Taylor )1951) 15 Conv.(N.S.) 428).

In order to see how the system of registration works in
practice let us take a look at one particular title showing
various types of entries in the register which are, of course,
fictitious.

Let us begin with 14 Langley Lane of which John and Jane
Thomas were registered as proprietors with absolute title on
February 16, 1956. The Title on the Register would have
looked as follows and a Land Certificate containing the
following entries would have been issued, though kept in the
Registry in view of the Registered Charge appearing below. A
detailed plan would also be filed at the Registry and be
reproduced in the Land Certificate.

---

### H.M. LAND REGISTRY

| Edition 1 | Title number RU 009818 |
|---|---|
| Opened 16.2.1956 | This register consists of three pages |

---

#### A. *Property Register*

containing the description of the registered land and
the estate comprised in the Title.

---

ADMINISTRATIVE AREA          PARISH or PLACE

(County, County Borough etc.)

Ruinshire                                    Pseudostock

THE Freehold land shown and edged with red on the plan of the above Title filed at the Registry registered on 16 February 1956 known as 14 Langley Lane

*Note*: A Conveyance of 12 Langley Lane (edged and numbered RU 0000816 in green on the filed plan) dated 22nd July 1949 and made between (1) Arthur Jones and (2) Joseph Brown contains the following exception for the benefit of the land edged red on the filed plan:

"Excepting and reserving to the vendor and the owner or owners for the time being of 14 Langley Lane the full and free and uninterrupted running and passages of water oil gas and electricity in and through the pipes drains wires and cables now upon under in over or across the property hereby conveyed or any part thereof to and from the adjoining and neighbouring properties with right of entry upon the said property hereby conveyed for the purpose of maintaining repairing cleansing and removing such pipes drains wires and cables as and when the occasion may require doing thereby no unnecessary damage and making good all damage thereby occasioned"

---

*[Blank space for further entries]*

---

*B. Proprietorship Register*

stating nature of the Title name address and description of the proprietor of the land and any entries affecting the right of disposal thereof.

Title absolute

---

| Entry number | Proprietor etc. | Remarks |
|---|---|---|
| 1. | JOHN THOMAS, Engineer, | Price paid £6,500 |

| | | |
|---|---|---|
| | and JANE THOMAS, his wife both of 8 Ruddigore Road Swanton Blankshire registered on 16 February 1956 | |
| 2. | RESTRICTION registered on 16 February 1956: No disposition by one proprietor of the land (being the survivor of joint proprietors and not being a trust corporation) under which any capital money arises is to be registered except on an order of the Registrar or of the Court | |
| 3. | CAUTION in favour of Property Magnates Limited of 7 Smooth Mansions, Utopia, Blankshire registered on 24 August 1963 | 2345/63 |

*[Blank space for further entries]*

*C. Charges Register*

containing charges, incumbrances etc. adversely affecting the land and registered dealings therewith

| Entry number | The date at the beginning of each entry is the date on which the entry was made on this edition of the register | Remarks |
|---|---|---|
| 1. | 16 February 1956—A Conveyance of the land in this title dated 28 January 1956 | |

and made between (1) Arthur Jones (Vendor) and (2) John Thomas and Jane Thomas (Purchasers) contains the following convenants:

"The Purchasers hereby jointly and severally covenant with the Vendor to the intent that the burden of this covenant may run with and bind the land hereby conveyed and every part thereof and to the intent that the benefit thereof may be annexed to and run with each and every part of the Vendor's adjoining properties known as 16 and 18 Langley Lane aforesaid To observe and perform the stipulations contained in the First Schedule hereto

THE SCHEDULE before referred to

1. No further buildings shall be erected on the said land

2. No alterations or additions to the present building shall be made except in accordance with plans and specifications to be approved by the Vendor or his architect at the expense of the Purchasers or their successors in title

3. Not at any time to carry on or suffer to be carried on the said land or any part thereof any trade or business whatsoever or permit the same to be used for any purpose other than as a private

dwellinghouse and private garage in connection therewith and not to allow any portion of the property to be used for the purpose of advertising and not to do or permit or suffer to be done anything upon the land which may be or become a nuisance or annoyance to the adjoining houses or to the neighbourhood

4. The garden ground of the dwellinghouse shall at all times be kept and maintained in a neat and proper order and condition as flower or ornamental gardens and shall not be converted to any other use whatsoever

| | |
|---|---|
| 2. | 16 February 1956—CHARGE dated 28 January 1956 registered on 16 February 1956 to secure the moneys therein mentioned |
| 3. | PROPRIETOR: THE HOME-PROVIDER BUILDING SOCIETY of 6 Happy Lane Happyshire registered on 16 February 1956 |

[*Blank space for further entries*]

Any entries struck through in red are no longer subsisting

If the reader plays detective the significance of the entries will soon become apparent, except for the caution, the significance of which will appear on looking at the following transfer of the property (as *per* Form 19 in the schedule to the rules, except in the imposition of covenants for title):

---

## H.M. LAND REGISTRY
## LAND REGISTRATION ACTS 1925–1936
## TRANSFER OF WHOLE

District                 —Ruinshire
Title Number       —RU 009818
Property             —14 Langley Lane,
                          Pseudostock
Date                    —13 July 1964

1. In consideration of Seven Thousand Six Hundred Pounds (£7600) (the receipt whereof is hereby acknowledged) We JOHN THOMAS, ENGINEER and JANE THOMAS, HOUSEWIFE formerly of 14 LANGLEY LANE PSEUDOSTOCK RUINSHIRE but now of 8 HIGH ROAD MORRISTON MORESHIRE as Beneficial Owners hereby transfer to PROPERTY MAGNATES LIMITED of 7 SMOOTH MANSIONS UTOPIA BLANKSHIRE the land comprised in the title above mentioned

2. PROVIDED always and it is hereby declared that the covenants which are to be implied by reason of the said John and Jane Thomas hereby being expressed to grant as Beneficial Owners shall be in the terms set out in Part I of the Second Schedule to the Law of Property Act 1925 and shall extend to any liabilities rights and interests affecting the land hereby transferred which rank as overriding interests under the provisions of the Land Registration Act 1925 or any subsequent Act and of which prior to completion of this transfer the said Property Magnates Limited had no notice under the equitable doctrine of actual constructive or imputed notice as set out in section 199 (1) (ii) of the Law of Property Act 1925.

3. The said Property Magnates Limited with the object
   and intent of affording to the said John and Jane
   Thomas a full and sufficient indemnity in respect of
   the covenants and provisions referred to in entry no.
   1 of the Charges Register of the title above referred
   to but not further or otherwise hereby covenants
   with the said John and Jane Thomas and each of
   them and their and each of their representatives that
   it will at all times hereafter observe and perform the
   said covenants and provisions so far as they relate to
   the land hereby transferred and are now subsisting
   and capable of being enforced and will at all times
   keep the said John and Jane Thomas and each of
   them and their and each of their representatives
   effectually indemnified against all actions proceedings costs charges claims and demands whatsoever in
   respect thereof

[*Executed by all parties and attested*]

This transfer would have followed upon a fairly simple
contract for the sale of "the property comprised in title no. RU
009818 and known as 14 Langley Lane Pseudostock
Ruinshire." The contract would have expressly provided for the
vendors to sell as beneficial owners and not as trustees (for
sale), for an indemnity covenant to be entered into by the
purchaser (see *Cator* v. *Newton* [1940] 1 K.B. 415) and for the
cover given by the implied covenants to be extended to cover
overriding interests of which the purchaser had no notice.

As the need for such extended cover is doubted in many
quarters[1] and most cases on covenants for title have arisen out
of defects of title concerned with interests that are overriding
interests in registered conveyancing[2] it is worthwhile here to
have a short excursus on implied covenants in registered
conveyancing contrasting the position with unregistered
conveyancing.

In unregistered conveyancing section 76 (1) of the L.P.A.
1925 implies certain qualified covenants (*e.g.* full power to
convey, quiet enjoyment, freedom from incumbrances other

than those to which the conveyance is expressly made subject, and further assurance) where a vendor "conveys and is expressed to convey as beneficial owner." There is controversy as to whether the clause requires a vendor actually to have the capacity in which he is expressed to convey or whether the clause should be construed as "purports to convey and does expressly convey as beneficial owner."[3] To be on the safe side co-owners who are trustees for sale and wish to make title not "as trustees" but "as beneficial owners" should expressly incorporate the implied covenants set out in Part I of the Second Schedule to the L.P.A. 1925.

A vendor is liable on the implied covenants if there are incumbrances or defects on the title where the conveyance to the purchaser was not *expressly* made subject to those incumbrances or defects and despite the fact that the purchaser may, after but not before the contract, have known of such incumbrances or defects *e.g.* where they appear in the recitals on the conveyance: *Page* v. *Midland Rly.* [1894] 1 Ch. 11; *G.W.R.* v. *Fisher* [1905] 1 Ch. 316. A purchaser is entitled to assume that he is to have what is expressly conveyed to him pursuant to contract and that the vendor must somehow have cleared up the defects or is prepared, by giving an unqualified covenant, to guarantee the purchaser against the risk of defects materialising and causing damage. However, a vendor will not be liable on the covenants, since they are implied only "as far as regards the subject matter . . . expressed to be conveyed" (L.P.A., s. 76 (1)), where he conveys only such title as he has, *e.g.* "all the estate term and interest if any" or conveys without using words of limitation when the conveyance operates to pass only "the fee simple or *other* the whole interest which the grantor had power to convey in such land" (L.P.A., s. 60 (1)): *May* v. *Platt* [1900] 1 Ch. 616; *Stait* v. *Fenner* [1912] 2 Ch. 504; *George Wimpey & Co.* v. *Sohn* [1967] Ch. 687. The position is as if I say, "I'll sell to you for £1 whatever I've got in my closed hand", you give me the £1 and I open my hand to drop a dead worm into your palm. You cannot complain that I have not conveyed what I agreed to convey since you have received exactly what I said I was going to convey.

In registered conveyancing section 38 (2) and rules 76 and 77 import the covenants implied under the L.P.A. in

unregistered conveyancing,[4] though without facing up to the
special hiatus between execution of the transfer and actual
registration in registered conveyancing. You may wonder why
it is necessary to imply any covenants where land registered
with absolute title is concerned in view of the state guarantee
given to such titles. Because of this, section 16 (3) of the Land
Transfer Act 1897 (now repealed) did not require a vendor
with absolute title to enter into covenants for title and, indeed,
after 1925 this view is reflected by Brickdale and Stewart-
Wallace, p. 257. However, the state guarantee does not extend
to overriding interests since every registered title is *ipso facto*
always subject to such interests (ss. 5, 9, 20, 23, *Re Chowood*
[1933] Ch. 574) so the covenants for title are, indeed, most
necessary to afford protection against overriding interests
(recognised in Ruoff and Roper, pp. 289–290 and
*Encyclopaedia of Forms and Precedents*, Vol. 18, p. 313).

   Because it was felt wrong for a purchaser who had notice of
an overriding interest to have an action against his vendor in
respect of it under the covenants for title, rule 77 (1) (*b*)
provided that the covenants shall "take effect as though the
disposition was expressly made subject to . . . any overriding
interests of which the purchaser has notice and subject to which
it would have taken effect, had the land been unregistered."
This can be compared with the position in unregistered
conveyancing that a purchaser who at the time of the contract
had actual or constructive notice of a patent defect or actual
notice of a latent irremovable defect cannot sue for damages or
refuse to complete (*Ellis* v. *Rogers* (1885) 29 Ch.D. 661;
*Timmins* v. *Moreland Street Property Co. Ltd.* [1958] Ch. 110)
unless the contract expressly provided for sale of a good
marketable title or an unencumbered freehold interest (*Cato* v.
*Thompson* (1882) 9 Q.B.D. 616). Rule 77 was drafted at a
time when it was thought[5] (mistakenly as subsequent necessary
practice has shown[6]) that sales of registered land would often
occur without any formal contract preceding the transfer and
that such a rule was necessary to deal with such a situation: if
in the pre-transfer negotiations a purchaser came to know of an
incumbrance amounting to an overriding interest then he
should not be able after the transfer to have an action on the
covenants for title against his vendor.[7]

Anyhow, rule 77 (1) makes it beyond dispute, as accepted in *Hissett* v. *Reading Roof Co.* [1969] 1 W.L.R. 1757, that a vendor cannot be liable on the implied covenants in respect of overriding interests of which the purchaser had notice, since the disposition is deemed to be expressly subject to such interests. Notice normally has nothing to do with overriding interests as is shown in Chapter 6 but the concept has a pragmatic purpose here. Since overriding interests are supposed to approximate to patent defects it seems probable that notice covers actual or constructive notice of the purchaser or his agents (*cf.* L.P.A., s. 199 (1) (ii)).

By way of contrast with rule 77 (1) it would clearly seem that a vendor *can* be liable on the implied covenants in respect of overriding interests of which the purchaser had *no* notice and this is the view taken by Ruoff and Roper, p. 290, Key and Elphinstone (15th ed.), p. 128, Hallett's *Conveyancing Precedents*, p. 1248, and the Law Commission Published Working Paper No. 37, pp. 16–18. However, with respect, this view is too superficial as made clear by Professor Potter in (1942) 58 L.Q.R. 356, Professor Farrand in *Contract and Conveyance*, pp. 271–272 and *Emmet on, Title* (16th ed.), pp. 472–473. The covenants for title are only implied "as far as regards the subject-matter . . . expressed to be conveyed." In a transfer of—and a contract for the transfer of—registered land, all that is expressed to be conveyed or contracted for is "the land in the title above mentioned" (or some other very similar wording). The land in the title is in the case of a fee simple absolute, the fee simple absolute subject (1) to the incumbrances and other entries on the register and (2) to such overriding interests as may affect the land (ss. 5, 20 (1)). This is what the vendor is registered with and he is conveying whatever he is registered with. The position is analogous to the unregistered conveyancing position where the vendor is only conveying such title as he has (*May* v. *Platt* [1900] 1 Ch. 616). The purchaser cannot complain if he gets the land subject to some overriding interests of which he had no notice since he has got all that was supposed to be conveyed to him. As Russell L.J. said in *George Wimpey* v. *Sohn* [1967] Ch. 487, 509, "An obligation to convey only such title as the vendors have avoids covenants for title" and that is the obligation of a vendor of registered land conveying "the land in the title above mentioned."

Accordingly, for a purchaser to obtain full protection the contract should provide for an express extension of the implied covenants for title and the transfer should incorporate this extension: (1961) 105 S.J. 985. In practice where it is a seller's market, as will usually be the case, it will be unlikely that the vendor will agree to such an extension. To protect himself the purchaser before entering the contract will have to do his utmost on the lines suggested in Chapter 6 (*infra*) to discover all possible overriding interests. He may also be able to take advantage of other terms in the contract which do not merge in the conveyance or transfer[8] if the overriding interest amounts to a breach of such a term *e.g.* for vacant possession as in *Hissett v. Reading Roof Co.* [1969] 1 W.L.R. 1757 or to proceed under the Misrepresentation Act 1967.

To return to our specific transfer to Property Magnates Limited this company will need to register the transfer in the Land Registry in order to become registered proprietor. Until this is done John and Jane Thomas remain the legal owners by virtue of section 19 (1). Since Property Magnates Limited is a company and since the chargees, The Home-provider Building Society, have been paid off by John and Jane Thomas the following changes will occur in the Register upon registration:

(a) All three entries in the Proprietorship Register will be struck through in red and replaced by:

---

4. PROPERTY MAGNATES LIMITED of 7 Smooth Mansions, Utopia, Blankshire registered on 3rd August 1964          Price paid £7,600.[9]

---

5. RESTRICTION registered on 3rd August 1965: Except under an order of the registrar no charge by the proprietor of the land is to be registered unless a certificate signed by the secretary, the solicitor or director thereof has been furnished that such charge does not contravene any of the provisions of the memorandum and articles of the said proprietor.

---

(b) Entries 2 and 3 in the Charges Register will be struck
through in red.

As can be seen, after various dispositions of the land have
been made over a period of time the register will become
cluttered up with many old entries that have been struck
through. Accordingly, when the Registrar considers it
practicable and desirable he will clear the register by closing it
and making a new edition containing the subsisting entries only
(r. 17). The old land certificate will be called in by the
Registry, if not already in the Registry for giving effect to a
disposition, and a new land certificate issued.

Property Magnates Ltd. then granted a lease of the property
to John Jackson for 22 years from September 1, 1964. This, as
a disposition of a registered proprietor, needs to be completed
by registration and by being noted on the Charges Register of
the registered freehold (s. 19). Accordingly, there will be an
additional entry on the Charges Register as follows:

---

4. 10 September 1964—LEASE dated 1 September
1964 to John Jackson for 22 years from 1st September 1964 at the rent of £480. Registered under Title
number RU 087321.

---

John Jackson's title will be registered as follows:

---

### H.M. LAND REGISTRY

Edition 1              Title number RU 087321
Opened 10.9.1964    This register consists of two pages

---

#### A. Property Register

ADMINISTRATIVE AREA              PARISH or PLACE
(County, County Borough etc.)
   Ruinshire                                      Pseudostock
   The Leasehold land shown and edged red on the plan
of the above Title filed at the Registry registered on
10 September 1964.

*Short Description*

14 Langley Lane
SHORT PARTICULARS OF LEASE UNDER
WHICH THE LAND IS HELD
(The word lease includes a sub-lease)

| Date | Parties | Term | | Rent |
|------|---------|------|------|------|
| | | Years | From | |
| 1.9.1964 | 1. Property Magnates Ltd. | 22 | 1.9.1964 | £480 |
| | 2. John Jackson | | PREMIUM | |
| | | | | Nil |

*Note* 1: The lease contains a prohibition against alienation without licence during the last seven years of the term and all estates rights interests powers and remedies under the lease at any time arising upon or by reason of such alienation are excepted from the effect of registration.

*Note* 2: Lessor's Title registered under RU 009818.

The Proprietorship Register would then merely state that Title was Absolute and John Jackson was the proprietor and the Charges Register would contain details of the restrictive covenants entered against the freehold absolute title (Ruoff & Roper, p.444). It can be seen that it would still be vital for a purchaser from John Jackson to see the lease (which John Jackson would have in his possession) to obtain full particulars of the various rights and obligations.

In April 1968 Bronco Bank Ltd., the bankers to Property Magnates Ltd., demanded more security to cover the company's overdraft. Property Magnates Ltd. accordingly created an equitable mortgage by deposit which was protected by an entry on the Charges Register of Property Magnates Ltd.'s freehold title as follows:

> 5. 30 April 1968—NOTICE of Deposit of Land
> Certificate with Bronco Bank Ltd. of 6 Greenhorn
> Street Utopia Blankshire registered 30 April 1968.

By virtue of rule 239 (4) such a notice operates as a caution under section 54 and there we will leave the title to 14 Langley Lane.

It may appear that registered conveyancing is relatively simple and straightforward and whilst it is generally true to say that it is more simple and straightforward than unregistered conveyancing there are, unfortunately as we shall see, one or two traps for the unwary, bemused by all the form-filling necessary in registered conveyancing, and some difficulties that would not arise in the case of unregistered conveyancing.[10] There is the same underlying substantive law added to which there are the many and complex technical provisions in the Act and the Rules that though intended to provide a simple system do not always do so. Moreover, secreted in the interstices of the new procedures provided for by the Act and the Rules there is in fact some new substantive law. Conveyancing law is thus still fairly complex and must remain so while land continues to serve the multifarious economic and social purposes for which it now provides. However, as we shall increasingly see it need not be so complex as it is at present.

One thing however is clear. Once land has been registered, then conveyancing costs are usually cheaper though sometimes there is little difference: *Property & Reversionary Co. Ltd.* v. *Secretary of State for the Environment* [1975] 1 W.L.R. 1504, *Which?*, June 1975, pp. 164–165.

## Notes

[1] Ruoff and Roper, p. 314; Key and Elphinstone (15th ed.), p. 128; Hallett's *Conveyancing Precedents*, p. 124; Law Com. Published Working Paper No. 37, pp. 16–18.

[2] *Eastwood* v. *Ashton* [1915] A.C. 900 (squatter's rights—s. 70 (1) (*f*)); *Stoney* v. *Eastbourne R.D.C.* [1927] 1 Ch. 367 (public right of way—s. 70 (1) (*a*));

*Chivers & Sons Ltd.* v. *Air Ministry*[1955] Ch. 585 (chancel repairs—s. 70 (1) (c)).

[3] The better view is that the nature of the vendor's actual interest is immaterial: Megarry and Wade, p. 603, Farrand, p. 263, *David* v. *Sabin* [1893] 1 Ch. 523, *Re Ray* [1896] 1 Ch. 468, *Parker* v. *Judkin* [1931] 1 Ch. 475, *Eastwood* v. *Ashton* [1915] A.C. 900, *Butler* v. *Broadhead* [1975] Ch. 97. Contrast *Fay* v. *Miller, Wilkins & Co. [1941] Ch. 360, Pilkington* v. *Wood* [1953] Ch. 770, *Re Robertson's Application* [1969] 1 W.L.R. 109.

[4] Not very clearly (Farrand, p. 269) but a court could hardly be expected to hold otherwise.

[5] Brickdale and Stewart-Wallace, p. 28.

[6] Farrand, pp. 144–145

[7] There is thus a clear distinction between registered and unregistered conveyancing where after contract but before completion a purchaser obtains notice of an interest within the class of overriding interests. Can this be justified?

[8] Query whether merger may not occur until registration of the transfer: *cf. Montgomery* v. *Continental Bags (N.Z.) Ltd.* [1972] N.Z.L.R. 884.

[9] Since November 1, 1976, the price paid for, or value of, registered land has only been entered on the register where the registered proprietor has made a specific request (S.I. 1976 No. 1332).

[10] *e.g.* in *Hodgson* v. *Marks* [1971] Ch. 892 the transfer by the plaintiff to the vendor was expressed to be in consideration of love and affection. If this had been a conveyance of unregistered land this would have estopped the plaintiff from setting up an undisclosed trust against a subsequent purchaser: *Re King's Settlement* [1931] 2 Ch. 294. As the transfer of the registered land was no part of the title and thus was not seen by the defendant no estoppel arose. See also *London & Cheshire Insurance Co.* v. *Laplagrene* [1971] Ch. 499 indicating that even the defendant's sight of the transfer form would not have absolved him from his duty of inquiry under s. 70 (1) (g) so that no estoppel would have arisen in the absence of erroneous answers by the plaintiff occupier.

CHAPTER 6

## OVERRIDING INTERESTS

OVERRIDING interests, since they comprise a miscellaneous category of interests that do not appear on the register of title, provide a cavernous crack in the fundamental mirror principle under which the register is supposed to reflect accurately and irrefutably the current facts material to a particular title. This crack did not arise through accident or mistake but was deliberate as is made clear by paragraph 63 of the Royal Commission Report in 1857 upon whose recommendations registration of title was introduced:

> "The register will be a substitute for the documentary or parchment title. But the registered ownership . . . will remain subject, as the fee simple now is, . . . to such other rights as are not usually included in the abstract of title. . . . These are rights which are commonly evidenced by known usage or continued enjoyment or may be ascertained on the spot by inspection or inquiry; and the title to them is generally so independent of the documentary title to the property that they will necessarily form a partial exception to that which will constitute the registered ownership."

As Cross J. pointed out in *National Provincial Bank Ltd.* v. *Hastings Car Mart Ltd.* [1964] Ch. 9, 15, "As to such [rights] persons dealing with registered land must obtain information outside the register in the same manner and from the same sources as people dealing with unregistered land would obtain it."

It does, however, appear that the crack was not intended to be as cavernous as recent decisions have shown it to be, so that more inquiries are needed in respect of registered land than in the case of unregistered land. Moreover, there is still uncertainty over the types of interest that are capable of being overriding interests. It really is a most surprising and disconcerting state of affairs to find that overriding interests are not narrowly and exactly defined but constitute a broad uncertain category of interests for as Sir John Stewart-Wallace, a former Chief Land Registrar, wrote:

> 'Clearly such overriding interests are a stumbling block on the registration ot title. They may, perhaps, be described as *the* stumbling block. What purchasers want is that there should be a register to which they can look for proof of title and that they should have to look nowhere else. Any exception to the principle that they take free from anything not specifically set out on the register renders it useless over the field to which the exception extends. Absolute title becomes something of a misnomer."[1]

The position becomes even more surprising when it is realised that not only do overriding interests provide an exception to the mirror principle but they also provide an exception to the principle of no rectification against a proprietor in possession and to the principle of no rectification without indemnity. The theory is that since a registered proprietor holds his property subject to overriding interests in any event, he suffers no loss through the rectification: *Re Chowood's Registered Land* [1933] Ch. 574. A purchaser may thus find that, even though he has been registered as proprietor, he is bound by an overriding interest which he could not reasonably be expected to have discovered, that the register can be rectified against him so as to give effect to the overriding interest, that he cannot obtain any indemnity by way of compensation from the funds provided by Parliament for this purpose, and that he probably cannot, as shown in Chapter 5, obtain any damages from his vendor under the covenants for title or at all.

Most surprising is the overlap of overriding interests with registrable interests, with easements and profits registered in the property register of the dominant land and noted in the charges register of the servient land, and with minor interests. Thus any registrable interest may, until it is registered, rank as an overriding interest if its owner is in actual occupation of the land since "the rights of every person in actual occupation of the land" can constitute overriding interests within section 70(1) (*g*). Interests that would normally be minor interests, and, as such, requiring protection by notices, cautions or restrictions, can rank as overriding interests *e.g.* actual occupiers' options to purchase freehold reversions [2] or liens for unpaid purchase moneys [3] or rights under a bare trust or a trust for sale.[4] It is not beyond doubt whether easements not properly registered and noted under sections 19 (2) and 22 (2) may rank as overriding interests within section 70 (1) (*a*) *infra*.

It is, however, fundamental to appreciate that once an interest capable of ranking as an overriding interest appears on the register in any way it then *ipso facto* ceases to be an overriding interest for by section 3 (xvi) overriding interests mean "interests . . . *not entered* on the register but . . ." A conundrum arises if the interest is protected by a caution, so ceasing to be overriding and becoming a minor interest, and the caution is then "warned off." Then "upon the caution so ceasing the registered land may be dealt with in the same manner as if no caution had been lodged" (s. 55 (1)). If no caution had been lodged then the interest would have been an overriding interest and all dispositions would have been subject to it! It would be remarkable is this logic prevailed so it is to be hoped that "the interpretation of the Act as a whole or the doctrine of estoppel would prevent the incumbrancer then claiming an overriding interest."[5]

A final surprising defect in the legislation is the failure to make clear the connection between the scheme of overriding interests and general land law principles, relating to the distinction between legal and equitable interests, the relevance of the doctrine of notice and the nature of "rights" within section 70 (1) (*g*).[6] This creates many problems as we shall see if we proceed to examine the statutory provisions dealing with overriding interests.

### LIST OF OVERRIDING INTERESTS

(a) Rights of common, drainage rights, customary rights (until extinguished), public rights, *profits à prendre*, rights of sheepwalk, rights of way, watercourses, rights of water, and other easements not being equitable easements required to be protected by notice on the register;

(b) Liability to repair highways by reason of tenure, quit-rents, crown rents, heriots, and other rents and charges (until extinguished) having their origin in tenure;

(c) Liability to repair the chancel of any church;

(d) Liability in respect of embankments, and sea and river walls;

(e) ... payments in lieu of tithe, and charges or annuities payable for the redemption of tithe rent charges;

(f) Subject to the provisions of this Act, rights acquired or in course of being acquired under the Limitation Acts (now the Limitation Act 1980);

(g) The rights of every person in actual occupation of the land or in receipt of the rents and profits thereof, save where inquiry is made of such person and the rights are not disclosed;

(h) In the case of a possessory, qualified, or good leasehold title, all estates, rights, interests, and powers excepted from the effect of registration;

(i) Rights under local land charges unless and until registered or protected on the register in the prescribed manner;

(j) Rights of fishing and sporting, seignorial and manorial rights of all descriptions (until extinguished), and franchises;

(k) Leases for any term or interest not exceeding 21 years, granted at a rent without taking a fine (see Chapter 3);

(l) In respect of land registered before the commencement of this Act, rights to mines and minerals, and rights of entry, search, and user, and other rights and reservations incidental to or required for the purpose of giving full effect to the enjoyment of rights to mines and minerals or of property in mines or minerals, being rights which, where the title was first registered before January 1, 1898, were created before that date, and where the title was first registered after December 31, 1897, were created before the date of first registration:

This list is found in section 70(1) but subsequently included are:

(1) Adverse rights, privileges and appurtenances appertaining to other land or reputed to do so (r.258).

(2) Redemption annuities charged on land out of which extinguished tithe rentcharge formerly issued (Tithe Act 1936, s.13(11)).

(3) All rights and title conferred on the National Coal Board (Coal Act 1938, s.41; Coal Industry Nationalisation Act 1946, s.5).

Needless to say it would make life much easier if all overriding interests were listed in section 70, the text being amended appropriately to cover any addition or variations in subsequent legislation.


## Noting Such Interests on the Register

Before examining the types of overriding interests in detail it should be emphasised that interests capable of being overriding interests may, in fact, be mentioned on the register, in which case, by virtue of the definition in section 3 (xvi) of overriding interests, they cease to be overriding interests but become registered interests or minor interests. Indeed, section 70 (2) specifically is intended to make the register reflect the title deeds by making it mandatory for the Registrar to note on the Charges Register at the time of first registration any easement or profit created by an instrument and appearing on the title that adversely affects the land. It was only after *Re Dances Way* [1962] Ch. 490, 508 that the obligatory nature of section 70 (2) was recognised, for until then the Registrar claimed to have a discretion to enter a notice "if the registrar thinks fit" under rule 41: Curtis and Ruoff (1st ed.), p. 135.

Rule 41, however, coupled with section 70 (3) and rule 197, gives the Registrar a discretion, not confined to first registration, nor to matters appearing on the title nor to easements and profits, to note any overriding interest on the Charges Register of the land adversely affected, whenever the existence of the overriding interest is proved to the Registrar's satisfaction or admitted by the owner of the land adversely affected. If full advantage is taken of these provisions then very many overriding interests could be brought on to the register thereby ceasing to be overriding: registered conveyancing would then be quite an improvement upon unregistered conveyancing.

Finally, it is possible under rule 197 to have an entry made in the Property Register of freedom from an overriding interest where it can be shown that an overriding interest of the type "mentioned in section 70" once existed but that this "liability right or interest" has been discharged. The normal case envisaged by the rule and by Diplock L.J. in *Re Dances Way* [1962] Ch.490, 510 will be where there has been a previous entry of the existence of an overriding interest of the type mentioned in section 70 and where evidence is then produced to show that such a liability has been discharged but, with all due respect to the view of Diplock L.J. (as he then was) there seems no justification for confining the operation of the rule to such cases. One final point about rule 197 that reveals the dangers of creating overriding interests otherwise than by extending section 70: should rule 197 really be confined (as at present) to those overriding interests mentioned in section 70?

## Overriding Interests and Purchasers of Registered Land

Prolonging the suspense a little longer before examining the specific types of overriding interests, it is worthwhile to remember that a disposition of registered land *when registered* vests in the transferee the legal estate and appurtenant rights subject to the interests, if any, protected by some entry on the register and to the overriding interests, if any, affecting the estate transferred *at the time of registration i.e.* the date of the delivery at the Registry of the application (r.83 (2)).[7]

Since this is the relevant date (as established by *Re Boyle's Claim* [1961] 1 W.L.R. 339 and *London & Cheshire Insurance Co.* v. *Laplagrene* [1971] Ch. 499) and not the earlier date of the actual disposition, when the completion moneys would have been handed over, the position is different from the unregistered conveyancing position. In unregistered conveyancing, purchasers take subject to the legal rights existing at the date of completion when the title deeds and banker's drafts are exchanged. In registered conveyancing, purchasers take subject to overriding interests existing at the date of registration (*i.e.* the date the application for registration is delivered at the Registry) which is bound to be some time after the purchase has been completed.

Dangers lie here for purchasers since overriding interests, such as leases not exceeding 21 years and the rights of persons (*e.g.* co-owners) in actual occupation or in receipt of rents and profits, may arise between the date of the actual disposition and the date of registration (see pp.104–105, 125–129). Dangers also lie for those with overriding interests which may cease to be such as where persons go out of occupation or let a daughter or a son occupy the premises rent free in their own right (*Strand Securities Ltd.* v. *Caswell* [1965] Ch. 958). However, so long as such persons have an overriding interest at the relevant date, the date of registration at present, that interest continues to bind the registered proprietor as an overriding interest at the date of registration, despite the fact that subsequently the interest ceases to be an overriding interest, as where persons go out of occupation a month after the date of registration: *London and Cheshire Insurance Ltd.* v. *Laplagrene* [1971] Ch. 499. This accords with the principle that once priorities have crystallised, then, subsequent events cannot alter the order of priorities so established: *c.f. Randeo Mahabir* v. *Payne* [1979] 1 W.L.R. 507. However, where a person has gone out of actual occupation after the date of registration, then, though his interest binds the then registered proprietor, it will not bind a subsequent transferee, if by the time of registration of the subsequent transfer the person has not gone back into actual occupation.

As in unregistered conveyancing, to be completely safe and not to have to rely on an action for damages against the vendor (and there are difficulties in relying on the covenants for title where registered conveyancing is concerned as has been seen in Chap.5) purchasers should inspect the property on the day of completion or, indeed, have completion take place on the property itself and, for the present, where registered conveyancing is concerned, ensure that no one else occupies the property before the registration is effected.

## Section 70 (1) (a)

This paragraph with its specificity and yet its generality is very jumbled primarily due to its history. It started life as section 18 of the Land Transfer Act 1875, had additions made in the 1897 Land Transfer Act, and, then, as section 70 (1) (*a*) had these additions inserted in its middle and further bits tacked on to its end!

The paragraph is primarily concerned with "*profits à prendre . . .* and easements not being equitable easements required to be protected by notice on the register." The reference to "equitable easements" creates a problem straightaway, leading one to assume that legal easements and legal and equitable profits can be overriding interests. But how is one to determine whether an easement or profit is legal or equitable: upon registered or unregistered land principles? In unregistered land an easement or profit will be equitable if created otherwise than "for an interest equivalent to an estate in fee simple absolute in possession or a term of years absolute" or by an instrument not under seal. In registered land the express grant of an easement, legal upon the above principles, will operate only in equity unless and until completed by registration in the form of entries on the dominant and servient titles (sections 19 (2) 22 (2): Ruoff & Roper, pp. 98 and 278).

It would seem that since overriding interests take effect outside the registration system the categories within such interests should be ascertained according to unregistered land law principles except where registered legislation provides otherwise. Thus easements and profits existing at the date of first registration of title must be legal or equitable according to unregistered land principles, whilst easements and profits created after first registration must be legal or equitable according to registered land principles.

However, our problems are not yet over for what is meant by "not being equitable easements *required to be protected by notice* on the register"? There are no provisions in the Act or the Rules *requiring* equitable easements to be protected by notice. They *may* be protected by notice (ss. 59 (2). 49 (1) (*c*), 48 (1), r. 90) but they may be protected by a caution. Thus, no equitable easements are excluded from paragraph (*a*) so all equitable easements are capable of being overriding interests as held in a county court case, *Payne* v. *Adnams* [1971] C.L.Y.

6486. However, on this basis the last 13 words in paragraph
(*a*) are ignored as being of no application: but the draftsman
must surely have intended his 13 words to have some effect. He
probably ought to have written, "not being equitable easements
that are required to be protected (*e.g.* by a notice) if they are to
bind a subsequent purchaser for value under a registered
disposition" (*cf.* s. 101 (2)). Accordingly, Ruoff and Roper, pp.
97, 720 are probably correct in their view that equitable
easements are not capable of being overriding interests. It is
anomalous that equitable profits are so capable.

It would be a useful reform if Parliament were to enact that
easements and profits, expressly granted or reserved out of
registered land and whose creation should be completed by
entry on the Property Register of the dominant land and also
noting on the register of the title of the servient land, should
not be capable of ranking as overriding interests.The position
will then be assimilated to the unregistered land position where
equitable easements and profits if not registered as land charges
under the Land Charges Act are void as against purchasers of
a legal estate for money or money's worth (*cf.* s. 101 (2) of the
Act providing that dispositions of registered land as if it were
unregistered shall take effect as minor interests capable of being
overridden by registered dispositions for value: since the section
does not say "minor interests *only*" it seems it does not oust
section 70 especially in the light of *Webb* v. *Pollmount* [1966]
Ch. 584 and *Bridges* v. *Mees* [1957] Ch. 475 holding that
section 59 (1) and (2) do not oust section 70). This would
certainly help the register become, so far as possible, a true
mirror of the title, especially if the prescriptive acquisition of
easements and profits is abolished as recommended by the
majority of the Law Reform Committee in its 14th Report
(1966) Cmnd. 3100. The New Zealand Torrens system, where
easements and profits cannot be acquired by prescription,
works well in this respect and, after all, there is no reason why
a person who wishes to have an easement over his neighbour's
land should not adopt the straightforward course of asking for
it. In the case of implied easements under section 62, Law of
Property Act 1925 it seems that practical problems require
them to be allowed to be overriding interests: sections 3 (xxiv),
5,9,19 (3),20(1),22(3),23(1) and rules 251–258.

## Section 70 (1) (f)

So long as under ordinary substantive principles rights are capable of arising by adverse possession the land registration system must provide for this contingency. Accordingly, this paragraph preserves the rights of an adverse possessor as an overriding interest. Moreover, if the experiences of Victoria, Western Australia, South Australia and New Zealand are anything to go by it will always be necessary to cater for adverse possession by preserving the rights of adverse possessors as overriding interests.[8]

Thus, whether land is registered or unregistered, as a matter of practical and expedient social engineering it is necessary to recognise title acquired by adverse possession. One distinction, though, must always exist. Where unregistered land is concerned, 12 years' adverse possession automatically confers a legal title on the adverse possessor and extinguishes the "owner's" title. Where registered land is concerned, the "owner" on the expiration of the period is still on the register as registered proprietor invested with the legal title. Accordingly, he is deemed to hold the property on trust for the adverse possessor who may, on proving the relevant facts and after the Land Registry has served the necessary notices, be registered in his place (s. 75).[9]

## Section 70(1) (g)

As Lord Denning remarked in *Strand Securities Ltd.* v. *Caswell* [1965] Ch. 958, 979–980, paragraph (*g*) is:

> "an important provision. Fundamentally its object is to protect a person in actual occupation of land from having his rights lost in the welter of registration. He can stay there and do nothing. Yet he will be protected. No one can buy the land over his head and thereby take away or diminish his rights. It is up to every purchaser before he buys to make enquiry on the premises. If he fails to do so it is at his own risk."

At first sight it seems it can be said, as indeed Lord Wilberforce said in *National Provincial Bank* v. *Ainsworth*

[1965] A.C. 1175, 1259, that paragraph (*g*) is "a statutory application to registered land of the well-known rule protecting the rights of persons in occupation."

This well-known rule is the one in *Hunt* v. *Luck* [1902] 1 Ch. 428 where Farwell J. in a passage approved by the Court of Appeal (at p. 432) set out the rule as follows:

"(1) A tenant's occupation is notice of *all* that tenant's rights, but *not* of his lessor's title or rights;

(2) *actual* knowledge that the rents are paid by the tenants to some person whose receipt is inconsistent with the title of the vendor is notice of that person's rights."

In the case it was strongly submitted that if the proposed purchasers had inquired of the tenants, "To whom do you pay your rent?" they would have discovered that a person other than the vendor was the true owner and, therefore, since they had not made such inquiry, they were affected by constructive notice of the true owner's title. These submissions were rejected on the ground that it was not the duty of a purchaser or mortgagee to inquire of tenants to whom they pay their rents. In the words of Lord Denning M.R. in *Strand Securities* (*supra*, p. 980):

"Section 70 (1) (*g*) carries the same doctrine forward into registered land but with this difference. Not only is the actual occupier protected, but also the person from whom he holds. It is up to the purchaser to inquire of the occupier, not only about the occupier's own rights, but also about the rights of his immediate superior. The purchaser must ask the occupier: 'To whom do you pay your rent?' And the purchaser must inquire what the rights of that person are. If he fails to do so it is at his own risk for he takes subject to 'the rights of every person in actual occupation *or in receipt of the rents and profits thereof.*' "

It so happened in *Strand Securities* that a lessee allowed his step-daughter and her children to occupy his flat rent-free without himself residing with them. Since he was not in receipt of rents and profits he was not within the second limb of paragraph (*g*) and whilst a person can be in actual occupation through the agency of another person, such as a wife or a

aretaker or employee, that was not the case in the present
circumstances. There is a moral for benefactors to draw from
he case: lease or sub-lease at a nominal rent.

### Absolutist v. Constitutionalist view of Section 70 (1) (g)

On the absolutist view paragraph (g) brings about further
differences from the *Hunt v. Luck* rule: a person is absolutely
bound by the rights of every person in actual occupation of the
and or in receipt of rents and profits thereof (save where
nquiry is made of such persons and the rights are not
disclosed.) It matters not that it is unreasonably difficult to
ascertain the actual occupier or receiver of rents and profits; it
matters not that it is unreasonable to expect someone to
discover certain unusual rights of the occupier of receiver of
rents. Any traditional doctrine of notice is excluded from the
elf-contained paragraph.[10]

The constitutionalist view of those accustomed to traditional
conveyancing is that a person is only bound by the rights of
every person in actual occupation or in receipt of rents and
profits thereof (save where inquiry is made of such person and
the rights are not disclosed) so far as such rights are binding
according to traditional conveyancing principles (concerned
with legal interests, equitable interests and the doctrine of
notice, express, constructive and imputed) except as expressly
imited or extended by statue. The constitutionalists have to
admit that the position of those in receipt of rents and profits is
improved by paragraph (g).

The crux of the matter is whether paragraph (g) is self-
contained or whether there is still scope for the doctrine of
notice, more especially the doctrine of constructive notice
whereby a purchaser is under a duty to make those inquiries
and inspections that ought *reasonably* to be made.

Only in 1980 did it become clear that the absolutist view was
correct. Lord Wilberforce stated in *Williams & Glyn's Bank* v.
*Boland [1980]* 3 W.L.R.138 at p.143: "In the case of
unregistered land the purchaser's obligation depends on what
he has notice of—notice actual or constructive. In the case of
registered land it is the fact of occupation that matters. If there
is actual occupation, and the occupier has rights, the purchaser

takes subject to them. If not, he does not. No further element is material." Lord Scarman at p.149 stated "The statute has substituted a plain factual situation for the uncertainties of notice, actual or constructive, as the determinant of an overriding interest."

In *William & Glyn's Bank* v. *Boland* H, a sole registered proprietor, mortgaged the house to the bank when living there with W, who had an equitable interest as tenant in common under a trust to the extent of her contribution to the purchase of the house. The Lords rejected the bank's submission that it was not bound by W's interest since it did not have notice of her interest, it being entitled to assume that H alone was in occupation as the sole owner with W there merely *qua* wife, chief cook, bottle-washer and bed-warmer!

The Lords also rejected a submission of the bank based on section 74 of the Act: "neither the Registrar nor any person dealing with a registered estate or charge shall be affected with notice of a trust express implied or constructive, and references to trusts shall, so far as possible, be excluded from the register." The submission was that the Bank was only bound if it had notice of W's interest under a trust and section 74 prevented the Bank being affected by any such notice. This was rejected by Lord Wilberforce at p.146: " the doctrine of notice has no application to registered conveyancing and, as an administrative measure, entries may not be made in the register which would only be appropriate if that doctrine were available."

Other than actual physical presence what is covered by "actual occupation"? If a purchaser, P, only actually sees the sole registered proprietor, V, when visiting the house, is it possible for P to be bound by the equitable interest of W whom he never saw e.g. if W happened to be at a regular bridge evening, or at the hairdresser or the shops, or her relatives, when V arranged for P to call at the house where W normally resided. Is W not then in actual occupation? What if W was temporarily in hospital or on holiday visiting relatives in the U.S.A. What if W was an air hostess, thereby being frequently temporarily absent from the house? What if W 's job as a croupier takes her away on a liner for 3 months each year? *Williams & Glyn's Bank* v. *Boland* makes it clear that the

endor's occupation does not exclude the possibility of
occupation of others, so can W rely on outward visible signs of
her ordinary residence in the house, *e.g.* her clothes, her make-
up? However, V could hide these things, using cigar smoke or
an air freshener to remove any trace of perfume but can this
affect whether objectively W is in actual occupation?
Alternatively, if challenged V might pretend to be a "drag"
artiste, or a transvestite. However, a prospective purchaser
cannot rely on the "untrue *ipse dixit* of the vendor" [11] so that
the electoral roll should be inspected and inquiries of
neighbours would be necessary or a watch kept on comings and
goings for inquiry to be made of overnight visitors.

Where there are "outward visible signs" [12] of someone other
than the vendor being ordinarily resident on the premises, then
it seems fair, in striking the balance between the interests of
occupiers and the interests of purchasers, that the occupier
should be protected. The purchaser is thus under a strict
absolute duty to ascertain the rights of a person apparently
ordinarily resident on the premises but is seems he can also be
bound by rights of a person in actual occupation even though
such occupation was not reasonably discoverable.

Where the cunning of V is such that the ordinary residence
of W is not at all apparent to P, *e.g.* if W is imprisoned in a
secret cellar then on which of the two innocent parties, W and
P, should the loss fall? Policy dictates it should fall on the less
innocent party if there be one but it will be difficult to displace
the statutory weighting in favour of the occupier. What if
relations between V and W were so strained that it was (or
should have been) clear to W that V would be likely in
underhand fashion to take advantage of her absence (in
hospital, on holiday, on a job) to sell the house? Should not
W's "default" in failing to protect her interest on the register
(assuming she knew she had an interest) enure for the benefit
of P as more innocent than W so W should not be treated as in
actual occupation? It is true that a person may be in actual
occupation through a resident representative such as a caretaker
or housekeeper or wife [13] but it seem unlikely that W could
successfully claim that V was her resident representative when
V had not, or no longer, so agreed and when, indeed, his
actions totally denied such role. Moreover, if V were her

representative but denied she had any right, presumably this would bind her.

Further problems arise when one considers the rights of children. Take a case where a sole registered proprietor, V, four years ago declared that he held the house on trust for his three children now aged six, 16 and 20 years. No entry on the register protects their interests so will they be protected if a purchaser, P, had seen them on the premises but made no inquiry of them, assuming they were present *qua* children of the actual occupier, V, rather than as equitable co-owners themselves in actual occupation? Should P be bound by the adult 20 year old's rights but not by the younger children's rights on the basis that minors should never be treated as themselves in actual occupation—at least where living with a parent or guardian, since, presumably, a 16 year old married woman living with her sole registered proprietor husband can be in actual occupation? Yet more problems arise if the 20 year old is away at Cambridge University for 24 weeks a year and the 16 year old is at boarding school.

A final poser is whether a minor can be treated as in actual occupation through the residence of some adult. This may depend upon whether or not such adult (*e.g.* the minor's mother or eldest sister) has an independent right of occupation justifying residence. On the other hand, if as a matter of law it is held that an unmarried minor cannot be in actual occupation (a little hard on a seventeen-year-old woman cohabiting with a sole registered proprietor) one can argue that since such minor principal cannot be in actual occupation then neither can his adult agent: however, the fact of adult actual occupation should be sufficient to put a purchaser on inquiry of the right by which the adult is in occupation and so protect minors' rights.

It is most unfortunate—especially for purchasers—that the concept of actual occupation raises so many unresolved questions. There are cases on occupation in other contexts such as rating law, [14] landlord and tenant law [15], compulsory purchase law [16] and criminal law [17], but they cannot really be of much assistance in the context of registered land. In the end, actual occupation must be a question of degree in all the circumstances and thus very much depend on the court's view of the respective merits of the parties. As Russell L.J said in

*Hodgson* v. *Marks* [1971] Ch 892 at 932: "A wise purchaser or lender will take no risks. Indeed, however wise he may be he may have no ready opportunity of finding out; but, nevertheless, the law will protect the occupier. Reliance on the untrue *ipse dixit* of the vendor will not suffice." In *Strand Securitites Ltd.* v. *Caswell* [1965] Ch. 958 at 991 he had earlier stated: "If resort to general principles is required to solve the otherwise insoluble I prefer a result which accords with the principle that it is for the person who seeks to ignore an equitable interest to establish his right to do so." All in all, it seems that in cases of doubt the occupier (perhaps socially disadvantaged) will prevail over the purchaser (perhaps advantaged by the professional assistance of solicitors and estate agents). Lord Denning in *Williams & Glyn's Bank* v. *Boland* [1979] Ch. 312 at 333 made it clear that he did not want to see "monied might prevail over social justice." Furthermore, Lord Scarman on appeal stated at [1979] 3 W.L.R. 148 :

> "It is our duty to give the provision [in a statute] a meaning which will work for, rather than against, rights conferred by Parliament, or recognised by judicial decision, as being necessary for the achievement of social justice. The courts may not put aside as irrelevant the fact that if the wives succeed the protection of the beneficial interest which English law now recognises that a married woman has in the home will be strengthened, whereas if they lose this interest can be weakened and even destroyed by an unscrupulous husband. Nor must the courts flinch when assailed by arguments that the protection of her interests will create difficulties in banking or conveyancing practice. Bankers and solicitors exist to provide the service the public needs. They can adjust their practice if it be socially required."

### Receipt of rents and profits

Obviously, a person will be in receipt of rents and profits where his tenant or licensee is actually paying him for use of his land. But what if his tenant or licensee is not making the payments to which he is entitled? There are dicta of Sir John

Pennycuick and Buckley L.J. indicating that a person cannot be treated as in receipt of rents and profits if he is entitled to such but payment is being withheld: *Schwab* v. *McCarthy* (1975) 31 P & C.R. 196 at 213, 215.

Against this Russell L.J. in *Strand Securities Ltd.* v. *Caswell* [1965] Ch. 958 at 983 remarked "If instead he had received from or demanded of his stepdaughter [the occupier] a penny a week he would have had an unanswerable claim to his sub-lease as an overriding interest within section 70 (1) (*g*) as being in receipt of rents and profits." Moreover, in *Sheridan* v. *Dickson* [1970] 1 W.L.R. 1328 at 1332 Winn L.J., albeit in another context, made the general comment that "a landlord may comprise a man who is in receipt of i.e. entitled to receive rent." Surely, it is not whether the occupier is a good prompt payer, or a bad dilatory payer that ought to matter: it is the fact of his occupation that should produce an inquiry, eliciting his response that he is in occupation under a right arising from an obligation to pay £x a week to one L. "Receipt of rents and profits" is surely used in contrast to "actual occupation" to denote not actual possession but constructive possession [18] through another person obliged to pay for his actual possession. No sensible system of justice can allow a purchaser knowing of such person's presence on the premises to take advantage of the carpricious fact that such person had not paid the rent currently due to his landlord at the relevant time.

One tends to assume that if there is a receiver of rents and profits then there will be an actual occupier who will put a purchaser on inquiry, so leading to the ascertainment of the receiver. However, a receiver has the protection of an overriding interest even if the payer does not happen to be in actual occupation as might well be the case at the beginning or at the end of the payer's tenancy or licence.

Take V, who in 1980 granted a 21 year lease at a premium to L or in writing leased premises for 21 years to L. In June 1981 L agreed in writing to lease the premises to an Australian, T, a mature Ph.D. student from June 1981 until December 1984. It took T longer to wind up his affairs in Australia than he thought, so he did not arrive to take up occupation until August 30th 1981, though having paid 3 months' rent in advance. Meanwhile, V had sold to P who had become registered proprietor on July 31st. Here, L as a person in receipt of rents is protected by virtue of his overriding interest whilst T, not being in actual occupation, has no protection for his equitable lease. However, T could claim that L has a 21 year overriding interest valid as against P and that T's interest thus has derivative validity, like Mr. Attallah's leasehold interest derived out of Mrs. Hodgson's overriding interest in *Marks* v. *Attallah* (1966) 110 S.J. 709. Against this, P would claim that T's interest, unlike Mr. Attallah's interest, was subsisting at the time P became registered proprietor, whereupon P took subject only to the overriding rights of L and free from all other interests whatsoever under L.R.A., s. 20 (1): thus, P is entitled to use the property till T's interest expires in December 1984, though then L will be entitled till his interest expires in 2001. Even this occasions problems for P since T's interest could expire earlier by forfeiture or surrender: see *Fairweather* v. *St. Marylebone Property Co.* [1963] A.C. 510. It seems unlikely that L and T would have to resort to an arranged forfeiture or surrender since the court would probably see the force of T's derivative validity claim.

Since a purchaser's inspection of the property cannot assist him in cases like the above, there is much to be said in favour of such purchaser, who has done all that can reasonably be expected of him, that section 70 (1) (*g*) should be reformed so as only to protect a receiver of rents where the payer is in actual occupation.

Finally, since section 70 (1) (*g*) is not, on its face, limited to a person beneficially entitled to rents and profits, [19] can an agent's receipt of rents protect his rights (*e.g.* under an option)? It seems he could make out quite a strong case, expecially where he receives the moneys as his own and merely has to account to his principal for an amount equal to such sum less expenses.

### Rights within section 70 (1) (g)

It is at least clear that rights within paragraph (*g*) do not include any right of howsoever a personal character but only those "rights in reference to land which have the quality of enduring through different ownerships of the land, according to normal conceptions of title to real property" (*per* Russell L.J. and Lord Upjohn in *National Provincial Bank* v. *Ainsworth* [1964] Ch. 665, 696; [1965] A.C. 1175, 1237).

As Lord Wilberforce said (p. 1261):

> "To ascertain what 'rights' come within [para. (*g*)], one must look outside the Land Registration Act and see what rights affect purchasers under the general law. To suppose that [para. (*g*)] makes any right, of howsoever a personal character, which a person in occupation may have, an overriding interest by which a purchaser is bound, would involve two consequences: first, that this Act is, in this respect, bringing about a substantive change in real property law by making personal rights bind purchasers; second, that there is a difference as to the nature of rights by which a purchaser may be bound between registered and unregistered land. . . . One may have to accept that there is a difference between unregistered land and registered land as regards what kind of notice binds a purchaser, or what kind of inquiries a purchaser has to make. But there is no warrant for supposing that the nature of the rights which are to bind a purchaser is to be different, excluding personal rights in one case, including them in another. The whole frame of section 70 shows that it is made against a background of interest or rights whose nature and whose transmissible character is known or ascertainable, *aliunde, i.e.* under other statutes or under the common law."

Thus, rights in registered land within paragraph (*g*) which are capable of binding purchasers as overriding interests do not differ from the rights in unregistered land which are capable of binding purchasers *i.e.* legal interests, equitable interests and mere equities (not being those standing naked and alone but those ancillary to or dependent upon interests in land such as rights to set aside a disposition for undue influence or to rectify a deed [20]). On the absolutist view of paragraph (*g*) it matters not that in unregistered conveyancing a purchaser is only bound by an equitable interest registrable under the Land Charges Act if actually registered thereunder or by an equitable interest neither registrable nor overreached if he has notice thereof or by a mere equity if he has notice thereof. As Lord Wilberforce stated in *Williams & Glyn's Bank* v. *Boland* [1980] 3 W.L.R. 138, 143, "The land is so subject [*i.e.* to overriding interests] regardless of notice actual or constructive . . . the law as to notice as it may affect purchasers of unregistered land has no application even by analogy to registered land."

From *Smith* v. *Jones* [1954] 1 W.L.R. 1089 it is clear that a purchaser of unregistered land is only expected to make reasonable inquiries and, whilst he is expected to ascertain the terms of any tenancy, he is not expected to ask whether the lease correctly represents the tenant's rights or to go through the terms of a lease with the tenant occupier to see if they conform to what the tenant and the landlord agreed so as to negative any equity of rectification. However, in registered conveyancing there is an absolute duty cast upon a purchaser, who buys at his peril, since the rights within paragraph (*g*) are not restricted to "reasonably discoverable rights." Whether or not equities can be overriding interests was fully argued in *Lee-Parker* v. *Izzet* (No. 2.) [1972] 1 W.L.R. 775 but Goulding J. expressed no view on the matter. For the present, a purchaser will only certainly be safe if he asks the tenant, "Does this lease correctly represent your rights?" and receives the answer, "Yes." (See also *Dovto Properties Ltd.* v. *Astell* (1964) 28 Conv. 270).

Purchasing, where there are tenants in occupation, is, indeed, fraught with danger. This is because paragraph (*g*) protects not just the rights by virtue of which someone is in occupation (*e.g.* a 30 year lease in writing taking effect as an agreement for a lease) but all his rights (*e.g.* an option to purchase the freehold reversion, an unpaid vendor's lien) so far as legal, equitable or, it seems, mere equities. Mortgagees have additional cause to worry through the effect of the doctrine of feeding the estoppel (see Chap. 8, p. 125).

Since it seems an equity to rectify can be an overriding right, what of the statutory claim to rectify the register under section 82 (1), since rectification will be ordered even against a proprietor in possession to give effect to an overriding interest and no indemnity is then payable except where forgery was involved? The position will be crucial for someone like Mrs.

Beaney in *Re Beaney* [1978] 1 W.L.R. 770 and for the victim
of a forgery or of double conveyancing (see pp. 57, 178) who
has only a claim under section 82 (1) (*g*). Such statutory claim
is unknown to general land law and is *sui generis* so it is
unlikely it was intended to rank as an overriding interest.
However, such claim seems capable in some circumstances of
affecting successive landowners who should, after all, be put on
enquiry by virtue of the actual occupation or receipt of rents
and profits of the above victim. The statutory claim should
therefore be capable or ranking within section 70 (1) (*g*).

From the case law it appears that the following rights fall
within paragraph (*g*):

(i) the right of occupation and of specific performance
under a contract for the purchase of a lease or a freehold:
*Woolwich Equitable B.S.* v. *Marshall* [1952] Ch. 1, *Grace
Rymer Investments Ltd.* v. *Waite* [1958] Ch. 831, *Bridges* v.
*Mees* [1957] Ch. 475;

(ii) the right to purchase the freehold reversion to a lease:
*Webb* v. *Pollmount* [1966] Ch. 584;

(iii) the right to an unpaid vendor's lien (held by a vendor
to whom the purchased land had been leased back by the
purchaser): *London & Cheshire Insurance Co.* v. *Laplagrene*
[1971] Ch. 499;

(iv) the right to a purchaser's lien for his deposit: *Lee-
Parker* v. *Izzet* [1971]1 W.L.R. 1088;

(v) the rights under the Rent Acts of tenants: *per* Lord
Denning M.R. in *National Provincial Bank* v. *Hastings Car
Mart Ltd.* [1964] Ch. 664, 689;

(vi) the equitable proprietary rights of a licensee arising
from expenditure on land: *per* Lord Denning, *supra*; this is
probably the real basis of *Re Sharpe* [1980] 1 All E.R. 198
(see [1980] Conv. 207);

(vii) the right of a tenant to make deductions (amounting
to the proper costs of repair) from future payments of rent
where the landlord was in breach of an express or implied
covenant to repair [21]: *Lee-Parker* v. *Izzet* (1971) 1 W.L.R.
1688;

(viii) the right of a tenant and his successors in title under

a waiver of rights by the landlord: *Brikom Investments Ltd.*
v. *Carr* [1979] Q.B. 467

(ix) the rights of a beneficiary under a bare trust:
*Hodgson* v. *Marks* [1971] Ch. 892; and

(x) the rights of a beneficiary under a trust for sale (see
below).

It is noteworthy that:

(i) the rights of a beneficiary under a Settled Land Act
settlement can only be a minor interest: L.R.A., s. 86 (2);

(ii) the rights of a tenant arising from a notice under the
Leasehold Reform Act 1967 of his desire to have the freehold
or an extended lease can only be a minor interest: section 5
(5) of that Act;

(iii) the rights of occupation of a spouse under the
Matrimonial Homes Act 1967 can only be a minor interest:
section 2 (7) of that Act.

(iv) a mortgage, not being by way of registered charge,
can only be a minor interest: L.R.A. s. 106 (2).

### Rights under trusts for sale

Only in 1980 did it become clear that rights under a trust for
sale can be overriding interests so as particularly to protect
equitable co-owners under a trust for sale of land having a sole
registered proprietor. Previously, the standard works of the
Chief Land Registrars (Brickdale, Stewart-Wallace, Curtis,
Ruoff and Roper) had assumed that rights under trusts for sale
could only rank as minor interests. They assumed that it could
never have been intended that rights under trusts for sale, and
thus interests in cash under the doctrine of conversion, could
rank as overriding interests in land thereby being dangerous
rights *in rem* binding the whole world, rather than
overreachable rights *in personam* as in unregistered land and as
envisaged by section 3 (xv) defining minor interests as
including interests under trusts for sale. The Law of Property
(Joint Tenants) Act 1964 also assumes that interests under a
trust for sale can only be minor interests, binding purchasers
only if protected by entry on the register, so that the problems
that the Act remedies in unregistered land cannot happen in
registered land, so the Act does not apply to registered land.

However, the House of Lords in *Williams & Glyn's Bank* v. *Boland* [1980] 3 W.L.R. 138, upholding the Court of Appeal's reversal of Templeman J., held that a person with an interest under a trust for sale can have an overriding interest in a house purchased for his occupation. Neither section 3 (xv) nor any other section (*cf.* s. 86 (2) which prevents interests under Settled Land Act settlements from being overriding interests) prevents interests under trusts for sale, when not protected by entry on the register, from falling within the broad terms of section 70 (1) (*g*). "Subsisting in reference to the registered land" was the wife's right of occupation under her equitable interest under a trust for sale imposed by statute (due to her contribution to the purchase price of the house making her a co-owner). Thus Mrs. Boland's interest bound the Bank, which had taken a mortgage from her husband, the sole registered proprietor.

Such a conclusion accords with social justice. Where a person acquires an interest under a trust for sale by virtue of a co-ownership interest acquired by some contribution to the purchase price or improvement of property, would not such person naturally expect that his occupation would sufficiently protect his interest? Could he or she reasonably be expected to know of the need to apply for an entry (*e.g.* of a caution or restriction) on the register? In unregistered land such a person seems fully protected by his occupation.[22]

The House of Lords placed much emphasis on the fact that the wife had *Bull* v. *Bull* [1955] 1 Q.B. 234 rights of occupation since the house had been bought to be lived in by her and her husband. It would seem to follow that if there is a trust for sale where the intention is that the beneficiaries are to have interests in the proceeds of sale and the net rents and profits till sale as in *Barclay* v. *Barclay* [1970] 2 Q.B. 677 then an occupying beneficiary cannot have an overriding interest.

In *Bull* v. *Bull* a mother and son bought a house which was put in the son's name. The house was intended to be a home for both of them. Later the son met and married a woman even more wonderful than his mother. His wife and mother did not get on so he claimed to be able to evict his mother as a trespasser. The Court of Appeal held the son held the legal estate on a statutory trust for sale for himself and his mother as equitable tenants in common. Her equitable interest entitled her to remain, each co-owner until sale being entitled concurrently with the other to the possession of the land and to the use and enjoyment of it. The house could not be sold with vacant possession unless she agreed to it. If she unreasonably refused the son could go to the court under section 30 of the Law of Property Act 1925 and obtain an order for sale, and in aid of it the court could order the mother to vacate the house.

In *Barclay* v. *Barclay* a testator left his bungalow on trust to be sold and the proceeds divided in five equal shares between his sons and daughters-in-law. One son, Allan, was living with the testator and after the testator's death continued to live in the bungalow. The testator's personal representative claimed possession against Allan so that there could be a sale with vacant possession. The Court of Appeal held that the prime object of the trust was the sale and division of the proceeds of the bungalow, no beneficiary having been given any right or interest in the bungalow itself. The beneficiaries were tenants in common not of the bungalow but of the proceeds of sale. Allan did not have a *Bull* v. *Bull* equitable tenancy in the land entitling him to remain in possession, subject only to any order that might be made by the court under section 30 of the Law of Property Act. The plaintiff was thus entitled to possession of the bungalow.

Trusts for sale created by will to enable the proceeds of sale of property to be distributed (rather than to enable beneficiaries to live in the property) are not the only instances where a right under the trust for sale may not be regarded as an overriding interest in land. A and B could purchase in A's name a pub with upstairs residential accommodation for the publican, intending not themselves to occupy the property but to be interested in the rents and profits till sale and ultimately the proceeds of sale. It could so happen that A as sole registered proprietor might sell the property at a time when B resided in it, *e.g.* as a friend of the publican upon separating from Mrs. B. or as temporary manager after the publican had suddenly left.

Mr. and Mrs. C might have purchased in Mr. C's name a house for their joint occupation. To raise cash urgently without letting her husband know, Mrs. C might have assigned her

equitable interest to her sister Miss D for £4,000 so that Miss
D was only interested in the proceeds of sale. Five years later
Mrs. C might have died. Miss D might have given up her job
and flat in Brussels to live in the house temporarily to assist
Mr. C, who might then sell the house as beneficial owner,
considering himself to be sole surviving joint tenant, not
realising that his late wife's action had created an equitable
tenancy in common. It could well be that no inquiry was made
of Miss D, the purchaser never seeing her and assuming that
the signs of a female presence related to the recently deceased
Mrs. C. It would seem that Miss D has a right in land capable
of being an overriding interest *only* if Mr. C could not remove
her except with the court's assistance under section 30 of the
Law of Property Act. It is hard to see any court affording a
secret assignee such as Miss D (or Tom, Dick or Harry) the
protection of being entitled concurrently with the resident
registered proprietor to possession and use and enjoyment of
the house subject only to the section 30 jurisdiction. On the
other hand, Miss D would have a right in land if she had
purchased Mrs. C's interest in circumstances where Mr. C had
agreed that Miss D was by virtue of such purchased interest
herself to be entitled to occupy the land whenever she wanted.

In the above examples we have been concerned with a sole
registered proprietor holding land under a trust for sale. Of
course, if there are two proprietors holding under a trust for
sale then the rights of equitable co-owners are overreachable
rights in the proceeds of sale where the moneys are paid to the
two trustee proprietors (see L.P.A., ss., 2, 27, T.A., s. 14) so
that the co-owner's equitable rights cannot bind the purchaser.
For further examples of the extent of "rights" under general
principles see pp. 138–139 *infra*.

## Rights of contractual licensees

Whether the rights of an occupier with an irrevocable
contractual licence are within paragraph (*g*) depends whether
or not they rank as equitable interests or mere equities so as to
be capable of binding third parties rather than being personal
rights binding only the contracting parties.[23] In *National
Provincial Bank* v. *Ainsworth* [1965] A.C. 1175 [1964] Ch.

665, 699, Russell L.J. considered legislation necessary if contractual licences were to be elevated to the status of an interest in land whilst Lords Upjohn and Wilberforce expressly reserved the question for later consideration. At present the better view seems to be that irrevocable contractual licences are not interests in land: see *King* v. *David Allen* [1916] 2 A.C. 54 and the remarks of Goff J. (as he then was) in *Re Solomon* [1967] Ch. 573, 582–586. The contrary view of Lord Denning in *Errington* v. *Errington* [1952] 1 K.B. 290, *Binions* v. *Evans* [1972] Ch. 359 (where he gives a misleading view of the facts in *King* v. *David Allen* [1916] 2 A.C. 54) and *DHN Food Distributors* v. *London Borough of Tower Hamlets* [1976] 1 W.L.R. 852 (where Goff L.J. surprisingly agreed with Lord Denning) must be treated with a great deal of caution.[24] Accordingly, the rights of an occupier with an irrevocable contractual licence probably do not fall within paragraph (*g*): he will need to go further and prove an equitable estoppel interest which is probably the best explanation of *Re Sharpe* [1980] 1 W.L.R. 219 (see Jill Martin in [1980] Conv. 207, 213). In reality, in a registered land context the receiver of rents and profits from the licensee should have an overriding interest binding a purchaser, so conferring a derivative validity upon the licence:*cf. Strand Securities Ltd.* v. *Caswell* [1965] Ch. 958, 983.

### *The proviso to section* 70 (1) (*g*)

A purchaser is bound by the rights of a person within section 70 (1) (*g*) "save where inquiry is made of such person and the rights are not disclosed." This proviso first appeared in the L.R.A. 1925, without having been in the Law of Property Act 1922 or the Law of Property (Amendment) Act 1924, and it does not appear in any of the other paragraphs in section 70 (1) though a purchaser, if misled as to rights within these other paragraphs by the owners of such rights, may be able to rely on some sort of estoppel or on the equitable principle that statutes must not be allowed to be the engine of fraud. It seems that inquiry must be made, so that it will not be open to a purchaser to say that if he had inquired of the ignorant

occupier he would have been told that the occupier had no
rights and so should be treated as if that had happened.

It is vital to note that inquiry of the vendor alone is
insufficient (*cf. Goody* v. *Baring* [1956] 1 W.L.R. 448 and
*Bailey* v. *Barnes* [1894[ 1 Ch. 25, 35 in unregistered
conveyancing): inquiry must be made of such persons as are in
actual occupation or in receipt of rents and profits. As Russell
L.J. remarked in *Hodgson* v. *Marks* [1971] Ch. 932, "Reliance
upon the untrue *ipse dixit* of the vendor will not suffice." The
only remedy against a vendor would be damages, which would
be of no avail if the vendor were insolvent and which, in any
case, would hardly compensate for the inconvenience of being
lumbered with various overriding interests.

In practice, to rely on the proviso it will be necessary to
show that the occupier received the inquiry. To this end all
inquiries should be sent by recorded delivery or by registered
post and, in the case of companies, be sent to the company's
registered office (Companies Act 1948, s. 437 (1)). It would
seem that to give efficacy to section 70 (1) (*g*) it must be
extended so as to read "and the rights are not disclosed *within
a reasonable time following the receipt of the inquiry.*" As ever,
what is "reasonable" depends on the circumstances and there
must be balanced the occupier's possible wish to consult his
solicitors and the purchaser's wish for a prompt reply so as to
be able to get on with the purchase. In his inquiry the
purchaser should stipulate a time limit *e.g.* four weeks.

If no reply is obtained from the occupier or a director or, in
the light of *Panorama Developments* (*Guildford*) *Ltd.* v. *Fidelis
Furnishing Fabrics Ltd.* [1971] 2 Q.B. 711, even the secretary
of the company, within the time, then the purchaser will safely
be within the proviso. If the occupier's reply on its face is
incomplete or indefinite then he should be pressed into replying
within a reasonable (but shorter) time. If he refuses to make
his new reply complete and definite or refuses to reply at all
then once again the purchaser will be within the proviso. If the
occupier's reply on the face of it is a proper complete reply
then, in the absence of any extraneous factors that might make
a purchaser suspect the accuracy and completeness of the reply,
the purchaser will be within the proviso. As between a person
who has done all he reasonably can to protect his interest and

someone who has not quite done all he reasonably can the former (*i.e.* the purchaser) should prevail. For this very reason if the occupier's rights change after his reply, but before registration of the purchase, then the purchaser should still fall within the proviso since the occupier, knowing of the intended purchase, should have informed the purchaser of the change of position. However, if some time has elapsed since the date of the reply, then, since the occupier will have expected the transaction to have been completed and thus, quite reasonably, will not expect to need to inform the purchaser of any change, the purchaser will not fall within the proviso. Instead, the purchaser will need to send a further inquiry to the occupier to check that no change in the occupier's rights has occurred.

So far it has been assumed that the purchaser knows of a specific occupier of whom he has then made inquiry. However, there is a danger that there might be some occupier whose presence has not been discovered by the purchaser. Can the purchaser protect himself by sending a recorded delivery letter to "The Occupier(s)" at the registered address inquiring what rights, if any, are claimed in respect of the property and requiring a written answer within, say, six weeks? Obviously, there can be no harm in trying this, but it seems that it will not be effective unless the particular occupier actually received it.[25]

The Chief Land Registrar, where a notice is required to be given, can send out such a letter and even state what will be the consequence of any omission to comply therewith: rules 311–314, which deem the letter to have been received by the person addressed unless returned by the Post Office. However, the Registrar's power only seems to cover notices required to be given under the Act or the Rules, *e.g.* section 30 and rules 25, 46, 48(2), 198, 218, 253, 276, 300. It does not seem that a prospective purchaser can require the Registrar to send out an appropriate notice. However, on prospective first registration with absolute or good leasehold title the Registrar may give such notices to tenants and occupiers as he may deem expedient (rule 25) so that if he wished he could thereby greatly assist purchasers by making inquiries on their behalf of occupiers.

It seems from *London & Cheshire Insurance Co.* v. *Laplagrene* [1971] Ch. 499, 505 that to come within the proviso to section 70 (1) (*g*) the relevant inquiry must have been deomonstrably made "by or on behalf of the intending transferee or grantee for the purposes of the intended disposition."[26]

It is also clear from this case and *Re Boyle's Claim* [1961]1 W.L.R. 339 that a purchaser takes subject to overriding interests affecting the purchased estate at the date of registration of the purchaser as new proprietor, *i.e.* the date of delivery of the application at the Registry (rule 83 (2)). Thus, if the purchaser does not take up actual occupation immediately he receives the transfer form in return for his banker's draft for the purchase price a watch must be kept for any occupiers. It will, however, be too late to do anything about any overriding interests that may then materialise so occupation by others after the purchase but before registration must be prevented at all costs.

However, a mortgagee, M, faces problems where a purchaser's wife (or other co-habitee) is concerned. Take Mrs. P who uses her £3,000 legacy for the deposit on a £30,000 registered house which she and Mr. P wish to buy. On June 1, 1981 a transfer form in Mr. P's name is given to him by V in return for a banker's draft for £27,000 (£2,000 from P and £25,000 from M). On June 15 the relevant documents are delivered to the Registry so that Mr. P as new registered proprietor and M as the registered chargee *(cf. Grace Rymer* v. *Waite* [1958] Ch 831) are subject to overriding interests then subsisting, *e.g.* the rights of Mrs. P in actual occupation as equitable tenant in common in equal shares with Mr. P.

In practice, it is thus up to M to make inquiry not just of actual occupiers living with the vendor but also to make inquiry of the purchaser as to whether or not any persons will be occupying the property with him and, if so, whether they are contributing to the purchase money in any way that might make them equitable tenants in common. Problems will still arise if the purchaser is untruthful since one cannot rely on his untrue *ipse dixit*. If Mr. P truthfully admits Mrs. P will be contributing to the purchase price, then M should persuade them to become joint proprietors and joint chargors or else have Mr. P as sole proprietor charge the house as sole beneficial owner and have Mrs. P join in the charge in such manner that she is estopped from claiming any beneficial equitable interest as against M and his successors in title, having held out Mr. P as sole beneficial owner: on general principles her "rights" will not be capable of binding M and his successors in title.

Where inquiry reveals that an occupier, O, has rights under a trust for sale then a purchaser, P, should insist that sale be made by two trustees for sale, so satisfying L.P.A., s. 27 and Trustee Act 1925, s. 14, so that O should become registered as co-proprietor with V or at least sign a joint receipt, having been appointed trustee. A sale by them will then overreach everyone's rights under the trust for sale (trustees' *mortgaging* powers are limited unless unlimited in the trust deed but may a mortgagee presume the powers unlimited in the absence of a contrary entry in the register)? An alternative approach is to get a written undertaking from each occupier in the following terms.[27]

> "In consideration of V and P entering into a contract with each other for the sale and purchase with vacant possession of the property known as Blackacre [or of V and P proceeding to complete such a contract] I, John Smith, undertake that as from the date of payment to or to the use of V of all the purchase moneys due under the said contract I shall not seek to enforce against the said P or his successors in title any right that I may have or may in the future have arising by virtue of any statute or by reason of any equitable interest or otherwise to the intent that the said P and his successors in title shall from the date of payment aforesaid enjoy the said property freed and discharged from all claims or rights that I may have or may in the future have arising as aforesaid."

Ideally in cases such as of multiple occupation, where even the vendor may find it difficult to ascertain the identity of all occupiers, the vendor should be prevailed upon to give a warranty as to the identity of the occupiers. Furthermore, if the vendor is pressing for completion of a sale so that time does not allow of the making of direct inquiries of occupiers the vendor should be prevailed upon to give a warranty not only as to the identity of the occupiers he has specified but also as to their rights. An extension of the covenants for title in relation to overriding interests would also be advisable as has been seen in Chapter 5.

Of course, as ever, it is the relative bargaining strengths of the parties that count, so that purchasers may find that they cannot cover themselves as much as they would like. Moreover, the making of the novel and full inquiries and requisitions, that really need to be made to cover purchasers properly, will certainly meet with opposition from conservative and time-and-trouble-conscious solicitors acting for vendors. The answer, apart from any reforms simplifying the present parlous position, only lies in the co-operation of solicitors either through their local law societies or the Law Society.

### *Caveat solicitor*

As can be seen from the earlier material in this chapter, the situation of a solicitor acting for a purchaser or a mortgagee is not to be envied. The width of section 70 (1) (*g*) is such that a solicitor has to be very much on his guard in case any client, finding himself bound by an overriding interest, might try to bring an action for professional negligence. Moreover, it is no defence to show that he has been doing what the great majority of other men of his profession have been doing: the courts will not allow what they consider to be bad professional practice to become good law (*cf. Goody* v. *Baring* [1956] 1 W.L.R. 448; *Lloyds Bank* v. *Savory* [1933] A.C. 201; *Cavanagh* v. *Ulster Weaving Co.* [1960] A.C. 145; *Brown* v. *Rolls Royce Ltd.* [1960] 1 All E.R. 577; *Simmons* v. *Pennington* [1955] 1 W.L.R. 448).

In order for a client to succeed in such an action he would need to show that there was such a want of skill or care on the part of his solicitor as to amount to a breach of contract or to the tort of negligence.[28] In this respect it is vital to remember that it is part of a solicitor's duty to his client that he "should consult with his client in all questions of doubt which do not fall within the express or implied discretion left him, and should keep the client informed to such an extent as may be reasonably necessary according to the same criteria" (*per* Scott L.J. in *Groom* v. *Crocker* [1939] 1 K.B. 194, 222).

In the first place, of course, the solicitor must make sure that

his client is aware of all overriding or minor interests affecting
the property that have been discovered by the solicitor (*Lake* v.
*Busby [1949] 2 All E.R. 964; Piper* v. *Daybell, Court-Cooper*
(1969) 210 E.G. 1047; *Sykes* v. *Midland Bank* [1971] 1 Q.B.
113). Then, whenever it is impossible or impracticable to take
all those steps that, ideally, should be taken to protect his client
completely against the risk of being bound by overriding
interests, the solicitor should explain the ideal steps and the
reasons why they ought to be taken and go on to make clear
why these ideal steps are impossible or impracticable, and also,
most importantly, the risks which might ensue from failure to
take such steps (*cf. Buckland* v. *Mackesy* (1968) 112 S.J. 841
on risk of exchanging contracts before a mortgage is arranged,
*Morris* v. *Duke Cohan & Co.* (1975) 119 S.J. 826 on danger of
exchanging contracts for a new house before deposit was paid
by prospective purchaser of old house and *Buckley* v. *Lane
Herdman & Co.* [1977] 10 C.L. 290 on danger of exchanging
contracts for sale of clients house without simultaneously
exchanging contracts for purchase of new house). He should
then obtain clear instructions to press on without taking such
steps (perhaps after one final attempt to carry out some of the
steps) or to resile from the proposed transaction. Some steps,
such as the close inspection of the property, will have to be left
to the client himself or some agent such as a surveyor
appointed by the client. The solicitor should make it clear to
the client which are the steps and what is the particular
purpose of taking these steps, such as to discover the identity of
any occupiers and any rights they may claim and any defects
patent to the eye or a necessary consequence of something
which is patent to the eye. *Yandle & Sons Ltd.* v. *Sutton* [1922]
2 Ch. 199, 210. Where there is to be a contract, which is
normally the case except for mortgages, then the solicitor
should see that full inquiries and inspections are made
beforehand and that the contract is appropriately drafted to fit
the particular circumstances. Finally, it should be remembered
that a solicitor who is unfortunate enough to be sued for
negligently investigating title cannot compel his client to
mitigate his damages by embarking on anything but the most
straightforward litigation: *Pilkington* v. *Wood* [1953] Ch. 770.
  A solicitor thus has an exacting and tiring task if he is to

perform his job properly. Indeed, it will not be surprising if some solicitors try an easy way out by attempting to make it a term of their contract with their clients that they are not to be responsible, in any way, for loss occasioned by overriding interests. It is significant that since *Wilson* v. *Bloomfield* (1979) 123 S.J. 860 indicated that a vendor's solicitor could be liable in negligence to a purchaser for replies to inquiries before contract, the disclaimer on the Oyez form of "Enquiries before Contract" now commences "These replies *are given* on behalf of the proposed vendor and *without responsibility on the part of his solicitors their partners or employees.*"

## REFORM

As the Royal Commission on Land Transfer of 1870 recognised in paragraph 64 of their Report:

> "The problem [which s. 70 (1) (*g*), in particular, tries to resolve] is not to find a perfect system of land transfer, recording with mathematical accuracy the nature and extent of the land and every interest in it, so that the record shall absolutely dispense with the necessity of ordinary examination and enquiries, but to find a system which, not impairing the personal security of owners or purchasers and not exonerating a purchaser from the easy and obvious task of looking on the outward and visible side of the property and making enquiry of persons in outward and visible possession of it, shall enable the legal ownership to be readily passed from hand to hand and dispense with the necessity of enquiry for invisible equities and interests whose only evidence is contained in private documents."

As we have seen, this problem has not yet been resolved, primarily due to the uncertain width of section 70 (1) (*g*) which, by no means, provides a purchaser with an "easy and obvious task." The absolutist nature of paragraph (*g*) and its apparent coverage of mere equities immediately suggests that the paragraph should be restricted to "The reasonably discoverable legal and equitable rights of every adult person appearing to be in actual occupation (whether on his own or with others) of the land or any part thereof, save where

enquiry is made of such person and such rights are not
disclosed within a reasonable time of the receipt of the
enquiry."

It will be noted that "or in receipt of the rents and profits
thereof" is omitted. It is thought that a non-occupying lessor
with a registrable interest should be protected only if his
interest is registered. A non-occupying lessor with an
unregistrable interest in the form of a head-lease should be
protected by an extended section 70 (1) (k), "leases or
agreements for leases for any term or interest not exceeding
[10]?[29] years together with the legal and equitable rights arising
therein."

*Overriding interests and registrable interests*

As a general rule it is thought that there should be as little
overlap as possible between registrable interests and overriding
interests. Is it not most surprising that at present any
registrable interest may, until it is registered, rank as an
overriding interest if its owner is in actual occupation of the
land in question? Is it right that a person in occupation with a
registrable transfer or lease which he ought to have registered
under a system specially created for the purpose, but which he
has failed to register, ought to have complete protection for that
interest as an overriding interest? Surely, the proper operation
of the system requires that all registrable interests should be
promptly registered? Surely, any provision which makes it
unnecessary to register land and discourages registration should
be avoided as a matter of principle? Accordingly, no registrable
interest should be capable of being an overriding interest. This
would also prevent occupation under a registrable instrument
amounting to adverse possession under the Limitation Act 1980
from ranking as a section 70 (1) (f) overriding interest. Of
course, it will be necessary as a matter of social policy to
ensure that the category of registrable interests is closely
defined so as not to include instances where the owners of such
interests are not likely to be legally represented or to appreciate
the need for registration (see Chap. 3).

It might be argued that protection as an overriding interest
ought to be available for the *interregnum* before the purchaser
of an interest in registered land actually registers that interest.

However, protection is already afforded under the Land Registration (Official Searches) Rules 1978. A purchaser, entitled as of right under section 110 to an authority to inspect the register can, by obtaining an official search certificate, gain full priority for his interest over intervening minor interests providing he lodges his documents in the prescribed time—and an extension of that time can be obtained.

The position of a person who is taking not a fee simple but a lease of registered land is different as he is not, at present, entitled to an authority to inspect the register of his lessor's titl and can only obtain such an authority if his lessor consents. If authority is given he will be able to obtain the protection afforded by a search certificate whilst, if authority is not given, if he has gone into occupation, he will have the protection of an overriding interest, otherwise he will need to deliver the relevant documents for registration to the Registry as soon as possible. It will be best to put prospective lessees on the same footing as prospective purchasers by entitling them to an authority to inspect the register so that the protection of an official search certificate may be obtained: the proposals concerning inspection of the register already canvassed in Chapter 2 cover this.

It should be noted that there is a clear distinction between cases of dispositions of land already registered and cases of the first registration of a registrable interest.

A person entitled to apply for registration as first proprietor of the land is in a privileged position. He may protect himself by a caution against first registration (s. 53) or he may reserve priority for his application by a priority notice under rule 71 (which, confusingly, has nothing to do with priority cautions or priority inhibitions, which regulate priorities as between assignees of minor interests under trusts and are entered in the Minor Interests Index which, confusingly, is not a register of minor interests as will be seen in Chap. 8). Furthermore, he is protected against dealings taking place between the date of the instrument necessitating registration and the date of registration by rules 42 and 73, which provide that the date of registration is to be the date of delivery of the application to register and that such dealings shall take effect as if they had taken place after the date of registration.

Since a prospective first proprietor is in such a strong position there is no justification for allowing his interest as an overriding interest.

## Overriding interests and minor interests

We now reach the remarkable overlap between overriding interests and minor interests. Basically, minor interests, despite their lengthy, confusing definition section comprise the two categories of equitable interests that are fundamental to unregistered land. We have already seen in Chapter 2 that the 1925 legislation did away with most of the old doctrine of equitable notice by creating (1) overreachable "family" interests that, notice or no notice, do not bind the land if the purchaser of the land pays his money to the proper trustees and, in the case of settled land, complies with the Settled Land Act 1925 and (2) registrable "commercial" incumbrances that, if registered, bind everyone and, if unregistered, bind no one except volunteers.

In general, it can be said that in the case of registered land the first class comprise minor interests protected by restrictions, whilst the second class comprise minor interests capable of protection by a notice or a caution depending on the availability of the proprietor's land certificate (s. 64). In the first case, the interests are overreached upon compliance with the terms of the restriction that the Registrar will have entered upon examining the title, whilst, in the second case, the interests will continue to bind the land if they have been protected by an entry on the register but if they have not been so protected then they will be overridden by a disposition for valuable consideration.

Now, if any of these two classes of interest can be overriding interests automatically binding the land without further ado, like legal interests, then registered land law is radically different from unregistered land law.

However, there *are* radical differences since the "rights of every person in actual occupation of the land or in receipt of the rents and profits thereof" constitute overriding interests (s. 70 (1) (*g*)). Such rights will include (1) overreachable equitable interests and (2) incumbrances of the class registrable as land charges under the Land Charges Act in unregistered conveyancing, unless the Act somewhere provides that such interests and incumbrances shall not take effect as overriding interests. Indeed, section 86 (2) specifically provides that overreachable equitable interests under Settled Land Act settlements shall take effect as minor interests and not otherwise. However, there is no corresponding provision for overreachable equitable interests behind trusts for sale: such interests are expressly included in the definition of minor interest in section 3 (xv) but they are nowhere made exclusively minor interests so, as held in *Williams & Glyn's Bank* v. *Boland* [1980] 3 W.L.R. 138, they are within section 70 (1) (*g*).

The courts have already held that the following equitable interests registrable as land charges in unregistered conveyancing fall within section 70 (1) (*g*): an agreement for a tenancy,[30] a contract for sale,[31] an option to purchase the freehold reversion,[32] an unpaid vendor's lien,[33] a purchaser's lien.[34] The fact that such interest could have been protected by entry of a notice or a caution was held to be immaterial so long as the interest was protected by the occupation of the owner of the interest. At first sight this is surprising when in unregistered conveyancing a registrable land charge is void against a purchaser even when protected by the occupation of the owner: *Hollington Brothers Ltd.* v. *Rhodes* [1951] 2 All E.R. 578 (more fully reported in [1951] 2 T.L.R. 691),[35] Land Charges Act 1925, s. 13 (2), Land Charges Act 1972, s. 4. However, it has already been pointed out at p.16 that it was a draftsman's consolidation mistake that inadvertently took away from the owner of a land charge the protection formerly afforded him by L.P.A. 1922, s. 33 if in actual occupation.

In *Hollington Brothers Ltd.* v. *Rhodes* a firm called D. Ltd. contracted to buy from the defendants a head-lease "subject to and with the benefit of the several leases and agreements for tenancies as described in the schedule hereto annexed." The schedule showed the plaintiffs as having a lease of the rooms they were occupying for seven years from April 29, 1945, at £612 10s. a year. The contract with D. Ltd. was completed by an assignment of the head-lease "subject to and with the benefi of such leases and tenancies as may affect the premises." In fact, the plaintiffs had no lease but only an agreement for a lease which they had not registered as an estate contract. Accordingly D. Ltd. gave the plaintiffs notice to quit as merely yearly tenants forcing the plaintiffs to negotiate a new lease at a higher rent with D. Ltd. This led the plaintiffs to sue the defendants for damages for breach of contract.

Harman J. held that the plaintiff's agreement[36] for a seven year lease was void against D. Ltd. by reason of non-registration despite the fact that D. Ltd. had express, actual notice or clear, constructive notice. He said, at page 696, "There is, after all, no great hardship in this. The plaintiffs could at any time right up to the completion of the assignment to D. Ltd. have preserved their rights by registration just as the defendants could have fulfilled their obligations by completing the lease of which D. Ltd. could not have complained as they knew all about it." As far as the morality of D. Ltd.'s actions was concerned, in the words of Lord Cozens-Hardy M.R. in *Re Monolithic Building Co. Ltd.* [1915] 1 Ch. 643 (where the Court of Appeal held that a mortgage not registered under the Companies Act was void against a subsequent registered mortgage even though the subsequent mortgagee had express notice of the prior mortgage at the time when he took his own security), "It is not fraud to take advantage of legal rights, the existence of which may be taken to be known to both parties."

This is the crux of the matter. It may well be that where the companies were concerned in *Hollington Brothers Ltd.* v. *Rhodes* they could reasonably be expected to know of their legal rights so that a fair result was reached on the merits of the case, D. Ltd. having been the better businessmen and had the best advisers. A fair result, however, would not be reached if some old spinster, or bachelor girl, or working-class family man or foreigner had informally, without bothering with solicitors, gone into occupation under a four year lease in writing (taking effect as an agreement for a lease owing to the lack of a formal deed). Such persons would naturally expect that their occupation was sufficient protection and they could not reasonably be expected to know that they ought to register an estate contract. They would have good cause to feel badly done by if their landlord sold out to a company which then gave them notice to quit as merely monthly periodic tenants, so forcing them to negotiate a new longer lease at a higher rent with greater obligations or to give up their home.

In fact, nowadays the Landlord and Tenant Act 1954 and

the Rent Acts would often provide the protection otherwise denied tenants by the general land law, but it is an indictment of the general law that it allows such injustice. Registered land law with the protection section 70 (1) (*g*) confers does achieve more social justice. An often socially disadvantaged occupier should be able to rely on his occupancy to protect all his rights: someone with the money and ambition to purchase a house or lend money on mortgage can reasonably be expected to have professional advice to ensure that an occupier is asked what rights he claims.

A final example may help. Let us say that V bought several properties with the assistance of a mortgage and, before the execution of the mortgage, he had agreed in writing to sell one property to a purchaser P, who was a foreigner who was neither particularly bright nor literate. Basically P wished to find a home for himself and his family and intended to rent an unfurnished house. However, V, who wished to make as large a profit as possible and to avoid the Rent Acts, persuaded P that P would be better off buying the house outright. P pointed out that he could never obtain a mortgage to cover the £9,500 purchase price though he could just manage, with some borrowing, to put down the £950 deposit. V said he had some friends who most probably would be able to provide the other £8,550 but this would take some time and he could not guarantee that he would be successful. If he were not successful then he would return P's deposit. Meanwhile P, after paying the £950 deposit, should move in as licensee and, pending completion, see to any repairs and pay 14 per cent. per annum interest on the outstanding purchase money, payable weekly. The contract was concluded and the deposit handed over and P moved in the day before V's mortgage was executed. The completion date was fixed two months hence. However, V, for one reason or another, never managed to find a person prepared to provide mortgage moneys to help P acquire the house from V: V was quite happy not to insist on the completion date. P was too busy working to maintain his family to bother further with the matter. He trusted that V would see him all right. V, however, was in difficulties himself, so much so that he defaulted on his own mortgage payments and the mortgagee decided to exercise his power of sale.

Now, if the land were unregistered the mortgagee would have no problems, since P's estate contract and lien would be void for want of registration under the Land Charges Act 1972, whilst if the land were registered, the mortgagee would have many problems since the contract and lien would constitute overriding interests: *Lee-Parker* v. *Hassan Izzet* [1971] 1 W.L.R. 1688. However, it is surely the mortgagee (normally wealthy and with professional advisers) who should have problems for failing to make simple inquiries of P. It is just that P should be entitled to rely on his occupancy to protect his rights for it would be expecting far too much of him to know of a need to enter a notice or a caution [*cf.* the position of occupiers under rental purchase or instalment "mortgages": B.M. Hoggett (1972) 36 Conv. 325 and Shutt & Stewart [1976] New L.J. 217].Of course, if P in agreeing to buy the house had taken the house subject to a friend of V occupying a room in it, then it would be equally just that P should be subject to the rights of V's friend.

It is thus unregistered land law that is out of touch with social reality: registrable land charges should bind purchasers, though unregistered, if protected by the occupancy of the owner of the land charges. Any reforming legislation should also make it clear that rights of preemption can be equitable interests in land [37] ranking as Class C (iv) estate contracts in unregistered conveyancing and as minor interests, if protected by a notice or caution or restriction, but otherwise as possible section 70 (1) (*g*) overriding interests in registered conveyancing.

It would also be useful if legislation were passed to provide that for the purposes of section 70 (1) (*g*) if a clear affirmative or negative reply is not received within five weeks of a written inquiry then the reply shall, in favour of a purchaser, conclusively be presumed to be in the negative: this will avoid the trouble and expense of an appointment of a co-trustee where it leaves the registered proprietor as apparent sole beneficial owner.

If the legislature could be moved by reforming zeal to enact a new Law of Property (Miscellaneous Provisions) Act it might also usefully include a provision (after Lord Denning's heart) elevating contractual licences of occupiers to the status of an equitable interest. Persons like ex-employees, who are given a particular house or cottage to live in rent-free for the rest of their days under an arrangement not constituting a tenancy but a licence would thus be protected as any purchaser from the employer would be bound to honour the arrangement: *cf. Foster v. Robinson* [1951] 1 K.B. 149; *Binions* v. *Evans* [1972] Ch. 359 noted (1972) 36 Conv. 277; *Re Sharpe* [1980] 1 W.L.R. 219.

## Notes

[1] *Principles of Land Registration* (1937), p. 32.

[2] *Webb* v. *Pollmount* [1966] Ch. 584.

[3] *London & Cheshire Insurance Co. Ltd.* v. *Laplagrene* [1971] Ch. 499.

[4] *Hodgson* v. *Marks* [1971] Ch. 892, *Williams & Glyn's Bank* v. *Boland* [1980] 3 W.L.R. 128

[5] F. R. Crane (1958) 22 Conv. 17–18. What are the s. 70 (1) *(g)* "rights"?

[6] See D. C. Jackson (1972) 88 L.Q.R. 93; (1978) 94 L.Q.R. 239.

[7] ss. 5, 9, 20, 23, 69.

[8] Ruoff: *An Englishman Looks at the Torrens System*, pp. 22, 23, 44.

[9] Further see *Fairweather* v. *St. Marylebone Pty. Co. Ltd.* [1963] A.C. 510, 78 L.Q.R. 541 (H. W. R. Wade), 88 L.Q.R. 116–119 (D. C. Jackson).

[10] See (1971) 35 Conv. 255 (I. Leeming), 2nd edition hereof, pp. 91–95.

[11] *Per* Russell L.J. in *Hodgson* v. *Marks* [1971] Ch. 932. Further see p. 101 *ante*.

[12] See *Brown* v. *Bush* [1948] 2 K.B. 247, 254 (continuing occupation for Rent Act purposes).

[13] *Strand Securities Ltd.* v. *Caswell* [1965] Ch. 958.

[14] *Re Briant Colour Printing Co.* [1977] 1 W.L.R. 942.

[15] *Brown* v. *Bush* [1948] 2 K.B. 247, *Morrisons Holdings Ltd.* v. *Manders* [1976] 1 W.L.R. 353.

[16] *Laundon* v. *Hartlepool B.C.* [1979]Q.B. 252, *Heron* (1980) 255 E. G. 65

[17] *R.* v. *Tao* [1977] Q.B. 146.

[18] See also L.R.A., s.3 (xviii), L.P.A., ss. 14, 205 (1) (xix).

[19] *Cf. Arsenal Football Club* v. *Smith* [1979] A.C.1.

[20] See *National Provincial Bank* v. *Ainsworth* [1965] A.C. 1175, 1238; (1976) 40 Conv. 209 (A. R. Everton). A right of a purchaser to rescind for misrepresentation is purely personal and cannot be transferred unlike a vendor's equity to rescind for undue influence: *Gross* v. *Hillman* [1970] Ch. 445; *Brikom* v. *Carr* [1979] Q. B. 467

[21] On this see (1976) 40 Conv. 196 (P. M. Rank).

[22] *Hodgson* v. *Marks* [1971] Ch. 892 shows that a purchaser has notice of the rights of persons other than wives who occupy property with the sole legal owner and *Williams & Glyn's Bank* v. *Boland* [1980] 3 W.L.R. 138 (H.L.) [1979] Ch. 312 (C.A.) contains dicta indicating that nowadays a purchaser of unregistered land will have notice of the rights of wives.

23. This is a vexed question: Megarry and Wade, pp. 782–783 and articles there cited; *Re Sharpe* [1980] 1 W.L.R. 219

24. See [1977] Camb. L.J. 12, (1977) 93 L.Q.R. 170.

25. See [1980] Conv. 313. There is an obvious danger that the proprietor will open the letter and destroy it before it can be seen by any other occupier.

26. Thus the inquiries made by the trustee in bankruptcy in *Re Sharpe* [1980] 1 W.L.R. 219 of the occupying aunt preparatory to offering the house for sale with vacant possession would not protect the purchaser.

27. See (1974) 38 Conv. 110 (D. J. Hayton).

28. *Midland Bank Trust Co.* v. *Hett* [1979] Ch. 384; *Ross* v. *Caunters* [1979] 3 W.L.R. 605.

29. See Chap. 3 *supra*.

30. *Woolwich Equitable B.S.* v. *Marshall* [1952] Ch. 1.

31. *Bridges* v. *Mees* [1957] Ch. 475.

32. *Webb* v. *Pollmount* [1966] Ch. 584.

33. *London & Cheshire Insurance Co.* v. *Laplagrene* [1971] Ch. 499.

34. *Lee-Parker* v. *Izzet* [1971] 1 W.L.R. 1688.

35. Also see *Coventry Permanent Economic B.S.* v. *Jones* [1951] 1 All E.R. 901. The vendor may be liable: *Wright* v. *Dean* [1948] Ch. 686.

36. Ultimately he held no final contract had been concluded.

37. Overturning *Pritchard* v. *Briggs* [1980] Ch. 388 in light of *Birmingham Canal Co.* v. *Cartwright* (1879) 11 Ch.D. 421; *L. & S. Rly. Co.* v. *Gomm* (1881) 20 Ch.D. 562; L.P.A. 1925, s. 186; L.C.A. 1925, s. 10; L.C.A. 1972, s. 2 (4) (iv); Perpetuities and Accumulations Act 1964, s. 9 (2).

# Chapter 7

# MORTGAGES

## Unregistered Land

IN unregistered land legal mortgages of freeholds may be effected by (i) a demise by deed for a term of years absolute (3,000 years) subject to a proviso for cesser on redemption or (ii) a charge by deed expressed to be by way of legal mortgage,[1] whilst legal mortgages of leaseholds may be effected by (i) a sub-demise by deed for a term of years absolute (at least one day, and usually 10 days, shorter than the term vested in the mortgagor) subject to a proviso for cesser on redemption or (ii) a charge by deed expressed to be by way of legal mortgage.[2] There seems little reason why the second method with its versatility should not be made the exclusive method for creating legal mortgages.

An equitable mortgage of freeholds or leaseholds may be effected merely by deposit of the title deeds or, as is usually the case, by a memorandum under seal supported by deposit of the title deeds. It may also be effected by any writing manifesting an intent that the property should constitute a security for the discharge of some debt or other obligation.

## Registered Land

For registered land we have already seen that most land is usually mortgaged by way of a registered charge (s. 26). A charge is registered when an entry showing the charge (but not the amount of the charged sum) and the name of the proprietor of the charge is entered in the charges register of the title to the land that is mortgaged. The proprietor of the charge is issued with a *charge certificate* which contains a copy of the filed plan and of the subsisting entries on the register of the title of the mortgaged land and also contains the original mortgage deed. The registered proprietor's *land certificate* is retained at the Registry until the cancellation of the registered charge (s. 65).

Registered charges, unless made or taking effect by demise or sub-demise, correspond to charges by way of legal mortgage in unregistered land since they take effect as charges by way of legal mortgage, subject to any provision to the contrary contained in the charge (s. 27). One would have expected that all mortgages not capable of such registration (*e.g.* equitable mortgages) would rank as minor interests capable of protection by entry of notices so as to bind everyone (s. 49 (1) (*c*) and (*f*)). Priorities would then be determined simply by a rule that the register is everything so that charges rank in order of registration (under s. 26) or of protection by the entry of a notice, except that where simultaneous applications were delivered to the Registry, with no special priority under the 1978 Official Searches Rules, then resort would have to be made to "the principles that between equities the first in time prevails and that it is for the person who seeks to ignore an equitable interest to establish his right to do so."[3] This would be quite an advance on the complex and cumbersome rules of priorities in relation to unregistered land. Unfortunately, these expectations are not realised. However, the position has been improved by Administration of Justice Act 1977, s. 26 which substitutes a new section 106 L.R.A.

In the first case on mortgages of registered land to reach the courts, *Re White Rose Cottage* [1965] Ch. 940, Harman L.J. said at page 952:

> "The preface to Mr. Fortescue-Brickdale's [one-time Chief Land Registrar] work on the Act claims . . . that the system of land registration 'provides plain and simple methods for effecting transfers and charges.' It cannot be said that either of these policies emerge from the facts of the present case. No doubt the system has worked very well since 1925 by the efforts of the land registrars and the practice of the office but the present case shows there are difficulties and pitfalls in the way of comparatively

> simple transactions which would not have arisen with
> unregistered land."

The Registry officials certainly have a difficult task as the
draftsmanship of the Act and the Rules is particularly bad in
respect of mortages and charges, *e.g.* the latter part of section
25 (3) (*i*) which really is concerned with the proprietor of the
land rather than of the charge as drafted, and rule 154 (2)
where it is necessary to read "charge certificates" for "land
certificates"; (see also rule 245 (*b*) and (*c*) in relation to section
65 discussed by Ruoff and Roper at pp. 553–554).

However, even the practice of the Land Registry has not
been able to cope with every deficiency in the Act, as a
practising solicitor, Mr. H. J. Hartwig pointed out in an
instructive article in (1962) 26 CONV.(N.S.) 169. Whilst in
unregistered conveyancing a legal mortgage can be created and
protected as a puisne mortgage *after* an earlier equitable
mortgage protected by deposit of title deeds this, most
inconveniently, is not possible in the case of registered
conveyancing. This is because of the Land Registry's ruling
that the strength of section 65 (requiring the land certificate to
be deposited *at the Registry* for the duration of a registered
charge) is such that if the land certificate is deposited *with an
earlier equitable mortgagee*, whether or not supported by a
notice of deposit under rule 239, then a subsequent charge
cannot be registered and so cannot be a legal charge.[6]
Subsequent legal charges are thus only possible if there is a
prior registered charge when the land certificate will already be
deposited at the Registry under section 65. The mortgagor will
thus usually be pressurised by the prospective second
mortgagee, seeking a registered legal charge, to persuade the
first mortgagee to become a registered chargee.

It is important to realise that where the land certificate is
deposited with a first equitable mortgagee then since the second
(necessarily equitable) mortgagee cannot get himself registered
he cannot realise his security by selling the land to a purchaser
subject to the first mortgage *unless* the first mortgagee is
prepared to lodge the land certificate with the Registry, so
enabling the second mortgagee to become registered, a vital
prerequisite for the exercise of a mortgagee's powers of sale,

etc.: sections 110 (5), 34, 59 (2) pp. 123-125 *post* and *Lever Finance Ltd.*v. *Needleman's Trustees* [1956] 1 Ch. 375. Of course, with unregistered land, a second legal mortgagee can simply convey the land subject to the first mortgage, even thought the first mortgagee retains the title deeds.

Let us now proceed to examine the methods available for mortgaging registered land.

## By Registered Charge

A mortgage by deed in legal form may be registered as a registered charge under section 26 if the land certificate is deposited at the Registry. Until completed by entry on the register of the mortgaged land of the mortgagee's name and of the particulars of the mortgage (s. 26 (1)) no legal interest is created (ss. 19, 20; *Lever Finance Ltd.* v. *Needleman's Trustees* [1956] Ch. 375, *Schwab & Co.* v. *McCarthy* (1976) 31 P. & C.R. 196). Section 27 (3), stating that a charge "shall take effect from the date of delivery of the deed containing the same," only gives the chargee protection *inter partes* from that date and not the legal interest: *Grace Rymer Ltd.* v. *Waite* [1958] Ch. 831. It would seem from the framework of the Act (*e.g.* ss. 2, 18 (4), 25–36) that it is only mortages that are intended to be legal that are registrable as Lord Denning opined in *Re White Rose Cottage* [1965] Ch. 940, 949, disagreeing with Wilberforce J., who had briefly expressed the view in passing in the court below that sections 25–36 and 106 covered equitable as well as legal mortgages. There is nothing expressly in those sections that would confine the benefit of registration to legal mortgages since sections 27 and 34, which presuppose registered charges taking effect as legal mortgages, do allow for contrary provisions in the registered charge and entered on the register which could limit the registered charge to take effect as an equitable mortgage. However, it is most unlikely that the draftsmen would have let in equitable mortgages as capable of registration in such an indirect fashion.

*Mortgages*

*As a Minor Interest*

Instead of using the classic registered charge a proprietor may mortgage his registered land in any of the ways permissible for unregistered land: section 106 (1). Until the mortgage becomes a registered charge it takes effect only in equity and is capable of being overriden as a minor interest unless protected: section 106 (2).

Section 106 (3) makes it clear that a mortgage which is not a registered charge but only a minor interest may be protected on the register of the mortgaged land by entry of (a) a notice under section 49 requiring production of the Land Certificate under section 64 (1) (c) or (b) a notice of deposit (or intended deposit) under rules 239–242 where the Land Certificate is (or is to be) deposited with the mortgagee by way of security but such notice only operates as if it were a mere caution against dealings (rr. 239 (4) and 242 (1)) or (c) a caution against dealings under section 54.

It would seem from *Barclays Bank* v. *Taylor* [1974] Ch. 137 that a mortgagee can rely to some extent on the *de facto* protection afforded by having possession of the Land Certificate of the mortgaged property. It was there held that as against subsequent competing equitable interests the earlier equitable mortgage protected by deposit of the Land Certificate will have priority as first in time. Retention of the Land Certificate by the mortgagee also prevents someone subsequently becoming new registered proprietor of freehold land or becoming a registered chargee and thus prevents the minor interest from being overridden by such a subsequent registered disposition. However, it gives no protection against a subsequent lessee for 21 years or less since such a lease takes effect as a registered disposition under section 19 (2), enabling the lessee to take free from minor interests not protected by entry on the register: sections 18 (3), 20 (1), 21 (3), 23 (1), 59 (6). Indeed, there are even more worries for a mortgagee protected only by possession of the Land Certificate if the freehold mortgagor grants a registrable lease exceeding 21 years at a rent without taking a fine. The lease can be registered without the freehold Land Certificate needing to be produced: *Strand Securities Ltd.* v. *Caswell* [1965] Ch. 958. Under section 20 (1) the lessee takes subject only to entries on the register and overriding interests but free from all other interests whatsoever. If the equitable mortgage had initially been created merely by deposit, rather than by deed supported by deposit, the mortgagee might try to rely on section 66 for protection.[4]

By section 66 a proprietor

> "may, subject to overriding interests and to any interests registered or protected on the register at the date of the deposit, create a lien on the registered land by deposit of the Land Certificate; and such lien shall, *subject as aforesaid*, be equivalent to a lien created in unregistered land by the deposit of documents of title."

Arguably, the mortgagee thus takes subject only to overriding interests and interests on the register at the date of his lien by deposit and so is free of the subsequent registered lease. However, section 66 does not state "subject *only* as aforesaid" and if a lien by deposit of the Land Certificate is to be equivalent to an equitable mortgage of unregistered land by deposit of title deeds then since such a mortgage would be postponed to a subsequent lease (the legal lessee having no notice of the equitable mortgage, not being able to see the freehold title: L.P.A. 1925,s.44) so the lien by deposit should be postponed to the subsequent lease. Moreover, should a court really strive to create a distinction between a mortgage created by deposit under section 66 and a mortgage created under section 106 (1) but supported by deposit?

It is thus clear that a mortgagee should never rely merely on protection by possession of the Land Certificate.

### *The Position of a Registered Chargee*

As a general rule it is only a registered chargee who has the usual powers of a mortgagee to deal with the mortgagor's legal estate, *e.g.* to sell the mortgaged property or appoint a receiver of rents and profits(s. 34). Thus mortgagees (other than registered chargees) upon seeking to enforce their security must become registered chargees, and a prospective purchaser of the mortgaged property is entitled to require the mortgagee to become a registered chargee or procure a disposition from the registered proprietor of the mortgaged property to the purchaser: section 110 (5). By section 27 (3) a registered charge is "subject to the estate or interest of any person (other than the proprietor of the land) whose estate or interest (whenever created) is registered or noted on the register before the date of registration of the charge." The word "noted" clearly covers protection by entry of a notice: Ruoff and Roper, p. 616. Protection by other entries may be afforded under sections 18 (4) (5), 20 (1), 21 (4) (5), 23 (1).

The creation of a registered charge is a registered disposition of the land by the registered proprietor and so takes effect subject to overriding interests and to minor interests then protected on the register: sections 20 (1), 23 (1). What then of the common situation where there is an equitable mortgage by deed supported by deposit of the land certificate and entry of a notice of deposit? The deed is in common form, expressly charging all estates both legal and equitable in the property and expressly creating a power of attorney, whereby is conferred on the mortgagee the power to vest the legal estate in a purchaser free from any right of redemption.[5] Subsequently, a caution is placed on the register *e.g.* in respect of a charging order relating to a judgment debt of the registered proprietor. The proprietor's money difficulties then become such that the mortgagee seeks to enforce his security. He therefore applies to become registered chargee but the cautioner objects except on condition that his minor interest remains protected on the register against any subsequent purchaser.

The cautioner makes the point that if the registered proprietor were himself to sell the property he could only transfer the legal estate encumbered by the equitable mortgage and by the equitable charging order. The equitable mortgagee stands in the shoes of the proprietor if he exercises the power of attorney so he can only transfer the legal estate subject to the equitable charging order. However, against this, as held by Wilberforce J. in *Re White Rose Cottage* [1964] Ch. 483, 495–496 (endorsed in this respect by the Court of Appeal [1965] Ch. 940), the equitable mortgage, as first in time and properly protected, has priority over the equitable charging order. The over-reaching effect of sections 2 (1) (iii), 101 (1) (3) and 104 (1) of the Law of Property Act 1925, coupled with the mortgage charging the legal and equitable interest in the property and conferring the power to vest the legal estate in a purchaser free from any right of redemption, is then sufficient to enable the mortgagee to transfer the unencumbered legal estate to a purchaser. Accordingly, the mortgagee is entitled to become registered as registered chargee so that in that capacity such a transfer can be made to a purchaser. The caution is thus cancelled. In practice, there is no need for the equitable mortgagee to become registered chargee for, without becoming so registered, his over-reaching powers enable him to make good title to a purchaser. This is the exception to the general rule that only a registered chargee can deal with the legal estate of the chargor.

It should be noted that a sale by a registered chargee under the statutory power of sale operates (subject to any alterations on the register affecting the priority of the charge) as a transfer for value by the proprietor of the land *at the time of the registration of the charge* would have operated: section 34 (4). A mortgagee who only protects his mortgage as a minor interest may thus have problems if he cannot take advantage of the above power of attorney method or if priority problems cannot be resolved in his favour under the rules discussed in the next chapter.

## *Danger from Tenancies by Estoppel and Section 70 (1) (g) Rights*

A registered chargee has particular cause to worry about the overriding interests to which he may be subject, especially when the effect is considered of the doctrine of feeding the estoppel.[6] If, for example, a tenant merely has a tenancy by estoppel, because his landlord has not yet acquired the legal estate in the freehold or superior leasehold which the landlord has contracted to purchase, then when the landlord does acquire the legal estate the estoppel is forthwith fed. This gives the tenant a legal estate a split second before the landlord's mortgagee obtains his legal interest[7]: *Church of England B.S.* v. *Piskor* [1954] Ch. 553. The tenancy thus binds the mortgagee, thereby diminishing his security.

Take the case of P, purchasing property with the assistance

of a mortgage, who is allowed possession of the property by V some time after contracts have been exchanged. P purportedly grants a 21-year lease by deed to T within section 70 (1) (*k*) or allows T to go into occupation under a 21-year lease in writing within section 70 (1) (*g*) and also (*k*) as a periodic yearly tenancy. A week later P executes the mortgage, pays V the purchase moneys and obtains a transfer from V. A fortnight thereafter (all relevant documents then being delivered to the Land Registry) P becomes registered proprietor with the legal estate and the mortgagee becomes a registered chargee with a legal mortgage. Upon P becoming registered proprietor the 21-year tenancy by estoppel or yearly periodic tenancy by estoppel (probably protected by the Rent Acts) as the case may be, is fed, so becoming a proper legal lease of overriding effect a split second before the mortgagee obtains the legal interest: *Woolwich Equitable B.S.* v. *Marshall* [1952] Ch. 1, *Mornington P.B.S.* v. *Kenway* [1953] Ch. 382. The mortgagee is also bound by the agreement for a tenancy within section 70 (1) (*g*): *Grace Rymer Ltd.* v. *Waite* [1958] Ch. 831. Would the position under section 70 (1) (*k*) be any different if P, prior to granting the tenancy, entered into a binding contract with the mortgagee to obtain a mortgage on completion in consideration of paying interest thereon and paying the balance of the purchase price? Not, if the contract were unprotected, it seems, unless the tenant knew this and was fraudulent: *De Lusignan* v. *Johnson* (1973) 230 E.G. 499, see p. 19, *supra*, and p. 135, *infra*, and for unregistered land see *Security Trust Co.* v. *Royal Bank of Canada* [1976] A.C.503, *per* Lord Cross at p. 519.

Would the position be any different if the tenancy by estoppel were created *after* completion in the ordinary conveyancing sense when the mortgage was executed but *before* registration of P as proprietor and of the mortgagee as registered chargee? Let us assume that the mortgage deed contains the customary term excluding the mortgagor's powers of leasing. In such a case Danckwerts J. in *Woolwich B.S.* v. *Marshall* [1952] Ch. 1, 6 and Harman J. in *Hughes* v. *Waite*[8] [1957] 1 W.L.R. 713 treated it as axiomatic that the mortgagee could not be bound by the tenancy within section 70 (1) (*k*) or (*g*) since in unregistered conveyancing a mortgagee would not be bound in such circumstances.

However, if they had bothered to examine the Land
Registration Act properly it is likely that they would have come
to a contrary conclusion as far as section 70 (1) (*k*) is
concerned. After all, the mortgagee only had an equitable
interest upon completion, and upon registration of P as
proprietor the tenancy by estoppel was forthwith fed, so
becoming a legal overriding interest a split second before the
mortgagee became a legal registered chargee subject to
overriding interests and minor interest then protected on the
register: sections 18 (3) (4), 19, 20, 70 (1) (*k*). The tenancy
thus binds the mortgagee.

The conclusion could be the same for rights within section
70 (1) (*g*) if the absolutist view[9] of paragraph (*g*) as a self-
contained paragraph were taken fully to its logical conclusion
so that rights within paragraph (*g*) are to be enforceable by
virtue of their own overriding nature rather than according to
general land law principles concerned with the enforceability of
"legal" and "equitable" interests. In the words of Russell L.J.
in *Hodgson* v. *Marks* [1971] Ch. 892, 934, "An overriding
interest is just that." It could, however, be argued that, whilst
the registered charge is subject to any overriding interest
created between completion and registration and the absolutist
view shows that notice is immaterial, the "rights,"
masquerading as overriding interests, are on general land law
principles subordinated to the rights created by completion of
the mortgage, which crystallised rights later become
consummated in the registered charge.

An example may help. P executes a mortgage in M's favour,
pays V the completion moneys and obtains a transfer from V.
Next day P in writing leases the premises to T for 21 years, T
forthwith going into occupation and paying the rent. T has an
equitable 21-year lease, the lease being in writing and P not
having any legal title, and a periodic yearly tenancy by estoppel
at common law. The day thereafter P grants T an option to
purchase the freehold for £x. Ten days later (all relevant
documents then being delivered to the Land Registry) P
becomes registered proprietor with the legal estate and M
becomes registered chargee with a legal mortgage.

The equitable rights of T under the lease in writing and the
option are equitable rights within section 70 (1) (*g*). M takes

his registered charge subject to overriding interests existing at
the date of registration (*Re Boyle's Claim* [1961] 1 W.L.R.
339, *London & Cheshire Insurance Co.* v. *Laplagrene* [1971]
Ch. 499, the date of the writ approach of Buckley L.J. in
*Schwab & Co.* v. *McCarthy* (1976) 31 P. & C.R. 196, 215
being erroneous) save where inquiry is made of the rights of a
person in actual occupation and the rights are not disclosed.[10]
M is thus bound by T's rights if he made no inquiry of T.
Against this M might well argue that he is subject to T's
"rights" but what exactly are T's "rights"? Surely M's
equitable interest arising at the date of execution of the
mortgage (an equitable right to be in the same position as if he
had a 3,000 year term) prevailed over T's subsequent equitable
rights under the written lease and the option, as first in time
and further strengthened by becoming legal upon becoming a
registered charge when T's rights remained equitable. Thus,
whilst M takes his interest subject to T's "rights," such rights
on general principles are incapable of binding him. There is
much to be said for this solution as recognised by Oliver J. in
*Schwab & Co.* v. *McCarthy* (1976) 31 P. & C.R. 196, 205,
"The fact that the defendant had an overriding interest [within
s. 70 (1) (*g*)] does not convert it into something more than it
was before registration of the estate or the interest which is
alleged to be subject to it." See further Chapter 8, pp. 138–139.

In our example it is still necessary to consider T's periodic
yearly tenancy by estoppel and this has implications for what
the position would be if T had had a 21 -year tenancy by
estoppel by deed. A tenancy by estoppel is not a legal estate so
T could not claim as equity's darling to take free of the earlier
equitable interest of M arising at the date of execution of the
mortgage. Thus, until registration M's rights prevail but on
registration T obtains a legal estate a split second before M
obtains a legal registered charge. In unregistered land law T
can take advantage of this superior legal estate on *tabula in
naufragio* principles, unless he had notice of the earlier
equitable interest when first taking his interest or unless when
taking the legal estate he had notice that P held the legal estate
on trust for M.[11] Thus, even treating the lease within section
70 (1) (*k*) as a bundle of rights in the same way we examined
"rights" within paragraph (*g*), T's legal lease should, it seems,

have priority over M's mortgage, M's mortgage when registered being subject to T's then subsisting paragraph (*k*) lease.

All in all, study of section 70 (1) (*g*) and (*k*) indicates that for reasons of social policy the interests of tenants (and co-owners) in their homes is generally to be preferred to the interests of mortgagees in the securities for their moneys, especially as the risk of fraudulent purchasers is very small. Building societies, in particular, ought to be able to bear this risk or insure against it. Moreover, whilst moneys can make up for loss of moneys they cannot make up for loss of a home.

## Priorities of Registered Charges

The provisions of the Act regulating the priorities of registered charges *inter se* are very clear since section 29 provides, "Subject to any entry to the contrary in the register, registered charges on the same land shall as between themselves rank according to the order in which they are entered on the register, and not according to the order in which they are created." This parallels the provisions of section 97 of the Law of Property Act for mortgages of unregistered land. In similar relationship to section 94 of the Law of Property Act, section 30 goes on to provide for charges made for securing further advances. Where the proprietor of a charge is under an *obligation* noted on the register to make further advances, then, any subsequent registered charge takes effect subject to any further advances made pursuant to the obligation. Where there is no such obligation, but the charge is expressed to cover such further advances, if any, that may happen to be made, then the Registrar[13] has to give notice to the chargee of any subsequent charge that is about to be entered on the register. If, after the date when this notice ought to have been received in due course of post, the chargee does make further advances, these further advances do not have priority over the subsequent charge of which notice had, or ought to have, been sent to the chargee. If, by reason of any failure on the part of the Registrar or the Post Office in reference to the notice, the proprietor of the charge suffers any loss he is entitled to be indemnified.

Where charges are minor interests the position as to priorities is more complex and is dealt with in the next chapter.

## Discharge of Registered Charges

A registered charge has to be discharged by deletion from the charges register, the Law of Property Act provisions not applying: L.P.A. 1925, s. 115 (10). The charge certificate together with Form 53 (or other satisfactory evidence such as an indorsed receipt under the Building Societies Act 1962, s. 37 (1)) must be delivered to the Registry. The charge certificate is cancelled, the charge is deemed to have ceased, and any term or sub-term granted by the mortgage is extinguished and merges in the registered estate without any surrender: section 35, rule 267.

## Notes

[1] L.P.A. 1925, ss. 85, 87.

[2] *Ibid.* ss. 86, 87.

[3] *Per* Russell L.J. in *Strand Securities Ltd.* v. *Caswell* [1965] Ch. 958, 996; *cf. Clements* v. *Ellis* (1934) 51 C.L.R. 217.

[4] In *Re White Rose Cottage* [1964] Ch. 490–491 Wilberforce J. pointed out that s. 66 covered only mortgages created by deposit and not mortgages created by deed and supported by deposit. Either situation may be protected by notice of deposit under rules 239 & 240: *Re White Rose Cottage* [1965] Ch. 940 (C.A.).

[5] See Megarry and Wade. pp. 922–923.

[6] For a useful general article, see A. M. Prichard (1964) 80 L.Q.R. 370.

[7] What really matters is that the mortgagee does not take his legal interest, excluding powers of leasing, a split second before the legal lease is created.

[8] A very unsatisfactory case ignoring s. 70 (1) (*g*) and fundamental registration principles: contrast *Grace Rymer* v. *Waite* [1958] Ch. 831.

[9] See pp. 87–91.

[10] No protection is afforded by an official search certificate since such only protects against entries on the register, not overriding interests outside the register.

[11] See Megarry & Wade, *The Law of Real Property* (4th ed.), pp. 979–981; Snell, *The Principles of Equity* (27th ed.), pp. 48–49.

[12] In unregistered land law it is up to the subsequent chargee to give notice to the prior chargee: L.P.A. 1925, s. 94 (2), Megarry and Wade, p. 985. Law Com. Working Paper No. 67, para. 117, recommends that this should also be so for registered land.

CHAPTER 8

PRIORITIES

IN the matter of priorities registered conveyancing is rather
unsatisfactory: the position has to be gleaned from various parts
of provisions scattered amongst the Act and the Rules. At least
there is no difficulty where registered charges are concerned
since as between themselves they rank according to date of
registration (s. 29) and a sale by a chargee under his statutory
powers operates as a transfer for value by the proprietor of the
land at the time of the registration of the charge would have
operated (s. 34 (4)). Neither is there any difficulty where the
Minor Interests Index is concerned (except as to its ambit).
However, this Index is not what it appears to be *viz.* a register
of minor interests. Instead, it merely regulates priorities as
between assignees and incumbrancers of interests arising under
trusts as of date of entry in the Index.[1] It arises only out of the
provisions found in section 102 (2) providing for the lodgment
of priority cautions and priority inhibitions for dealings in
equitable interests - such priority cautions and inhibitions must
not be confused with ordinary cautions and inhibitions as even
Russell L.J. seems to have done in *Barclays Bank* v. *Taylor*
[1974]Ch. 137.[2]

*Registered Dispositions*

To move from the specific to the general, one fundamental
principle underpins the Act. A person taking an interest under
a registered disposition for value takes such interest subject to
overriding interests and interests entered on the register but
free from all other interests whether he "has or has not notice
thereof express, implied, or constructive": sections 3 (xv), 5, 9,
18 (5), 2O, 21 (5), 23, 59 (6), 74. As Plowman J. pointed out

in *Parkash* v. *Irani Finance Ltd.* [1970] Ch. 101, 109, "One of
the essential features of registration of title is to substitute a
system of registration of rights for the doctrine of notice."[3]
Moreover, Walton J. in *Freer* v. *Unwins Ltd.* [1976] Ch.288,
298 said "The general scheme of the Act is that one obtains
priority according to the date of registration, and one is subject
or not subject to matters appearing on the register according to
whether they were there before one took one's interest or after
one took one's interest." The registered land "registrar's
darling" equivalent of "equity's darling" is thus a purchaser
acquiring title under a registered disposition for value without
there being any entry on the register.[4] Where a disposition is
made without value the volunteer takes subject to any minor
interests binding the transferor but in all other respects the
disposition has the same effect as if for value: section 20(4),
23(5).

Allowance must be made for overriding interests as recognised
by Cross J. in *Strand Securities Ltd.* v. *Caswell* [1965] Ch.
373, 390 where he emphasised, "It is vital to the working of
the land registration system that notice of something which is
not on the register of the title in question shall not affect a
transferee unless it is an overriding interest." In the Court of
Appeal [1965] Ch. 958,987 Russell L.J. was prepared to accept
the general argument, "that a purchaser of registered land
searches the register of the title which he is acquiring and must
be able to rely on that search and (apart from matters such as
overriding interests) must surely be entitled to rely on a title
free from all that does not actually appear on that title before
completing."[5] Indeed, both Cross J. and the Court of Appeal
would have held a long lease not binding on a purchaser with
express knowledge of it but for the fact that the lessee was
protected in a particular way. In *De Lusignan* v. *Johnson*
(1973) 230 E.G. 499 Brightman J. actually held that a person
acquiring a registered charge with express knowledge of a then
existing but unprotected estate contract took free of the estate
contract in the absence of fraud.[6] In *Hodges* v. *Jones* [1935] 1
Ch. 657, 671 Luxmoore J. took the view, "Notice of the
existence of a restriction which is not registered does not affect
the property alleged to be subject to it."

This is not at all surprising when one considers that cases like

*Coventry Permanent Economic B.S.* v. *Jones* [1951] 1 All E.R.
901, *Hollington Brothers Ltd.* v. *Rhodes* [1951] 2 All E.R. 578,
*Sharp* v. *Coates* [1949] 1 K.B. 285, and *Greene* v. *Church
Commissioners* [1974] Ch.469 show that in unregistered
conveyancing where land charges registrable under the Land
Charges Act are concerned the Land Charges Register is
everything. Thus if such charges are not registered before
completion of a purchase then they are void against any
purchaser even if he has express notice of such charges.[7]
It should perhaps be mentioned that purchaser in the Land
Charges Act (s. 20 (8) of 1925, s. 19 (1) of 1972) is defined as
"any person (including a mortgagee or lessee) who, for
valuable consideration, takes any interest in land or in a charge
on land." The omission of the words "in good faith" which
appear in the definition of "purchaser" in the other 1925
Property Acts, prevents a court from holding that a purchaser
is bound on the footing that his express notice prevents him
from being a purchaser in good faith.
By section 3 (xxi) of the Land Registration Act "purchaser",
unless the context otherwise requires, means "a purchaser in
good faith for valuable consideration and includes a lessee,
mortgagee, or other person who for valuable consideration
acquires any interest in land or in any charge on land."

   Thus at first sight, there is some scope for the argument that
express notice of an unprotected minor interest prevents a
purchaser being in good faith, so that he cannot claim to take
free from the minor interest. However, sections 5, 9, 20(1),
23(1) and 74, which provide the statutory basis for the
"registrar's darling" principle, do not mention "purchaser" but
only "person" or "transferee." Section 59(6) states: "A
*purchaser* . . . shall not be concerned with any . . . matter . . .
not protected by a caution or other entry on the register
whether he has or has not notice thereof express, implied, or
constructive," but since the subsection makes express notice
immaterial it is clear that the context requires purchaser not to
mean purchaser in good faith if express notice precludes good
faith. Indeed, if express notice is to preclude good faith one
would expect the Act expressly so to provide as in section 61(6)
where a purchaser with express notice of an act of bankruptcy
is specifically deemed to take not in good faith. The definition

of minor interests in section 3(v) as "capable of being overridden (whether or not a purchaser has notice thereof)" and the provision in section 74 that no "person dealing with a registered estate or charge shall be affected with notice of a trust express implied or constructive," when taken together with sections 5, 9, 20(1), 23(1) and 59(6), clearly envisage that a new registered proprietor for value will take free of unprotected minor interests even if he has express notice of them.

As Lord Wilberforce stated in *Williams & Glyn's Bank* v. *Boland* [1980] 3 W.L.R. 138, 142: "In place of the lengthy and often technical investigation of title to which a purchaser [of unregistered land] was committed, all he has to do is to consult the register; from any burden not entered on the register, with one exception [overriding interests], he takes free. Above all, the system is designed to free the purchaser from the hazards of notice, real or constructive, which, in the case of unregistered land, involved him in inquiries, often quite elaborate. The Law of Property Act 1925 contains provisions limiting the effect of the doctrine of notice, but it still remains a potential source of danger to purchasers. By contrast, the only provisions in the Land Registration Act 1925 with regard to notice are provisions which enable a purchaser to take the estate free from equitable interests or equities whether he has notice or not. The only kind of notice recognised is by entry on the register."

Thus, in 1973 Brightman J. in *De Lusignan* v. *Johnson* 230 E.G. 499 had held that a person acquiring a registered charge with express knowledge of a subsisting unprotected estate contract took free from such contract. In 1976 Graham J. in the much-criticised[8] *Peffer* v. *Rigg* [1977] 1 W.L.R. 285 (where *De Lusignan* v. *Johnson* was not cited) held that to take free of an unprotected minor interest a transferee-purchaser had to be in good faith and he "cannot in my judgment be in good faith if he has in fact notice of something which affects his title as in the present case"—where a minor interest under a trust for sale was unprotected. This reasoning must be wrong, though the actual decision can be justified on the basis that the transferee's conduct was sufficiently fraudulent to cause the equitable in personam jurisdiction to be invoked. Accordingly, " purchaser" or "transferee" cannot in context be treated as meaning a purchaser or transferee in good faith so as to bring in by the back-door the doctrine of express or actual notice.

In the light of the above discussion it also seems that a case can be made out for the statutory context requiring "purchaser" in the Land Registration (Official Searches) Rules not to have the prima facie meaning of purchaser in good faith. However, Plowman J. in *Smith* v. *Morrison* [1974] 1 All E.R. 957 held that purchaser had such a prima facie meaning but then took the sting out of such a holding by going on to hold that a purchaser acts in good faith so long as he acts honestly and without any ulterior motive: thus, express notice of an earlier contract, as to the validity of which a later purchaser had honest doubts, did not prevent the later purchaser being in good faith so as to be able to take advantage of the priority period afforded by a search certificate.

The registered conveyancing position thus seems to be that a minor interest not protected at the date of registration of a registered disposition (or of the commencement of a priority period under a search certificate pursuant to which registration occurs within the period) is void against the disponee even if he had express notice of it as in *De Lusignan* v. *Johnson* (1973) 230 E.G. 499. A disponee can honestly take advantage of this rule for, "It is not fraud to take advantage of legal rights" *per* Lord Cozens-Hardy M.R. in *Re Monolithic Building Co. Ltd.* [1915] 1 Ch. 643 (where the Court of Appeal held that a mortgage not registered under the Companies Act was void against a later registered mortgage even though the later mortgagee had express notice of the earlier mortgage at the time when he took his own security).

On the other hand, a statute may not be used as an instrument of fraud. Thus, if A is contractually bound to sell his land to B, A cannot for ulterior motives transfer the land for value to the A Co. Ltd. and then claim that the A Co. Ltd. takes free of B's unprotected minor interest: *Jones* v. *Lipman* [1962] 1 W.L.R. 832. The A Co. Ltd. holds the land on constructive trust for B subject to B paying the purchase moneys outstanding. Further see p.19 above.

By section 3 (xxii) "registered dispositions" are defined as "dispositions[9] which take effect under the powers conferred on

the proprietor by way of transfer, charge, lease or otherwise
and to which (when required to be registered) special effect or
priority is given by this Act on registration." The following are
definitely registered dispositions: (1) those dispositions required
to be completed by registration (and sometimes also by notice
on the freehold title), e.g. transfers of registered freeholds or
leaseholds, grants of registrable rent-charges or leases, (2) those
dispositions required to be completed by entry of a notice on
the servient title, e.g. registered charges, legal easements and
profits, (3) one type of disposition taking effect as an overriding
interest, namely, legal leases granted for a term not exceeding
21 years granted at a rent without taking a fine: sections 18
(3), 19 (2), 22 (2).

It would seem that restrictive covenants created in any
registered disposition (e.g. the transfer of a registered estate)
have the protection afforded to the registered disposition. Other
restrictive covenants (*e.g.* created independently in a deed solely
drawn up for the purpose) are protected as minor interests (ss.
2 (1), 3 (xv)) which under section 40 take effect subject to "the
rights of persons entitled to overriding interests (if any) and to
any incumbrances entered on the register." A lien created by
deposit of the land certificate under section 66 is protected as a
minor interest with its priority governed by section 66 so that it
takes effect "subject to the overriding interests if any and to
any estates interests charges or rights registered or protected on
the register at the date of the deposit."[10] A lien created by deed
supported by deposit of the land certificate is not within section
66 (see *per* Wilberforce J. in *Re White Rose Cottage* [1964]
Ch. 490—491) and depends for its protection on a notice of
deposit under rule 239, an ordinary notice under section 49, or
a caution against dealings under section 54 or the *de facto*
protection of the deposit.

Oddly enough, the word "dealing" is nowhere defined in the
Act. It seems to be a wider expression than registered
dispositions, so covering applications for notices to protect
restrictive covenants (s. 50) and equitable mortgages (s.49).
The date of a registered disposition is the date the application
for registration or for entry of a notice is delivered at the
Registry (r. 83)[11] except that in the case of a legal lease not
exceeding 21 years granted at a rent without taking a fine the

date is the date of the grant of the lease: *Freer* v. *Unwins Ltd.* [1976] Ch.288. At such date—and only then—does the legal interest arise or pass.

## Overriding Interests

Overriding interests are analogous to legal interests in unregistered conveyancing. As we have seen registered dispositions all take effect subject to overriding interests existing at the date of registration, just as conveyances of unregistered land all take effect subject to legal interests existing at the date of conveyance. As Ruoff and Roper state at page 9, "Although only some overriding interests are legal interests they all have the character of legal interests in that they bind even a purchaser for value without notice of them." Their priority crystallises at the date of registration of the registered disposition. However, if an overriding interest ceases to be such by the date of a subsequent disposition, as where an occupier goes out of actual occupation, then the subsequent disponee is unaffected by it (unless it is then protected by some entry on the register): *London & Cheshire Insurance Co. Ltd.* v. *Laplagrene* [1971] Ch.499. But so long as he holds an overriding interest such a person is entitled to sit back and do nothing in reliance upon sections 20 (1) and 23 (1) except for making proper answers to any inquiries put to him. As Russell L.J. said in *Hodgson* v. *Marks* [1971] Ch. 899, 934, "An overriding interest is just that."

To determine what interests qualify for section 70 as overriding interests such as legal leases and legal easements it appears necessary to discover whether the land was registered or not at the date of creation of the interest. If the land was not registered at that time general land law criteria should determine whether the interest is legal or equitable. If the land was registered at the time then it seems that registered land law criteria should determine whether the interest is legal or equitable: thus perpetual easements granted by deed can only be equitable if not completed by entry of a notice on the servient title, leases for a term not exceeding 21 years granted by deed (or orally or in writing if not exceeding three years) at a rent without taking a fine are legal (ss. 19 (2), 22 2, 18 (3),

21 (3)) whilst other leases can only be equitable (unless, of course, registered with a separate land certificate).

Once an interest is within the category of overriding interests it seems that the label of "overriding" should dictate the quality of enforceability of the interest so categorised, especially in light of the absolutist view of section 70 (1) (*g*) (see p. 87). An equitable profit within section 70 (1) (*a*) thus binds a purchaser under a registered disposition even though the purchaser had no notice of such equitable interest.
It seems, however, that general law criteria (other than the doctrine of notice) must be taken into account in considering exactly what are the "rights" of a person claiming an overriding interest under section 70 (1) (*g*). Thus, if H and Ware registered proprietors, with no restriction on the register since they are joint beneficial owners, and H assigns his equitable share to S, and H and W as trustees for sale sell to P, receiving the purchase money from him, then P, even if S is in actual occupation, will take free from S, since S's rights are in the proceeds of sale and not in the land, being overreached under L.P.A. 1925, ss. 2 and 27. Take also the following sequence of events: (1) T has a lease within section 70 (1) (*k*); (2) L, the registered freehold proprietor mortgages the house by an equitable charge by deed supported by deposit of the land certificate but otherwise unprotected: the deed confers the usual power of attorney enabling a sale *qua* mortgagee to cover the whole legal and equitable estate in the house[12] subject to the tenancy; (3) L contracts to sell an unincumbered freehold to T; (4) the mortgagee *qua* mortgagee transfers the legal and equitable estate, subject to the tenancy, to P who becomes registered as proprietor in L's place. It is clear that P takes subject to T's lease within section 70 (1) (*k*) and to T's "rights"within section 70 (1) (*g*). However, under the general law a contract to sell made by the mortgagor L has no effect on the mortgagee's overreaching power of sale: *Duke* v. *Robson* [1973] 1 W.L.R. 267. Since L had no power to contract to sell the unincumbered freehold to T, T has no "rights" capable of binding P. [Further see p. 128 *supra* and *Schwab & Co.* v. *McCarthy* (1976) 31 P. & C.R. 196, 205.]

Another example may help. (1) RP contracts to sell to A who pays the 10 per cent. deposit; (2) RP contracts to sell to his brother, B, for half its value, and B pays the 10 per cent. deposit; (3) A pays over the balance of purchase moneys in return for the land certificate and a transfer; (4) B moves into actual occupation, RP having vacated the premises; (5) A becomes registered proprietor. A takes subject to B's "rights" within section 70 (1) (*g*). However, under the general law since RP by virtue of the contract with A held the house as trustee for A he could not effectively by a later contract with B hold the house also as trustee for B so B's "rights" are not such as to be capable of binding A. B's rights are against RP for breach of contract or for the proceeds of sale in RP's hands: *Lake* v. *Bayliss* [1974] 1 W.L.R. 1073. The position would be similar if, after contracting to sell to A, RP had declared himself trustee of the house for his thirty-year old son, B, who happened to be in actual occupation when A became registered proprietor.

As between competing overriding interests it seems that the analogy with legal interests and the inapplicability of the doctrine of notice to section 70 (1) (*g*) rights on the absolutist view are such as to indicate that a first overriding interest as first in time overrides a second overriding interest. It should thus be unnecessary to consider whether the first interest is equitable and the second legal and whether the second person had notice of the first.

### *Derivative Validity and Invalidity*

If a new registered proprietor takes property subject to an overriding interest (*e.g.* Mrs.Hodgson's absolute interest under a bare trust as in *Hodgson* v. *Marks* [1971] Ch. 892) then he will be subject to any interests granted out of such overriding interest whether before or after he became registered proprietor and even though unprotected when he became registered proprietor: *Marks* v. *Attallah* (1966) 110 S. J. 709. Interests granted out of a valid overriding interest thus have derivative validity: no complaint can be made of what the overriding interest owner has done with his overriding interest.

Correspondingly, there appears to be scope for a doctrine of derivative invalidity. Take the facts of *Hodgson* v. *Marks* [1971] Ch. 892 altered by Mrs. Hodgson not having an absolute interest but a mere life interest under the Settled Land Act, which can rank only as a minor interest (section 86(2), L.R.A.). Such minor interest is not proctected by an entry on the register. She then grants a 21 year lease to T just before P, the purchaser from her rogue lodger (to whom she had transferred the freehold title) became registered proprietor. P takes free from Mrs.Hodgson's unprotected minor interest under section 20(1) so that, just as an underlease derived from a void lease is void, so T's lease derived from a void minor interest should be void.The fact that T was in actual occupation paying rent when P became proprietor should not avail T since T's "rights" within section 70(1)(g) are on general principles void against P.

## Minor Interests

Minor interests take effect as equitable interests (sections 2(1), 101(3)) and are capable of protection by a caution, a notice, a restriction, or inhibition. Essentially, cautions and notices protect commercial-type interests like those registrable under the Land Charges Act in unregistered conveyancing, whilst restrictions protect overreachable interests under trusts for sale or under settled Land Act settlements. Whether a caution or a notice is used to protect a minor interest depends upon whether the land certificate is held by the Land Registry since a notice can only be used if such be the case (s.64(1)(c) and where land is subject to a registered charge, the typical form of mortgage in registered conveyancing, the certificate has to be deposited with the Registry (s.65). Of course, mere entry of a caution or a notice does not automatically validate the interest protected by such an entry and the extent to which an interest is valid depends upon the interest itself[13] and not whether it is a caution that protects it or fortuitously, a notice that protects it. Section 52 specifically states that dispositions are subject to rights protected by a notice "but only if and so far as such rights may be valid" and the Court of Appeal in *Kitney* v. *M.E.P.C.* [1977] 1 W.L.R. 981 held that sections 5 and 20 must be harmonised with section 52 so that a new proprietor takes subject to interests entered on the register only so far as they are valid.

*The promised land*

One might have expected that a system of registration of title placing such emphasis on the register of title would expressly provide for priorities of competing minor interests to be determined according to date of entry on the register of the cautions, notices, restrictions and inhibitions as is the position for Northern Ireland under section 40 of the Land Registration Act (Northern Ireland) 1970 and also for Alberta and Manitoba.[14] But not a bit of it! Whilst machinery is provided for settling disputes, nothing is said of the principles upon which disputes are to be decided. Section 56 (2) of the Land Registration Act 1925 provides "A caution lodged in pursuance of this Act shall not prejudice the claim or title of any person and shall have no effect whatsoever except as in this Act mentioned." This last reference is to the machinery for "warning off" cautions and the provision for compensation to be paid where a caution is lodged without reasonable cause.[15] Section 52 provides, "A disposition by the proprietor shall take effect subject to all estates, rights and claims which are protected by way of notice on the register at the date of the registration or entry of notice of the disposition *but only if and so far as such estates rights and claims may be valid and are not independently of this Act) overridden by the disposition."* R.J.Smith has argued in (1977) 93 L.Q.R. 541 that this introduces a first in time of protection principle for interests protected by notice (instead of a caution) but in the light of the italicised words this seems unlikely: see Ruoff & Roper, p. 124 and the approach of the court in *Barclays Bank* v. *Taylor* *[1974] Ch. 137* and in *Kitney* v. *M.E.P.C.* [1977] 1 W.L.R. 81

In "warning off" proceedings rule 219 provides "the cautioner or his personal representatives may show cause why the caution should continue to have effect or why the dealing should not be registered" and rule 220 directs the Registrar to "make such order as he shall think just" providing that he "may refer the matter at any stage for the decision of the Court." Such "general discretionary power"[16] could have enabled a bold Registrar and a bold Court to treat the Land Registration Act as a self-sufficient constitution for registered land, to treat the Act as erecting an edifice of revolutionary design though built with ordinary land law bricks. After all, it is revolutionary for someone with no title to land at all, but who somehow manages to have himself registered as proprietor of the land, to be able to sell the land on to X and to confer upon X an indefeasible title,[17] the register being conclusive as to X's title (except for overriding interests).If the register is so conclusive and since it is designed to mirror all the minor interests affecting the land then, surely, there is scope for minor interests to rank according to date of entry of the relevant caution or notice.[18] Surely it should not be necessary to apply general equitable principles (whereby an equitable interest only loses its priority to a subsequent equitable interest if its owner's conduct amounts to fraud or negligence or raises an estoppel, such conduct being sufficient to induce the later claimant to act to his prejudice)[19] and so to investigate questions off the register concerning negligence, estoppel and constructive notice[27] with all the difficulties and uncertainties that entails.

Judicial support for this may be found in a dictum of Cross J. (as he then was) in a reserved judgment in *Strand Securities Ltd.* v. *Caswell* [1965] Ch. 373, 390, "It is vital to the working of the land registration system that notice of something which is not on the register of the title in question should not affect a transferee unless it is an overriding interest" and in a *dictum* of Plowman J. in a reserved judgment in *Parkash* v. *Irani Finance Ltd.* [1970] Ch. 101, 109, "One of the essential features of registration of title is to substitute a system of registration of rights for the doctrine of notice." There is further support in the approach of Lord Denning in a reserved judgment in *Re White Rose Cottage* [1965] Ch. 940 concerning a competition between (1) a notice of deposit of an equitable charge protected by deposit of the land certificate, which takes effect as a caution under rule 239 (4) and (2) two subsequently entered cautions to protect two later equitable charging orders securing a judgment debt. Speaking of the interests protected by these entries on the register Lord Denning said at page 949 "Prima facie, their respective priorities were governed by the order of the date of those entries." On the other hand Harman L.J. approached the case by treating the order of creation of the equitable charges as prima facie governing priorities: [1965] Ch. 954. Salmon L.J. merely agreed with both judgments, both approaches leading to the same solution.However, Russell L.J. in giving the reserved judgment of the Court of Appeal in *Barclays Bank v Taylor* [1974] Ch. 137 has endorsed Harman L.J.'s approach.

The need to protect one's minor interest on pain of losing priority emerges from sections 66, 40, 48, 107 and 27 (3). By section 66 "The proprietor of any registered land or charge may, subject to the overriding interests, if any, to any entry to the contrary on the register, *and to any estates, interests, charges or rights registered or protected on the register at the date of deposit,* create a lien on the registered land or charge by deposit of the land certificate; and such lien shall, *subject as aforesaid,* be equivalent to a lien *created* in the case of unregistered land by the deposit of documents of title or of the mortgage deed by an owner entitled for his own benefit to the registered estate, or a mortgagee beneficially entitled to the mortgage, as the case may be." The clear implication is that such a lien by deposit is not to be subject to earlier minor interests not protected on the register at the date of deposit— the reverse of the unregistered land position indicated in *McCarthy & Stone Ltd.* v. *Hodge Ltd.* [1971] 1 **W.L.R.** 1547.[21]

Section 40 (1) has a similar effect to section 66 in the case of a registered proprietor creating restrictive covenants, though they should be protected by entry on the register under section 40 (3). In both cases priority is accorded on the creation of the lien or the restrictive covenant. However, it is the date of the protective entry that is crucial under sections 107, 27 and 48. By section 107:

> "The proprietor of any registered land or charge may enter into any contract in reference thereto in like manner as if the land or charge had not been registered, and, *subject to any disposition[22] for valuable consideration which may be registered or protected on the register* before the contract is completed[23] or protected on the register, the contract may be enforced as a minor interest against any succeeding proprietor[24]."

The implication[25] is that an earlier contract may be subject to a later equitable mortgage by deposit protected on the register by a notice of deposit, or to a later restrictive covenant noted against the proprietor's title, or if it amounts to a disposition, to a later option protected by a caution, before the contract had been completed or protected by a caution or a notice.[26] Solicitors should thus adopt the practice of protecting their clients' contracts as soon as possible.[27]

By section 27 (3) a registered charge "shall take effect from the date of delivery of the deed, but subject to the estate or interest of any person . . . whose estate or interest (*wherever created*) is registered or noted on the register before the date of registration of the charge." The italicised words in parenthesis reveal that date of entry of a notice is to be relevant and not the date of creation of the interest procted by the notice.[28] Similarly, by section 48, where a lease is protected by entry of a notice against the superior title, the proprietor and person deriving title under him are bound unless having an incumbrance registered or protected on the register *prior to entry of the notice.*

### The realities of registered land

However, despite the statutory support in section 82, which confers a deferred indefeasibility on a registered title subject only to overriding interests, and in sections 66, 40, 107, 48 and 27 (3) for supplying the principle that the register is to be everything (except for the case of overriding interests) it was inevitable that the Chancery Division, and the division of the Court of Appeal hearing Chancery appeals, would apply general equitable principles to problems of priority in the absence of specific statutory provisions ousting such principles: *Barclays Bank* v. *Taylor* [1974] Ch. 137. After all, the traditional English approach to statutory interpretation is to interpret statutes so as to affect general common law and equitable principles as little as possible and to fill gaps in statutes by such principles rather than novel principles ascertainable only by implication, but not strictly necessary implication, from the broad scheme of a statute.

Indeed, on a conceptualist as opposed to an instrumentalist view of law, it is only proper to take the view that the very fact that sections 66 and 40 give express guidance for priorities involving equitable mortgages created by deposit and restrictive covenants, that section 107 gives express guidance for priorities

between contracts and dispositions for value, that sections 27
(3) and 29 determine priority for registered charges, that
section 48 provides guidance for priorities between certain
leases and incumbrances, and that section 102 determines
priority of assignments of equitable interests, all signify that
other priorities must be determined on general equitable
principles. If it were otherwise then there would be statutory
provisions saying so, corresponding to sections 66, 40, 107, 27
(3), 29, 48 and 102, and cautions would be expressly stated to
have greater effect that they currently have under section 56
(2).

Unfortunately, general equitable principles lead to an
uncertain and unsatisfactory state of the law. Whilst this is true
of unregistered conveyancing where there are gaps in the Land
Charges Act[29] it is even more true of registered conveyancing.

### *Contract or Class F Charge* v. *Contract*

Take the case of an ordinary contract for the purchase of
land or of a Class F charge, followed by another contract,
where the earlier minor, and therefore equitable, interest is
protected by a notice or caution after the creation of the later
contract but before completion of the later contract. Since it is
not standard conveyancing practice to protect such interest by a
notice or a caution it cannot be said that the earlier equitable
incumbrancer is responsible for leading the subsequent
incumbrancer to believe that the registered proprietor has the
apparent power to deal with the land as if it were
unencumbered so as to estop the earlier incumbrancer from
taking advantage of his priority in time.[30] Moreover, if the
second incumbrancer has followed normal practice and
exchanged contracts and paid over the customary 10 per cent.
deposit *before* searching the register, then the first
incumbrancer's failure to enter a caution or a notice cannot
have had the effect of inducing the second incumbrancer to act
to his prejudice.

Even if the second incumbrancer has been able to take the
most unusual step of searching the register before contracting to
purchase the property[31] this alone should not have the effect of
depriving the first incumbrancer of his priority in time. After
all, if it had this effect it would mean that a prior unprotected

Class F charge or contract would lose its priority not, according
to the terms of the Act, upon the date of registration of the
purchaser as registered proprietor under sections 20 and 23,
but upon the earlier date when the purchaser exchanged
contracts pursuant to the clear search certificate.

On its own, failure to protect a Class F charge or a contract
should thus not occasion loss of priority against a subsequent
estate contract or other equitable interest (other than a lien
created by deposit[32] or a restrictive covenant[33] or, in the case of
a contract, a subsequent disposition for value within s. 107[34]),
though it might if combined with other circumstances. Thus, in
*Wroth* v. *Tyler* [1974] Ch. 30, where a Class F charge was not
protected by a notice until after the registered proprietor had
contracted to sell the property but before completion, Megarry
J. indicated that a wife's priority could be lost on estoppel
principles if her positive conduct in showing the contractual
purchasers round the house and explaining how various
gadgets worked amounted to a representation that she was
concurring in the sale and so deferring to the purchaser's
interest.[35]

In *Watts* v. *Waller* [1973] 1 Q.B. 153 it was assumed by the
Court of Appeal that although the purchasers' solicitors paid
over the purchase moneys and completed the purchase on May
24, which was within a search certificate's priority period
expiring at 11 a.m. on May 25, the house was taken subject to
the vendor's wife's Class F charge protected by a notice entered
during the currency of the priority period and so springing up
only at 11 a.m. on May 25, since by then the solicitors had not
delivered the relevant documents to the Land Registry. The
wife's appeal against an order for vacation of her notice was
thus allowed, the Court of Appeal holding that her right as a
wife out of occupation of the house, being a conditional right to
enter and occupy with the leave of the court, was properly
registrable as a Class F charge before such leave had been
given.

From the reported submissions of counsel it appears that the
statement of junior counsel for the wife[36] that her equitable
interest, having priority in time as of January 1, 1968,
prevailed over the purchasers' later equitable interest was not
disputed, despite the fact that, in reliance upon a clear search

certificate, the purchasers had paid over all the purchase moneys, which must be a most significant circumstance to be taken into account.

It is submitted that counsel for the purchasers, and the court in reserving their judgment, should at least have considered whether this circumstance was sufficient to displace the wife's priority in time. The leading authority is *Abigail* v. *Lapin* [1934] A.C. 491, a Privy Council appeal from the High Court of Australia.

*Australian authorities*

The Lapins, the registered proprietors of two properties, handed over their title certificates and executed transfers expressed to be in consideration of a money payment in favour of Mrs.Heavener. In reality the transaction was not one of sale but one of mortgage to secure a debt due to Mr. Heavener, a solicitor. It was quite common for mortgages to be effected in this way, the mortgagee or his nominee being put on the register as registered proprietor, the better to be able to exercise his remedies if the mortgagor defaulted. Upon payment of the debt and interest the properties were to be retransferred to the Lapins. After Mrs. Heavener was registered as proprietor she raised a £5,500 loan from Abigail and executed a mortgage in registrable form in his favour. Abigail lent the money without searching the register, though even if he had he would have discovered nothing to indicate the Lapins' interest. Abigail lodged a caveat (equivalent to an English caution) but before he delivered the mortgage for registration the Lapins at last lodged a caveat to protect their right to call for a retransfer.

Who then had priority?[37] The Lapins' equity of redemption was prior in time to Abigail's equitable mortgage (equitable because not registered) but the Privy Council held that the Lapins were bound by the natural consequences of their acts in arming Mrs. Heavener with the power to go into the world as the absolute owner of the properties and thus execute transfers or mortgages of the properties to other persons, so the Lapins had to be postponed to Abigail's equitable mortgage. Since their conduct in so arming Mrs. Heavener had induced Abigail to act to his prejudice it was immaterial that he had failed to search the register.

In their judgment the Privy Council stated that they thought that *Butler* v. *Fairclough* (1917) 23 C.L.R. 78, another decision of the Australian High Court on priorities, was rightly decided. There, the registered proprietor of a lease, subject to a registered mortgage with the title certifcicate deposited at the Registry, agreed under seal on June 30 to charge the lease with the repayment of money lent him by Butler and upon Butler's request to execute a registrable charge. On July 2 the registered proprietor agreed to sell the lease (subject to the registered mortgage) to Fairclough. That very day Fairclough searched the register, finding that the title was clear except for the registered mortgage, so later that day he completed his purchase by handing over the purchase moneys and taking a transfer in registrable form. On July 7 Butler lodged a caveat to protect his equitable charge and on July 12 Fairclough delivered his instrument of transfer for registration.

Griffiths C.J. after stating that the time sequence prima facie governs priorities of competing equitable interests went on in a passage approved by the Privy Council[38] to say,[39] "The claimant who is first in time may lose his priority by any act or omission which had or might have had the effect of inducing a claimant later in time to act to his prjudice." Since Butler's omission to enter a caveat had induced Fairclough to part with the purchase moneys, believing, after his search of the register, that he was purchasing subject only to the registered mortgage and no other charge, Butler lost the priority prima facie given his interest as first in time. To Butler's submission that it was expecting too much of him to enter a caveat within two days of the creation of his equitable charge Griffiths C.J. replied,[40] "The person who does not act promptly loses the advantage which he would have gained by promptitude."

### Implications for Watts v. Waller

At first sight then the Court of Appeal in *Watts* v. *Waller* should have considered and applied *Butler* v. *Fairclough* so as to hold that Mrs. Waller's omission to enter a Class F notice had induced the purchasers to part with their purchase money in reliance upon a clear search certificate and so was sufficient to displace Mrs.Waller's original priority in time.

However, *Butler* v. *Fairclough* is distinguishable in a particular

factul respect. It concerned an earlier equitable charge not
protected by deposit of the title certificte and, of course, it is
standard conveyancing practice to protect such a charge by an
entry upon the register. Since a purchaser can thus be expected
to rely upon such practice being followed, so as properly to
assume that a registered proprietor has an unencumbered title
in the absence of an entry relating to such a charge, the earlier
equitable chargee is estopped from claiming priority for his
earlier charge. In contrast, it is, of course, not standard
conveyancing practice to protect a Class F charge by a notice or
caution unless relationships have become rather fraught. Thus
failure to enter a Class F notice or caution does not entitle a
purchaser searching the register to assume that no Class F
rights exist. Indeed, if he actually knows the vendor is married
he knows that Class F rights exist, though they are as yet
unprotected and so may be destroyed if he becomes registered
as proprietor before they are protected. Accordingly, failure to
enter a Class F notice or caution cannot deprive a wife of her
priority in time on estoppel principles. Of course, negligence
principles are available but, as apparent from *Wroth* v. *Tyler*,
no court would find that a wife's failure to enter a Class F
notice or caution before a contract is entered into amounts to
negligence sufficient to deprive her of her priority in time.
Indeed, a court is likely to be so jealous in guarding the rights
of socially disadvantaged wives that payment of the purchase
moneys before entry of a Class F notice or caution would
probably not be sufficient to displace the wife's priority in time
(*cf. Tadder* v. *Catalano* (1975) 11 S. Australia S.R. 492)
especially in the light of sections 20 and 23 which provide that
it is upon registration that a purchaser takes subject to minor
interests then protected on the register but free from
unprotected minor interests—and in the light of a failure to
take advantage of the priority period accorded by an official
certificate.

If the earlier interest were an ordinary contract and not a
Class F charge, so as to be a commercial interest, it is still
standard practice not to protect it by a notice or a caution so
estoppel principles are, it seems, not available, to displace its
original priority, though the availability of negligence principles
so to do is more feasible, assuming that failure to protect the

earlier contract has led the subsequent purchaser to pay over his purchase moneys in reliance on a clear search certificate, though the purchaser then failed to register himself as proprietor within the priority period afforded by the certificate.

Indeed, this leads us on to a significant distinction from the position in *Butler* v. *Fairclough* since the Land Registration (Official Searches) Rules 1978 allow a search certificate to have a priority period of 20 working days within which a disposition may be registered free from any entry made on the register during the priority period. Accordingly, a purchaser who pays over his purchase moneys in reliance upon a search certificate clear of any notice or caution protecting a Class F charge or a contract, will automatically have priority over any Class F charge or contract protected by entry of a notice or caution during the priority period, so long as he delivers the relevant registrable documents before the end of the priority period as originally laid down or as specifically extended for a further 15 working days under a Form 95 application in that behalf.

In the light of this English priority period of 20, or even 35, working days it was quite reasonable for Fairclough to take 12 days including Saturdays and Sundays to deliver the relevant registrable documents to the Registry. In contrast, in *Watts* v. *Waller* it was unreasonable for the purchasers to deliver the relevant registrable documents outside the priority period or rather outside an extended priority period which they would automatically have obtained upon a Form 95 application. The clear search certificate should only have led Mr. and Mrs. Watts to believe that they would obtain an unencumbered title if they delivered the relevant registrable documents to the Land Registry before the expiry of the priority period whether original or properly extended. They misled themselves if they believed that they would take free from an interest not noted on the search certificate but protected by entry on the register during the priority period even if they delivered the relevant documents outside the priority period. Thus at the end of the day it was right that the purchasers should have been bound by the wife's Class F rights.

### Other Competing Minor Interests

There is another case on priorities that requires examination:

*Parkash* v. *Irani Finance Ltd.* [1970] Ch. 101. On July 7 Irani Finance Ltd. obtained an equitable charging order against the registered proprietor to secure a judgment debt against him and on July 10 it entered a caution on the register. On July 26 Parkash's solicitors, acting for him in a proposed purchase of the property, applied for an official search certificate and they then received a search certificate dated July 27 which by mistake failed to mention the caution. On August 10 Parkash completed his purchase, paying over the purchase money and receiving a transfer of the property, and on August 14 all the relevant documents were delivered to the Land Registry. The Registry notified Irani Finance Ltd. which, naturally, objected to registration of the transfer until its charge had been satisfied and claimed that the charging order had priority over Parkash's equitable interest.

Of course, the first equitable interest had been properly protected before the second equitable interest came into being, though from the point of view of the second incumbrancer it appeared, by virtue of the clear search certificate upon which he had relied in completing his purchase, that he would take an unencumbered title. In this difficult situation Plowman J. based his judgment on the fact that since under section 59 (6) "a purchaser acquiring title under a registered disposition" is *not* to be affected by notice express, implied, or constructive of matters capable of protection by a caution or other entry on the register, and not so protected, it follows implicitly that a purchaser *is* to be affected by notice of matters capable of protection by a caution, which in fact, are so protected, even though the purchaser may not know of the caution due to a mistake, whether on the Registry's part or his own part.

Such reasoning, unfortunately, is completely vitiated by the fact that section 59 (6) could not possibly have been applicable where Parkash had not yet been registered as proprietor for only then would he acquire "title under a registered disposition."[41] The reasoning would thus only have been valid if the Registry had compounded their mistake by not notifying Irani Finance Ltd. of the documents lodged for registration so that Parkash had been registered as proprietor. Such reasoning would then have been contradicted by section 79 (4), "A purchaser shall not be affected by the omission to send any notice by this Act directed to be given or by the non-receipt thereof,"[42] though supported by sections 20 (1) and 23 (1) enacting that the effect of registration of a disposition of a freehold or a leasehold is to transfer such interest *subject to any entries appearing on the register* and to any overriding interests affecting the estate transferred, but free from all other interests whatsoever.

In any event, it is submitted that Plowman J. should have approached the case on the footing that the earlier incumbrancer should only lose priority if he had been guilty of conduct amounting to fraud or negligence or raising an estoppel and being sufficient to induce the later incumbrancer to act to his prejudice. Since Irani Finance Ltd. had done all it could to protect its equitable charge its priority could not be displaced. Parkash could have recourse under section 83 (3) to the Consolidated Funds for an indemnity against any loss suffered by reason of the official serach certificate erroneously omitting the caution of Irani Finance Ltd.

One thing is quite clear about Irani Finance Ltd.'s equitable charging order: if it had not been protected by a caution before Parkash's official search certificate then since Parkash delivered the relevant documents to the Registry within the priority period affected by the search certificate it would have been void against Parkash.[43] But what if a caution had been entered during the priority period so as to spring up on the expiry of such period and Parkash had delivered the documents to the Registry outside the priority period? It seems to be standard conveyancing practice to protect a charging order by a caution or notice and to protect equitable charges by obtaining the land certificate and entering a notice of deposit or by entering a notice or a caution, so that to leave the proprietor (or an earlier mortgagee) with the land certificate without entering a caution or a notice is tantamount to arming another with the apparent power to deal with the land as if it were unencumbered by the charging order or equitable charge. Accordingly, this should estop the incumbrancer with his charging order or equitable charge from taking advantage of his priority in time against the subsequent purchaser, who has obtained the land certificate and paid over the purchase moneys in reliance upon a search certificate clear of the earlier interest

Furthermore, where the subsequent incumbrancer searches the register to discover the apparently unfettered power of the proprietor and then pays moneys over for the purchase of an option or for the purpose of a loan secured by an equitable charge created by deed[44] it would seem that an earlier incumbrancer with an unprotected charging order or equitable charge should similarly be estopped from relying on his priority in time. From *Barclays Bank* v. *Taylor* [1974] Ch. 137 it seems that an equitable chargee by deed is sufficiently protected by deposit of the land certificate alone (except as against a subsequent 21 or fewer years' lessee within section 70 (1) (*k*): see ss. 18 (3), 19 (2), 20, 59 (6).)

Where an earlier incumbrance is not a charging order or an equitable charge but a long-term conditional contract or an option it is fairly common practice to protect it by a caution or a notice. Accordingly, where such protection occurs during the priority period under a search certificate taken out by a purchaser who, in fact, only delivers the relevant documents outside the priority period so as then to be faced with the earlier incumbrance springing up at the end of the priority period, a good case can be made out for the earlier incumbrancer losing his priority on estoppel principles. Failing that, reliance could be placed on negligence principles but a court might hold that the first incumbrancer's negligence was matched by the second incumbrancer's negligence in not registering within the priority period so that the quities were equal so that the first in time should prevail. To avoid all problems it is thus vital to register within the priority period as originally obtained or as extended upon a Form 95 application *e.g. Watts* v. *Waller* [1973] 1 Q.B. 153; *Elias* v. *Mitchell* [1972] Ch. 652.

## Circular Priorities

The unsatisfactory nature of the rules governing priorities clearly appears in certain circular priority situations. Suppose V contracts to sell to A and then (by mistake, fraud or accident) contracts to sell to B who protects his interest by a caution or a notice. V then executes a registered charge in C's favour, C not knowing of B's contract through the fault of the Registry or of C. As registered chargee C has priority over A (who is unprotected), but A has priority over B (assuming it has not become proper conveyancing practice to protect A's contract in which case A's first in time priority would be displaced), but B (who was protected when the charge was registered) has priority over C!

Suppose O charges his house to A, who does not protect his charge in any way. Later O charges his house by deed to B supported by deposit of the land certificate. Then A enters a caution. Subsequently, O , with some flimsy excuse, persuades B to let him have the land certificate and then charges the house to C by deed supported by deposit. A has priority over C (since protected when C took his charge), but C has priority over B (since B was unprotected when C took his charge), but B has priority over A (since A was unprotected when B took his charge). These problems would not arise if mortgages could not be protected by deposit of the land certificate alone, but had to be protected by entry on the register, and if priorities were determined by date of entry on the register.

## Reform

Whilst it may be too much to expect the Land Registration Act to be completely recast along more logical and comprehensible lines could not Parliamentary time be found for some simple short measures?Could there not be enacted some short provision affording priority amongst competing minor interests as of date of the entry protecting a minor interest on the register, except in the case of fraud but that notice of the existence of an earlier interest should not of itself be imputed as fraud? Rules could be made under section 144 to deal with auxiliary matters such as the assignability of cautions[45] and to allow interests that are initially protected by cautions, but which are subsequently protected by a notice or substantively registered, to retain priority as of date of the initial caution. This might be thought burdensome for solicitors and for the Land Registry staff but it will radically improve the position for consumers of the registration system. The former Chief Land Registrar has himself written,[46] "In matters of land transfer the customer is always right. . . . [His] requirements should receive consideration first, last and all the time."

However, if such a reform is thought too burdensome could

there at least, not be a short measure enacted providing for a purchaser on the conclusion of a valid contract to be unaffected (except in the case of fraud) by minor interests not then protected on the register? Indeed, since this would mean that P out of fear of a possible P2 would enter a caution or notice, it would after all be better to provide for P to be protected as from date of entry of the caution or notice, especially since the uncertain ambit of section 107 already makes it desirable for P to enter a caution or a notice.[47]

Recently, the Law Commission in Working Paper No. 67 have produced a worthwhile set of radical proposals, though it may well be several years before sufficient Parliamentary time can be set aside for them. It is difficult to do better than set out the Commission's own "Summary of Provisional Conclusions" as follows.

## SUMMARY OF PROVISIONAL CONCLUSIONS

*As to protection of interests in registered land*

(a) *Generally*

1. The purpose in a registered land system of having notices and restrictions on the one hand and cautions on the other is to enable a distinction to be drawn between entries which are contentious and those which are not. Under the existing law this distinction is not clearly drawn. Accordingly we suggest the adoption of a new procedure for protecting interests on the register based on the following principles:

  (i) an interest which is not disputed by the proprietor should always be protected by notice or, where appropriate, restriction;
  (ii) an interest disputed by the proprietor should be protected by caution; and
  (iii) consequently (subject to the exceptions mentioned in 3 below) there should be no interests which are protectable only by notice (or restriction), or only by caution.

2. Under the proposed new procedure the applicant would in all cases apply initially for the entry of a notice or, where appropriate, a restriction. A notice or restriction would be entered if the case is one covered by paragraph 3 below or (as appropriate) the proprietor consents or does not object following his being notified of the application by the Registry. If the proprietor objects, a caution will be entered. In the event of conflict between competing interests, such a caution would have the same effect on priorities as a notice or restriction would have had. In a doubtful case the Chief Land Registrar might require the applicant to make a statutory declaration in support of the application.

3. The consent of the proprietor is not a relevant consideration where the entry on the register is of rights under a charging order or rights of occupation of a spouse under the Matrimonial Homes Act 1967. Such rights should accordingly always be protected by notice (and never by caution).

4. A person who without reasonable cause causes a notice or restriction to be entered on the register should be liable to compensate anybody who thereby suffers damage.

5. It should be made clear that those "equities" which in relation to unregistered land, are not registrable land charges but are nevertheless enforceable against a purchaser with notice are similarly enforceable where the title to the land is registered even if they do not appear on the register.[48] A person claiming to be entitled to such an equity should be able to apply for notice of it to be entered on the register under the new procedure mentioned in 2 above.

6. The provisions contained in section 49 (1) (*d*) and the proviso to section 49 (2) under which certain matters are protectable by notice where a restriction would be more appropriate should be repealed.

(b) *Mortgages and Charges*

7. There should be a new scheme for the creation and protection of mortgages and charges of registered land. Under it there would be only one kind of charge which must be by instrument and any distinction between "legal" and "equitable" charges of registered land would cease to exist.[49] The charge would be capable of being registered but registration would, where the charge is not by deed, require the

leave of the court. When registered the proprietor of the charge would have the full powers of a legal mortgagee.

8. A registrable charge could, as a less expensive alternative to registration, be protected and obtain priority by being noted on the register. Before realisation a noted charge would have to be registered.

9. A charging order on registered land should be treated as a charge created under hand. It could thus be registered with the leave of the court.

10. A floating charge by a company would not be registrable until it crystallised but would be protectable by notice or, if disputed, by caution.

11. Deposit of a land (or charge) certificate should, by itself, no longer create a charge over the land (or charge) concerned.

12. The mortgage caution, the notice of deposit and the restriction[50] should no longer be available as means of protecting charges of registered land.

(c) *Production of certificates of title before entries can be made on the register*

13. Certificates of title should, as now, be produced to the Registry on the occasion of the registration of a transfer or where an entry is to be made of a derivative interest which is required by the Act to be completed by registration. But production of the certificate should no longer be required on an application to register a transfer or a charge where the certificate is known to the Registry to be in the hands of a prior mortgagee.

14. Production to the Registry of the certificate of title should cease to be essential where the application is for the entry of a notice or restriction to protect a derivative interest which does not have to be completed by registration.

15. The obligation on a proprietor (under section 110 of the Act) to lodge his certificate (if it is not already in the Registry) to meet an application to register certain derivative interests should be extended to cover all classes of derivative interest created for value out of registered land and for which protection on the register is necessary.

16. If an applicant is unable to proceed with an application to register an interest because the proprietor fails to comply with his obligation to produce his certificate to the Registry, the

applicant should, before the application is cancelled, be entitled to have a caution entered as of the date of the delivery of the application for registration.

17. Production of certificates should no longer be required before registration of certain financial statutory land charges (*e.g.* local land charges), which must be registered before they can be realised.

### *As to priorities of interests in registered land*

1. An unprotected financial charge of registered land should be postponed to any interest, whether financial or not, acquired for value and protected on the register.[51]

2. Where a financial charge, having initially been noted, is subsequently registered it should on registration have priority over any land charge which was not duly protected on the register before the financial charge was originally protected.[52]

3. A mortgagee who intends to protect his charge by notice under the new procedure should be able, by making an official search and lodging his application within the prescribed time, to obtain the same priority for his charge as if his application had been for the registration of the charge.

4. Where a registered charge is made for securing further advances, the Chief Land Registrar is by section 30 of the Act under an obligation to notify the proprietor of the charge before making any entry in the register which would prejudice the priority of any further advances. It is suggested that the Chief Land Registrar should no longer be under this obligation.[53]

### *Notes*

[1] Virtually everyone is agreed it should be abolished and priorities left to the usual *Dearle* v. *Hall* (1828) 3 Russ. 1 rule as extended by L.P.A. 1925, s. 137. Hardly any use is made of it. Further, see 1st ed., pp. 141—143, *Ruoff* and Roper, p. 129, Law Com. Working Paper No. 37, paras. 106—107.

[2] The reference to cautions or inhibitions at the end of s. 102 (2) is surely to priority cautions and priority inhibitions.

[3] See also *Miles* v. *Bull* (No. 2) [1969] 3 All E.R. 1585, 1590A *per* Bridge J.

[4] See also *De Lusignan* v. *Johnson* (1972) 230 E.G. 499.

[5] He wrongly qualified this in respect of pending applications: see *Law Society's Gazette* (1965), Vol. 62, p. 507 *per* the then Chief Land Registrar.

[6] *Cf.Jones* v. *Lipman* [1962] 1 W.L.R. 832.

[7] L.C.A. 1925, s. 13 (2), L.C.A. 1972, s. 4. In the absence of fraud a constructive trust cannot be imposed so binding the purchaser: *Miles* v. *Bull (No.2)* [1969] 3 All E.R. 1590

[8] See ]1977] Cambridge L.J. 227, (1977) 40 M.L.R. 602, (1977) 93 L.Q. R 341, (1977) 41 Conv. 207, [1978] Conv. 52, [1979] Conv. 235, (1979) 94 L.Q.R. 239.

[9] See the non-exhaustive definitions in ss. 18 (5) defining disposition as including any disposition authorised under ss. 18 and 21 respectively.

[10] Witness the contrast in s. 58 between disposing of land, dealing with land, and depositing the land certificate by way of security. Also the contrast in Form 73 between a disposition and the creation of a lien by deposit.

[11] See also *Re Boyle's Claim* [1961] 1 W.L.R. 339, *London & Cheshire Insurance Co. Ltd.* v. *Laplagrene* [1971] Ch. 499.

[12] As in *Re White Rose Cottage* [1965] Ch. 940.

[13] ss. 52, 56; *Watts* v. *Waller* [1972] 1 Q.B. 153, *Willé* v. *St. John* [1910] 1 Ch. 701, *Cator* v. *Newton* [1940] 1 K.B. 415.

[14] See Land Titles Act T.S.A. 1955, c. 170, s. 152 Real Property Act R.S.M. 1954, c. 220,s. 148 and Land Registraion (Scotland) Act 1979, s. 7.

[15] A reference also to s. 18 (3).

[16] See *per* Wilberforce J. in *Re White Rose Cottage* [1964] Ch. 483, 492, "These provisions . . . give to the Registrar . . . what appears to be a general discretionary power to do what is just without laying down any principle on which he is to act."

[17]. ss. 20, 23, 69; *Morelle* v. *Wakeling* [1955] 2 Q.B. 379, 411, *Att.-Gen.* v. *Parsons [1956] A.C. 421, 441, Haigh's Case* reported in Ruoff and Roper (3rd ed.), p. 853. As Barwick C.J. pointed out in *Breskvar* v. *Wall* (1971) 126 C.L.R. 371, 385 speaking of the analogous Torrens system. "It is a system of title by registration. That which the certificate of title describes is not the title which the registered proprietor formerly had or which but for registration would have had. The title it certifies is not historical or derivative. It is the title which registration itself has vested in the proprietor. Consequently, a registration which results from a void instrument is effective according to the terms of the registration."

[18]. *Cf. Clark* v. *Barrick* [1950] 1 D.L.R. 260 (reversed on other grounds in [1950] 4 D.L.R. 529).

[19]. *Shropshire Union Rly. Co.* v. *R.* (1875) L.R. 7 H.L. 496; *Taylor* v. *London Banking Co.* [1901] 2 Ch. 231; *Abigail* v. *Lapin* [1934] A.C. 491. The best discussion of these principles is in *Equity; Doctrine and Remedies* by Meagher, Gummow and Lehane pp. 193–204.

[20]. If the subsequent claimant has actual constructive or imputed notice of the earlier equitable interest then it is *his* conduct in acquiring the subsequent equitable interest that is responsible for him acting to his prejudice. He then has no grounds for displacing the priority of the earlier interest: *Bailey* v. *Barnes* [1894] 1 Ch. 25, *McCarthy & Stone Ltd.* v. *Hodge* [1971] 1 W.L.R. 1547, and the Australian cases, *Courtenay* v. *Austin* [1962] N.S.W.R. 296,

314, *I.A.C. Finance Pty. Ltd.* v. *Courtenay* (1963) 110 C.L.R. 550, 578. The onus is always on the person seeking to displace the priority of time sequence to prove his case: *Strand Securities Ltd.* v. *Caswell* [1965] Ch. 958, 991, *Shropshire Union Rly. Co.* v. *R.(supra)*.

²¹. If V contracts to sell to A and then creates in B's favour an equitable mortgage protected by deposit of title deeds (or unprotected and so registered as a Class C (iii) or a C (iv) charge) and A later registers a C (iv) charge, A is not deprived of his priority in time since B was not a purchaser of a legal interest in the land (within L.C.A. 1925, s. 13 (2) or L.C.A. 1972, s. 4 (6)) before A registered his C (iv) charge.

²². Disposition is a word of wide import and is not exhaustively defined by ss. 18 (5) and 21 (5). It seems likely that it covers not just dispositions authorised under ss. 18 and 21 but also dispositions under a proprietor's powers to create restrictive covenants (s. 40), to create a lien by deposit (s. 66) and to create an equitable mortgage by deed supported by deposit (ss. 101, 106). See also s. 109. It seems that disposition must be a specific transaction for value complete in itself, so as not to cover a spouse's Class F rights or a contract though it may, perhaps, cover an option authorised under s. 107: *cf. George Wimpey Ltd.* v. *I.R.C.* [1975] 1 W.L.R. 995 and [1976] *Current Legal Problems* at p. 29 (D.J. Hayton). But see note 10, *supra*.

²³. *Semble* in a registered conveyancing Act this means not completed in the ordinary conveyancing sense of handing over the purchase moneys in return for the vendor's conveyance or transfer but completed in the sense of completed by registration of the contractual purchaser as proprietor *e.g.* RP contracts to grant a 25 year lease to T and the contract is completed by RP granting the lease in return for a consideration. RP then agrees to transfer and transfers an unencumbered freehold to RP2 who becomes registered as proprietor (before T registers his lease or goes into occupation) and so takes free of T's minor interest by s. 20 (1). If s. 107 meant completed in the ordinary conveyancing sense so as to make RP2 take subject to T's interest it would conflict with the linch-pin s. 20 (1). Thus s. 107 means completed by registration as proprietor.

²⁴. If any interests are protected by cautions, the "warning-off" procedure will ensure that priorities are resolved before anyone becomes succeeding proprietor. If V contracts to sell to A and then to lease to B who protects his contract by a notice, and A then becomes registered proprietor it would seem under s. 52 that B's rights are invalid against A who obtained the legal estate pursuant to his prior equitable interest.

²⁵. The implication arises from the fact that if, according to s. 107 (1), in a conflict between A (*e.g.* to whom RP had contracted to grant an easement) and RP2 (a succeeding proprietor) A's rights bind RP2 subject to the rights of X and Y but not of Z, then A's position *vis-à-vis* X, Y and Z should be the same whether the conflict is with RP or RP2 or there is no conflict with them at all. In dealing with the position in the case of a succeeding proprietor the draftsman revealed what he assumed was implicity the position in the case of an existing proprietor.

²⁶. A conflict arises between s. 66 and s. 107 where an unprotected contract (or option) is followed by a lien created by deposit (but otherwise unprotected) and the contract or option is subsequently protected since s. 66 appears to

afford priority to the lien and s. 107 by implication affords priority to the contract (or option). Presumably s. 66 is meant to prevail.

[27]. Whilst it may be that a court would strictly restrict s. 107 to a succeeding proprietor situation it may be a court might by implication apply the s. 107 principles to an existing proprietor situation (where a caution prevents there being any succeeding proprietor at the time of adjudication). "Safety first" is always a good motto.

[28]. See also *Freer* v. *Unwins Ltd.* [1976] Ch. 288, 297 on s.50 (2).

[29]. See D. J. Hayton [1976] *Current Legal Problems* at pp. 30–35, showing for example that where the sequence of events is (1) V contracts to sell P, (2) V contracts to sell to P2, (3) P2 obtains a clear search certificate but cautiously registers a C (iv) charge, (4) P registers a C (iv) charge, (5) P2 makes his pre-completion search and discovers P's C (iv) charge, it seems that P's equitable interest has priority over P2.

[30]. The position, of course, would change if it became standard conveyancing practice to protect a contract in the light of the views expressed in note 27, *supra*.

[31]. Normally the vendor will not give the written authority necessary for the purchaser to search the register until after the contract of purchase has been entered into.

[32]. s. 66.

[33]. s. 40.

[34]. See p. 143.

[35]. See also *Spiro* v. *Lintern* [1973] 1 W.L.R. 1002, *Re Sharpe* [1980] 1 W.L.R. 219.

[36]. [1973] 1 Q.B. 159, Matrimonial Homes Act 1967, s. 2 (1).

[37]. Priority as of date of *caveats* was not argued, possibly because of *dicta* of Dixon J. in the Australian High Court (1930) 44 C.L.R. 166, 205.

[38]. [1934] A.C. 491, 502.

[39]. (1917) 23 C.L.R. 78, 91.

[40]. *Ibid.* p. 92.

[41]. *Smith* v. *Morrison* [1974] 1 W.L.R. 659, 676.

[42]. ". . . by a person whose name is entered on the register as a proprietor of any land or charge, or as a cautioner or as entitled to receive any notice of in any other character" is implicit in light of s. 79 (1).

[43]. Land Registration (Official Searches) Rules 1969, r. 5.

[44]. If the equitable charge were a lien *created* by deposit of the land certificate it would have priority under s. 66. Query whether priorities then crystallise so protecting the chargee if he subsequently takes a deed (supported by deposit). This "short-cut" solution was not considered by the C.A. in *Barclays Bank* v *Taylor* [1974] Ch. 137.

[45]. Not presently assignable since there is no need where general equitable principles govern priority. If A first sells to B and B lodges a caution and A then sells to C who lodges a caution, then if B assigns his interest under the contract to D, whereupon B's caution is withdrawn and a fresh one is lodged by D, the first contract still retains its priority as first in time.

[46]. T. B. F. Ruoff, *An Englishman Looks at the Torrens System*, p. 59.

[47]. See p. 144 (*supra*). It is also advisable for P's solicitor since he may well

be held liable for professional negligence if P's contract became ineffective by P2 becoming registered proprietor: Farrand (2nd ed.); p. 231; Barnsley's *Conveyancing Law and Practice,* p. 226.

[48]. These "equities" are proprietary interests arising from acquiescence in expenditure like those in *Ives* v. *High* [1967] 2 Q.B. 379 and *Crabb* v. *Arun D.C.* [1975] 3 W.L.R. 847. Despite the *obiter dicta* of Cross J. in *Poster* v. *Slough Estates* [1969] 1 Ch. 495, 506–508 it seems they are protectable currently by a "caution" under s. 54 or a notice under s. 49 (1) (*f*). The Law Commission view that unprotected proprietary interests may well not be comprehended currently by the words in ss. 20 and 23, "but free from all other estates and interests whatsoever" seems a little optimistic. However, where an equitable interest arises under the principle "he who takes the benefit must also bear the burden" as in *Ives* v. *High* the equitable in *personam* jurisdiction, operating outside the registered land scheme, should be available.

[49]. After all equitable chargees invariably have a complex deed executed giving them full powers to get in and deal with the legal estate: Megarry and Wade, pp. 902, 922–923 and p. 124, *supra.*

[50]. Under s. 106 (3) substituted by Administration of Justice Act 1977, s. 26 the mortgage caution and the restriction are no longer available.

[51] This would clarify the position though this already appears to be the case, the earlier financial chargee being estopped from claiming his priority in time: paras. 103 and 107 of the Working Paper are too alarmist.

[52]. This and the previous proposal encourage a person with an estate contract to protect it so as to take priority over unprotected financial charges and protect himself against subsequent financial charges.

[53]. The onus should be on the subsequent mortgagee to give notice to the registered chargee as in unregistered land law: L.P.A. 1925, s. 94 (2).

# CHAPTER 9

# RECTIFICATION AND INDEMNITY
## THE INSURANCE PRINCIPLE

WHEREVER a system of registration of title exists the conclusiveness of the register has to be considered. In some jurisdictions (and under the original English system under the Land Registry Act 1862) a title, once on the register, is indefeasible, but, as a result of this, far too much fuss is made over the process of first registration: "there are lengthy advertisements, a multitude of inquiries, vexatious requisitions, costly surveys and a meticulous and pessimistic scrutiny of every deed and event on the title."[1] Moreover, situations inevitably arise where, after a period of time, the register no longer accurately reflects the true position, *e.g.* where a person other than the registered proprietor has been in possession for many years. Thus,. if the register is conclusive the system is unduly inflexible, cumbersome and bureacratic.

Accordingly, in England and Wales the register is not conclusive: absolute title is not absolute but relative, since rectification, subject to some qualifications, is always a possibility. However, if a person suffers loss through rectification or non-rectification of the register he will, subject to some significant qualifications, be entitled to compensation out of funds provided for the purpose.

In essence, the Registrar is in charge of an insurance organisation in which the state insures all titles to land on a business-like basis. Basically, "the applicant for first registration enters into a contract with the State for insurance against defects overlooked by himself or his solicitors—or even defects known to him and candidly disclosed—and any profit made out of the fees he pays may be regarded as a premium."[2] Of course, it is unlikely that any defects (except those

concerning physical inspection of the land) will not be
discovered since sometimes three, though usually two, solicitors
will have scrutinised the title before the Registrar sees it,
namely the vendor's solicitor who will have deduced it, the
purchaser's solicitor who will have examined and approved it
and the mortgagee's solicitor also. Nowadays there is an
increasing tendency for the one solicitor to act for both the
purchaser and the mortgagee.

Where the land is of low value the Registrar can accept it
for registration, without any examination at all, simply in
reliance upon a certificate from the applicant's solicitor that he
has carried out the normal process of investigation (r. 29).
Moreover, in respect of land of any value, the title to which is
open to objection, the Registrar may still register it with
absolute title if he considers it to be a good holding title (s. 13
(*c*)) even though a solicitor in such circumstances would have to
advise his client that the title was not really a good marketable
title (Ruoff & Roper, pp. 227–228 but *cf.* C. T. Emery (1976)
40 Conv. 122). Finally, the Registrar is very much assisted by
the "curtain" principle. Rule 170 (5) for transmissions on
death provides "It shall not be the duty of the Registrar nor
shall he be entitled to consider or to call for any information
concerning the reason why any transfer is made, or as to the
terms of the will, and whether he has notice or not of its
contents, he shall be entitled to assume that the personal
representative is acting (whether by transfer, assent or
appropriation or vesting assent) correctly and within his
powers." Section 74 further provides that the Registrar is not
to be affected with notice of trusts express implied or
constructive.

The analogy with an insurance organisation, however,
cannot be pressed very far since the insurance fund first
established under the Land Transfer Act 1897 disappeared into
the Consolidated Fund on October 1, 1971, under the power
contained in that behalf in section 1 of the Land Registration
and Land Charges Act 1971 (S.I. 1971, No. 1489). Since 1936
(ss. 4 and 5 of the 1936 Act) there had been no direct
relationship between the size of the fund and the level of Land
Registry fees since hardly any contributions from those fees had
been made to the fund. Investments of a nominal value of

£100,000 had been kept in the indemnity fund and all excess
fee income had been paid into the Exchequer Consolidated
Fund to which there was a right of recourse if the indemnity
fund were insufficient. Remarkably the investments consisted of
undated government securities so that the market value of the
investments was only about half their nominal value![3]

At present, to the extent that the fee income of the Registry
exceeds the administrative costs of providing the system of
registration and sums paid by way of indemnity the Exchequer
alone benefits. Moreover the sums paid by way of indemnity
are relatively small: in the years 1977–78, 1978–79 and
1979–80 the sums paid out were £49,866 (98 claims) £54,669
(109 claims) and £61,173 (120 claims) respectively in relation
to fee income of over £29 million, over £36 million and over
£46 million respectively![4] There were surpluses of income over
expenditure of £592,064, £2,487,038, £6,490,677 and
£2,396,723 in the years 1970–71, 1971–72, 1972–73, 1973–74,
so benefiting the Exchequer. This led the Registry sensibly to
abate its fees so giving rise to deficits of £2,341,131 and
£3,094,978 and £2,615,965 in 1974–75 and 1975–76 and
1976–77 respectively, the Exchequer subsidising the Registry
and, indirectly, property owners. Accordingly, the fees were
increased resulting in surpluses of £1,631,425, £4,762,740 and
an estimated £7,500,000 in 1977–78, 1978–79 and 1979–80
respectively.[5]

Since 1975 there has been in operation a full system of
management accounting to provide better budgetary control and
improved management information, so it would not be difficult
to have a separate insurance fund or insurance account. It
could then be checked that the fees charged covered the
administrative costs and indemnity claims, whilst enabling an
adequate reserve to be built up once again, as in the period
1925–36, at the end of which the insurance fund consisted of
investments to the nominal value of £478,822.[6] Moreover, as
we shall see, indemnity should be more freely available,
bearing in mind that "the purpose of an insurance system is
not so much to prevent claims as to spread loss more equitably.
In any event, an actuarial assessment of the risks involved in a
genuine scheme of state-guaranteed titles would be sounder
than the present unscientific assessment of the position."[7]

## *Rectification Jurisdiction*

The original strict Land Registry Act 1862 did not allow for rectification of the register. Sections 95 and 96 of the Land Transfer Act 1875 allowed rectification on certain grounds but only if it would not affect "any estates or rights acquired by registration in pursuance of this Act." As Lord Hanworth M.R. said in *Chowood* v. *Lyall (No. 2)* [1930] Ch. 156 at p. 164, "It would appear that as the 1875 Act left the matter there was practically no effective power to order rectification."

Section 7 (2) of the Land Transfer Act 1879, however, provided that

> "where a registered disposition would if unregistered be absolutely void or where the effect of such error omission or entry [being an error or omission in the register or an entry made by or in pursuance of fraud or mistake] would be to deprive a person of land of which he is in possession or in receipt of the rents and profits the register shall be rectified and the person suffering loss be entitled [subject to certain safeguards] to indemnity".

It thus "provided for rectification in cases where the effect would be to destroy estates or rights acquired by registration" as opined by Vaughan-Williams L.J. in *Att.-Gen.* v. *Odell* [1906] 2 Ch. 47 at p. 74 and cited approvingly by Lord Hanworth.M.R. in *Chowood* v. *Lyall* [1930] 2 Ch. 156 at p. 165.

Under the Land Registration Act 1925, s. 82 (2) it is now clearly stated that rectification may occur "notwithstanding that the rectification may affect any estates, rights, charges or interests acquired or protected by registration, or by any entry on the register, or otherwise," *e.g.* a right protected as an overriding interest.

Thus a rectification claim may be for replacement of the registered proprietor by the claimant, for cancellation of a notice or caution wrongly entered on the register, for entry of a notice burdening the registered title, or for any other matter requiring the register to be altered to reflect the true position.

By section 82 (1) (*a*) and (*b*) the register may be rectified by the court alone where the court:

(a) has decided that any person is or is not entitled to any estate right or interest in or to any registered land or charge and, as a consequence of such decision, it orders rectification[8];

(b) on the application of any person, who is aggrieved by any entry made in or omitted from the register or by any default being made, or unnecessary delay taking place in the making of an entry in the register, orders rectification.

By section 82 (1) (*c*)—(*h*) the register may be rectified by the court or by the Registrar:

(c) in any case and at any time with the consent of all persons interested;

(d) where either is satisfied that any entry has been obtained by fraud;

(e) where two or more persons are mistakenly registered as proprietors of the same registered estate or charge;

(f) where a mortgagee has been registered as proprietor of the land instead of as proprietor of the charge and a right of redemption is subsisting;

(g) where a legal estate has been registered in the name of a person who, if the land had not been registered, would not have been the estate owner;

(h) in any other case where, because of error or omission in the register or any mistaken entry, it may be deemed just to rectify the register.

There is also a miscellaneous collection of instances of powers of correction which sometimes verge on full rectification. They are to be found in rule 13 (clerical errors), rule 14 (larger clerical errors), rule 131 (where the powers of disposition have become vested in some person other than the proprietor), rules 211 and 248 (relating to the transitional provisions of the 1925 Property Legislation) and rules 276–277 (fixing boundaries).

## *Implicit Restrictions on Rectification*

At first sight there seems to be an awesome—or awful—blanket discretionary jurisdiction to rectify conferred by section 82 (1), paras, (*a*) to (*h*). However, just as Lord Radcliffe in *Sharkey* v. *Wernher* [1956] A.C. 58 at p. 80 made it clear that

it is wrong to treat the Income Tax Act as if it made law but
could not itself contain principle so with the Land Registration
Act. Just as in unregistered land there is the fundamental
"equity's darling" principle, enabling a bona fide purchaser of
a legal interest for value without notice to take free of equitable
interests, so in registered land there is the fundamental
"registrar's darling" principle, enabling a purchaser of a
registered interest for value to take free of interests not then
protected as overriding interests or by entry as minor interests
(L.R.A. ss. 5, 9, 20, 23, 59, (6), 74; *Freer* v. *Unwins Ltd.*
[1976] Ch. 288) though what exactly amounts to a sufficient
entry on the register can raise problems: see p.175, infra.

In section 82 (1) (*a*) surely in deciding whether or not a
person is entitled to any interest in registered land the court
must decide on registered land principles. Thus, if someone has
a minor interest which is unprotected when a purchaser for
value becomes the new registered proprietor of the property the
court should not be able to ignore registered land principles
(and L.R.A., s. 20) and decide on unregistered land principles
that such person has an interest in registered land, enabling the
register to be rectified by entry of a notice or caution.[9]
However, even registered land principles are subject to the
equitable *in personam* jurisdiction (operating by a court order
personally compelling the defendant to do something, *e.g.*
execute a transfer in the plaintiff's favour) that prevents
statutes being used as instruments of fraud.[10] If, indeed, the
dealings between the minor interest holder and the new
registered proprietor are such as to invoke the equitable
jurisdiction then it seems the court may directly rectify the
register under paragraph (*h*). Generally, however, where there
is an omission within paragraph (*b*) or (*h*) that is the fault of
the claimant (in failing to protect his interest) rectification
should not be ordered. Indeed, even if the omission is the fault
of Registry officials, the new registered proprietor, the
Registrar's darling, should not be liable to rectification, an
indemnity instead being given to the aggrieved claimant.
"Having searched the register, the purchaser must be able to
rely on that search and (apart from overriding interests) must
surely be entitled to rely on a title free from all that does not
actually appear on that title before completing" as accepted by

Russell L.J. in *Strand Securities Ltd.* v. *Caswell* [1965] Ch.
958 at p. 987.

Paragraph (*d*) raises two questions: what is meant by
"fraud" and whose fraud is it that is material? It would seem
that fraud should be brought home to the person whose
registered title is being impeached or his agents so that an
innocent successor in title to a "fraudster" should not be liable
to rectification.[11] However, if it be shown that his suspicions
were aroused and that he abstained from making inquiries for
fear of learning the truth (*i.e.* he has Nelsonian, as opposed to
actual knowledge, through having turned a Nelsonian blind eye
to problems) then fraud might properly be ascribed to him.[12]
"Fraud" would seem to require some want of probity, some
personal dishonesty or moral turpitude [13] and be capable of
extending to a case of undue influence.[14] Mere notice of an
unprotected interest which the new registered proprietor then
claims to take free from should certainly not invoke rectification
under paragraph (*d*) *c.f. De Lusignan* v. *Johnson* (1973) 230
E.G. 49. "It is not fraud to take advantage of legal rights" said
Lord Cozens-Hardy M.R. in *Re Monolithic Building Co. Ltd.*
[1915] 1. Ch.643 where a later mortgagee with express notice
of an earlier unregistered mortgage had priority over the earlier
mortgagee. An essential feature of registration of title "is to
substitute a system of registration of rights for the doctrine or
notice"[15] so if the right is not registered then *cadit quaestio*
(unless it is an overriding interest or was not registered owing
to the fraud of the defendant registered proprietor).

Paragraph (*g*) at first sight is startlingly broad in apparently
allowing rectification wherever the registered proprietor is
someone who would not have been the estate owner if the land
had been unregistered land. Thus where, say, land has actually
been registered for 50 years one can treat the land
hypothetically as if it had been unregistered throughout the
period, and if unregistered land principles produce as estate
owner someone different from the registered proprietor then
rectification is possible! Obviously, unregistered land principles
cannot be allowed to be perpetually pervasive and so
undermine registered land law completely. The position of the
Registrar's darling must surely be sacrosanct.

It is further submitted that paragraph (*g*) should be

considered in the light of paragraph (*f*), also introduced for the
first time by the Law of Property (Amendment) Act 1924,
Sched.8, para.16, both of which were probably intended to
allow for changes to be made to the register to make it accord
with the system of mortgages and the vesting of legal estates
introduced by L.P.A. 1925, ss. 85 (2), 86 (2) and First
Schedule. Thus, in 1926 it was possible to rectify the register to
make the tenant for life of settled land the registered proprietor
and to make the mortgagor of mortgaged land the registered
proprietor. It seems, though, that rectification was not just to be
available to give effect to the transitional provisions of L.P.A.,
s.39 and First Schedule. It was also to be available where a
post 1925 purported outright transfer was in substance only a
mortgage and where a registered disposition was made in
favour of a minor[16] and, presumably, where a S.L.A. settlement
was not properly effected *inter vivos* by two deeds so that no
legal estate in unregistered land would pass by virtue of
S.L.A.s.4, *e.g.* if W transferred her house to S absolutely but
only upon S undertaking to allow her a life interest therein. If,
however, the first registered proprietor liable to a rectification
claim managed to transfer the property to the Registrar's
darling then it is submitted that no rectification claim should
lie.

Paragraph (*h*) also appears to give the court or the Chief
Land Registrar an enormous discretion to rectify the register.
However, just as if in unregistered land law there were such a
vast statutory discretion in the Court on grounds of error,
omission or mistake to alter a person's title to land then the
court's discretion would be subject to certain fundamental
principles, so with the position in registered land. It can never
be just to rectify the register if this would detrimentally affect
the Registrar's darling. It would seem sensible to limit
paragraph (*h*) just to the transaction immediately affected by
the error, omission or mistake.[17] It would be possible to submit
that the error or omission or mistake within paragraph (*h*)
refers only to some act or neglect or default of the Registry, *e.g.*
where a registration is not in conformity with the instrument
on which it was based. However, such a submission is more
likely to succeed in relation to paragraph (*b*), the court being
very happy to retain its sizeable discretion in paragraph (*h*); a

self-denying refusal of jurisdiction (and power) tends to go against human – and judicial – nature. Retention of jurisdiction can be justified on the ground that mistakes in paragraph *(h)* must surely extend to a transaction itself based on a mistake, though a person detrimentally affected by such a mistake might have an alternative remedy under the court's equitable in personam jurisdiction under which the person benefiting from the mistake could personally be ordered to take certain steps.[18] Jurisdiction under paragraph *(h)* might also be exercised to regularise an *Ives* v. *High* [1967] 2 Q.B. 379 situation where the defendant is bound on the *in personam* principle that he who takes the benefit must also bear the burden.

## *Statutory Restrictions on Rectification*

Although section 82 (1) provides that the register may be rectified in the cases we have already noted, section 82 (3) as amended goes on to provide that "The register *shall not* be rectified, except for the purpose of giving effect to an overriding interest or an order of the court, so as to affect the title of the proprietor who is in possession" except in two instances.

### A. *Rectification against proprietor in possession*

The expression "in possession" creates difficulty since it is defined by section 3 (xviii) as including the "receipt of rents and profits or the right to receive the same, if any" "unless the context otherwise requires." There is no doubt that physical occupation by the registered proprietor protects him under section 82 (3): *Re 139 High Street Deptford* [1951] Ch. 884, *Re Sea View Gardens* [1967] 1 W.L.R. 134, *Epps* v. *Esso Petroleum* [1973] 1 W.L.R. 1071. Of course, an Englishman's home should not be taken away from him by rectification, except in very special circumstances, for a financial indemnity is inadequate recompense.

There is doubt as to whether a proprietor merely in receipt of rents and profits has protection. After all, a financial indemnity is adequate recompense for rents and profits. Moreover, if such a proprietor does have protection then all proprietors have protection except those allowing others to live in their property rent free. At first sight, section 82 (4) seems to clinch the meaning of possession as physical occupation only since it provides:

> "Where a person is in possession of registered land in right of a minor interest, he shall, for the purposes of this section, be deemed to be in possession as agent for the proprietor."

Thus, a 21 year lessee, protected by a notice or caution on the proprietor's freehold title, is deemed to be in possession as agent for the proprietor, so that the proprietor is in posession for the protection afforded by section 82 (3). There would, obviously, be no need for this if the proprietor's receipt of rents meant he was already in possession for section 82 (3) purposes.

However, it is unlikely that the draftsman had the lease example in mind since section 19 (2) reveals that he considered that a lease not exceeding 21 years would normally take effect as a registered disposition ranking as an overriding interest and incapable of being protected by notice (ss. 19 (2) *(a)* , 48). Surely if he had the lease example in mind he would have extended section 82 (4) to cover a person in possession in right of an overriding interest as well as a person in possession in right of a minor interest. It seems more likely that he had in mind the case of trustees registered as proprietors who allowed a beneficiary under a settlement upon trust for sale either to occupy the property himself or himself receive the rents and profits under section 29 of the L.P.A. Section 82 (4) is clearly necessary.

The meaning of possession is thus left open by section 82 (4). Mind you, it is a little tough on 21 or fewer year lessees with overriding interests who have made their homes on the demised premises if their proprietor landlords are not in possession for section 82 (3) purposes (assuming their leases may suffer from derivative invalidity if the landlord's interest is invalid).To be on the safe side they should enter notices (if the Registrar allows: p. 44, *supra*) or cautions so as to have minor interests that by virtue of section 82 (4) enable them to have protection derivatively from their landlords then protected by section 82 (3). This does seem rather absurd so it does not seem that the context of the Act requires "possession" to exclude "receipt of rents and profits." Indeed, without argument, Walton

J. in *Freer* v. *Unwins Ltd.* [1976] Ch. 288 at 294 assumed that "possession" included the receipt of rents and profits.[19] It would seem that possession cannot include the right to receive rents and profits for *all* registered proprietors have this right by virtue of their registration and section 82(3) is clearly intended to apply not to all but just to *some* registered proprietors.

## B. *The four exceptional instances*

(1) *Rectification to give effect to a court order.* Does a proprietor in possession really have much protection if the shield of section 82 (3) can always be taken away to give effect to a court order? This depends on the number of circumstances in which a court may order rectification of the register, *e.g.* under section 82 (1). It has already been submitted that the astonishing width of application of section 82 (1) cannot be taken at face value since there must be some implicit restrictions in order to protect the Registrar's darling and to prevent all registered titles being precarious.

Nevertheless section 82 (1) allows much scope for rectification. Indeed, it is *the* statutory rectification provision, giving such scope for rectification that the restriction on rectification against a proprietor in possession is rendered almost nugatory if the restriction is always to be lifted to give effect to court orders under section 82 (1). Can a more sensible interpretation be put upon the court order exception?

This exception was first introduced as part of the Administration of Justice Act 1977, section 24 which was introduced at the final stage in the Commons on July 22, 1977 (Hansard, cols. 2117-2118). The section was barely discussed and no one perceived that the court order exception at face value took away most of the protection hitherto afforded to a proprietor in possession.[20] It would seem probable that this was not intended but that the words "order of the Court" were included to deal with orders of the court other than those made under the statutory jurisdiction in section 82 (1). Thus, rectification against a proprietor in possession might be directly ordered by the court where the court held a disposition to be void under section 42 of the Bankruptcy Act 1914 or where the court held that a defendant had personally been guilty of such inequitable conduct (*e.g.* using a statute as an instrument of fraud) that he should personally be ordered to execute a particular document in the plaintiff's favour and send it to the Registry but that it would be more expeditious for the court directly to order rectification in the plaintiff's favour under its inherent jurisdiction. It is hoped that a court would strive to place a restrictive interpretation upon the court order exception but, it may well be, that further legislation is needed.

(2) *Rectification to give effect to an overriding interest.* A registered proprietor's title is always subject to overriding interests by virtue of sections 5, 9, 20, 23, and 70 and so, in law, rectification to give effect to them cannot be prejudicial since it alters the legal position not at all. For this very reason, as we shall see, no indemnity is payable in such cases. It may, however, be possible to sue an earlier unregistered vendor on the implied covenants for title (*cf. Chowood* v. *Lyall (No.2)* [1930] 1 Ch. 426; [1930] 2 Ch. 156 and *Re Chowood's Registered Land* [1933] Ch. 574 with *Eastwood* v. *Ashton* [1915] A.C. 900 and s. 76 (6) of the Law of Property Act 1925). The uncertain width of interests capable of existing as overriding interests, as we have seen in Chapter 6, makes this a very serious exception. It should be noted that the time for ascertaining whether a proprietor is in possession is the date of the rectification hearing, whilst the time for ascertaining whether a person has an overriding interest is the date of the registration of the proprietor: *London & Cheshire Insurance Co.* v. *Laplagrene* [1971] Ch. 499.

3. *Rectification because proprietor caused or substantially contributed to error or omission by fraud or negligence.* Section 24 of the Administration of Justice Act 1977 most usefully and sensibly substituted a narrower exceptional case than that originally provided in L.R.A., s. 82 (3) (*a*). Originally, there could be rectification against a proprietor in possession if he had "caused or substantially contributed by his *act* neglect or default to the fraud mistake or omission in consequence of which" rectification was sought. Judicial interpretation [21] treated this as covering not just cases where the proprietor intentionally or negligently misled the Registry but also cases where the proprietor innocently lodged documents for first registration of title, which did not in fact convey the exact estate in the particular parcel of land in question, *e.g.* "a

conveyance which by itself is inoperative to pass title"[22] (where part of the land had earlier been conveyed to someone else, before registration of title had become compulsory, and this had been overlooked) or "a document which contains a misdesciption of the property."[23] This interpretation deprived a first registered proprietor in possession of the apparent protection of section 82 (3) if there were any defect in the conveyance to him which he lodged with the Registry.[24] Subsequent registered proprietors were safe since it was only the first proprietor who was treated as responsible for the mistaken registration of title.[25]

Under the new section 82 (3) (*a*) rectification against a proprietor in possession is only available if he "caused or substantially contributed to the error or omission by fraud or lack of proper care" as suggested in Law Commission Working Paper No. 45. It remains to be seen how rigorous is the standard of proper care but it would seem that failure to carry out the usual conveyancing inquiries and inspections should amount to lack of proper care, which probably should be judged objectively and not subjectively.

Take the case of a registered proprietor, V, who granted O an option to purchase his land, such option expiring on May 1, 1981 but containing a provision that upon payment of £500 O may before May 1, 1981 extend the option to May 1, 1982. Pursuant to rule 190 and Form 59 a notice is entered by the Registrar which, misleadingly, only states that the option is exercisable until May 1, 1981.

In October 1981 P becomes new registered proprietor for value, having been told by V that the option has expired so that the notice no longer protects a valid right under section 52. In fact, O had validly extended the option to May 1982 and in December 1981 he exercises the option, claiming the notice sufficiently protects him or, alternatively, the register should be rectified to refer to the option being exercisable till 1982 if the extension provision were invoked by O.

P claims he should be entitled to rely on the entry in the register so as to have to make no inquiries about the option and that, anyhow, O should have checked that the Registrar made the proper entry.

O maintains that, having sent in the basic application with a copy of the option, he should be able to rely on the Registrar making a proper entry and that no sensible purchaser should have proceeded without insisting on the vendor having the notice removed, an easy matter if the option had expired as alleged by the vendor.

This last point will probably carry the day for O—and prevent any indemnity being payable to P.

(4) *Where for any other reason, in any particular case, it is considered that it would be unjust not to rectify the register against the proprietor* (s. 82 (3) (c). The words "unjust not to rectify" show that it is necessary to show more than that it would be just to rectify the register. These provisions are indefinite and broad; indeed, broad enough to give a blanket discretion. They have only been considered in five cases.[26] A little guidance can be found in *Re 139 High Street, Deptford* [1951] Ch. 884, 892 where the following factors were considered relevant in not rectifying the register; the true owner had no genuine need for the land; he would be sufficiently compensated by an indemnity; the proprietor in possession had expended money on the land. In *Epps* v. *Esso Petroleum* [1973] 1 W.L.R. 1071 it was considered relevant to review the indemnity position of each party on the footing that the claimant obtained rectification or was refused rectification as the case may be, and to take into account the failure of the claimant to take all proper conveyancing precautions before purchasing the property.

In *Freer* v. *Unwins* [1976] Ch. 288 the new registered proprietor had in 1974 taken a transfer from the old registered proprietor when there was no notice or other entry on the register relating to a 1953 restrictive covenant. Walton J. expressed "very great surprise" that the Registrar had rectified the register under section 82 (3) (c) to enter a notice of the covenant and stated at p.295, "I cannot see that there was any ground whatsoever for rectifying the register against the freehold proprietor." After all, as he stated at p.298, "The general scheme of the Act is that one obtains priority according to the date of registration and one is subject or not subject to matters appearing on the register according to whether they were there before one took one's interest or after." It surely cannot be unjust not to rectify the register against the Registrar's darling.

Reliance may now be placed upon section 82 (3) (*c*) in situations covered by section 82 (3) (*b*) until repealed by Administration of Justice Act 1977, s.24. Rectification used to be possible under section 82 (3) (*b*) where the immediate disposition to the proprietor was void or the disposition to any person through whom he claimed otherwise than for value was void, *e.g.* for forgery or *non est factum* and see *Re Beaney* [1978] 1 W.L.R. 770. It seems section 82 (3) (*b*) was repealed on the basis that if the proprietor was himself guilty of fraud or negligence in relation to the void disposition then section 82 (3) (*a*) was available whilst, if he were innocent, rectification ought not *prima facie* to follow as a matter of course under section 82 (3) (*b*) (*e.g.* if he had spent £30,000 on building a house on the land "conveyed" under a forgery)[27] but should be left to the court's broad discretion under section 82 (3) (*c*)[28] This overlooks the fact that in the exceptional section 82 (3) instances there still remains the general discretion under section 82 (1) as will now be seen.

## Discretion to Rectify

Since (1) section 82 (1) gives a discretion to rectify in certain cases but (2) section 82 (3) states that the discretion must not be exercised against a proprietor in possession except in certain instances, it has (3) been judicially assumed that in those instances the discretion must be exercised so as to rectify the register against the proprietor: *Re 139 High Street, Deptford* [1951] Ch. 884, 889. However, this third step does not follow, for if one of the exceptional instances arises, so as to prevent the general rule in section 82 (3) applying, then, only the first step remains, i.e. there is a discretion which may be exercised for or against the proprietor in possession. Pennycuick J. seemed to appreciate this in *Re Sea View Gardens* [1967] 1 W.L.R. 134, 141 where he stated that, though one of the exceptions were established, it might not be just to rectify in certain special circumstances, *e.g.* where the "true owner" had knowingly stood by and allowed the proprietor to do work on the land. However, these special circumstances may amount to

proprietary estoppel interests,[29] which prevent the "true
owner" seeking rectification from being the "true owner" of
the whole interest in the disputed land. It was left to
Templeman J. in *Epps* v. *Esso Petroleum* [1973] 1 W.L.R.
1071, 1078—1079 to make it clear that the discretion remains
where any of the exceptional instances are established.
However, in the case of the new court order exception, of
course, effect must be given to the order, the court, in its
discretion having decided to make the order.

One area which has not yet been judicially explored is the
extent to which advantage might be taken of the rule in
*Saunders* v. *Vautier* [1841] Cr. & Ph. 240 to circumvent the
discretion to rectify conferred by the Act. The rule in *Saunders*
v. *Vautier* confers upon an absolutely entitled beneficiary the
right to call for a transfer of the legal estate vested in his
trustee. Thus, if a registered proprietor has the legal estate and
the victim, V, of a wrongful or mistaken first registration
arising from forgery or double conveyancing retains the
equitable interest, as he does according to Templeman J. in
*Epps* v. *Esso Petroleum,* V can call for the legal estate to be
transferred to him by the proprietor and can obtain a court
order to this effect. Upon complying with this (on pain of
committal for contempt or execution of a transfer by a
Chancery Master) the proprietor will find that he has no claim
to an indemnity since he did not suffer loss by reason of
rectification but by reason of himself transferring the title to V.
If he wishes to preserve his indemnity claim it appears that the
proprietor will have to force V to take him to court and will
then have to persuade the court to take the short cut of directly
rectifying the register under section 82 (1) (*a*) as Harman J.
seems to have done in *Bridges* v. *Mees* [1957] Ch. 475, though
there the plaintiff actually sought an order for the defendant to
transfer the property to him or a court order for rectification.
However, section 82 (1) (*a*) seems broadly drafted enough to
enable a court of its own motion to rectify thereunder, so
preserving a defendant proprietor's claim to an indemnity.

Of course, these problems do not arise if the views of
Templeman J. are erroneous and registration confers on the
first proprietor the whole legal and equitable estate even in
cases of forgery and of double conveyancing as has already been

submitted.[30] Registration confers the full legal and equitable
estate upon the proprietor, subject to minor interests then
protected on the register and to overriding interests: sections 5,
9. Thus, if the overriding interest is the full equitable estate
under section 70 (1) (*f*) or (*g*) (*e.g.* in Mrs. Hodgson's case in
*Hodgson* v. *Marks* [1971] Ch. 892 or where the victim of a
forgery is in actual occupation) then it is open to the person
with the overriding interest to take advantage of the rule in
*Saunders* v. *Vautier,* so circumventing any judicial discretion
under section 82: no indemnity claim lies in any event where
overriding interests are concerned: *Re Chowood's Registered
Land* [1933] Ch. 574.

## The Effect of Rectification

When the register is rectified it is the Registrar's practice to
issue a new edition of the register, all interests then bearing the
date of the new edition as in *Freer* v. *Unwins Ltd.* [1976] Ch.
288, the date being that of the rectification application rather
than of the resolution of the application: rule 83 as substituted
by Land Registration Rules 1978 (S.I. 1978 No. 1601). Thus,
when a successful claimant replaces the registered proprietor
the new register will reveal to what registered charges and
minor interests the land is then subject, though it must be
remembered that interests protected by a notice are only
effective to the extent that they are inherently valid (s. 52 (1)
and that cautioners will either be "warned off" or their
protection upgraded.

In *Re Leighton's Conveyance* [1936] 1 All E.R. 667 a
daughter, fraudulently using undue influence, had her mother
transfer the mother's house to the daughter, the mother being
too prepared to sign whatever the daughter put before her
without examining the documents at all. The daughter as
registered proprietor created charges upon the house in favour
of chargees who were ignorant of the fraud. The mother
obtained rectification by replacing the daughter as registered
proprietor but the charges were left on the charges register of
the property on the footing, it seems, that the mother was
estopped by her conduct in enabling the daughter to appear as

unincumbered proprietor from having priority over the chargees.

There can be no quarrel with this if the mother did not have an overriding interest, but prima facie she did have by virtue of her actual occupation, if her right to set aside the disposition for undue influence is a "right" within section 70 (1) (*g*), a case of undue influence assuming a transfer of the equitable interest but in circumstances which entitle the transferor to recall it: see *per* Russell L.J. in *Hodgson* v. *Marks* [1971] Ch. 892, 929 (distinguishing the case before him as one where Mrs. Hodgson and her lodger had expressly agreed that the beneficial ownership was to remain in Mrs. Hodgson).

However, if the mother had an overriding interest then "a person who remains in actual occupation does not do anything to abandon the rights which her actual occupation protects unless on inquiry she does not reveal them: that is what section 70 (1) (*g*) enacts. The [mother] did not arm [the daughter] with the apparent ability or power to deal with the property free from overriding interests" (*per* Russell L.J. in *Hodgson* v. *Marks* [1971] Ch. 892, 934).

Where a successful rectification claim results in entry of a notice on the register it seems that, whilst the registered proprietor will then be bound (as of the date of the rectification application) by the interest protected by the notice, earlier dispositions (*e.g.* leases for 21 years or less, charges, easements, restrictive covenants, liens created by deposit) will not be subject to the notice, the notice having no retrospective effect.

In *Freer* v. *Unwins Ltd.* [1976] Ch. 288, the plaintiff, a shop owner in a parade, had surprisingly obtained rectification against the freehold registered title of a nearby shop, of which the defendant was tenant, by obtaining entry of a notice relating to a valid restrictive covenant created in 1953.[31] Then the shops were unregistered land so the plaintiff had duly registered his covenant against the name of the nearby shop owner under the Land Charges Act. The nearby shop was later sold when the area had become a compulsory registration area, but somehow the new registered title omitted the burden of the covenant. The proprietor of the nearby shop in 1969 leased it for 21 years to S who, in 1974, assigned the lease to the

defendant. The proprietor, S, and the defendant had no actual
constructive or imputed notice of the covenant.

Having obtained rectification the plaintiff sued the defendant
to enforce the covenant, but failed, since Walton J. held that
the notice, though binding the proprietor, had no effect against
S or the defendant. By section 19 (2) the 1969 lease (though
not itself capable of being registered with a separate land
certificate and not noted on the freehold title) took effect as if it
were a registered disposition. Thus, by sections 20 (1) and 59
(6) the lessee, S, *then* took subject to minor interests protected
on the register and to overriding interests, but free from all
other interests whatsoever. The entry of the notice to protect
the covenant, a minor interest, was dated April 28, 1975,
pursuant to the successful rectification claim and took effect by
section 50 (2) subject to "incumbrancers or other persons who
at the time when the notice is entered may not be bound by the
covenant." Since the 1969 lease (with the benefit of sections 20
(1) and 59 (6)) was well prior to the 1975 notice the lessee, S,
took free from the covenant and the defendant assignee was "in
exactly a similar position" (*per* Walton J. at p. 617).

In essence the lessee was treated as if he had the rights of a
bona fide purchaser for value without notice under ordinary
land law principles and the defendant assignee as a *Wilkes* v.
*Spooner* [1911] 2 K.B. 473 type successor in title to such
"equity's darling." In registered conveyancing the "Registrar's
darling" seems to be merely a transferee for value without
there being any entry then on the register. It would thus seem
that even if the defendant somehow had notice of the plaintiff's
covenant when he took the assignment there is no reason why
he should not still have been able to take advantage of the
lease's priority according to the state of the register in 1969.
Presumably, if the 1969 lease had been for 22 years and so
registered with a separate title of which rectification was then
sought, in circumstances where the assignee somehow had
notice of the covenant when he took the assignment, the
assignee should also be able to rely conclusively on the register
(*cf. Hollington Brothers Ltd.* v. *Rhodes* [1951] 2 All E.R. 578,
*Miles* v. *Bull* (*No.* 2) [1969] 3 All E.R. 1585, *De Lusignan* v.
*Johnson* (1973) 230 E.G. 499, *Kitney* v. *MEPC* [1977] 1

W.L.R. 981). Rectification should thus not be ordered against him under section 82 (3) (*c*).

At least the freeholder in *Freer* v. *Unwins Ltd.* was bound by virtue of section 50 (2): "Where such a notice is entered *the proprietor* of the land and the persons deriving title under him (except incumbrancers or other persons who *at the time when the notice is entered* may not be bound by the covenant) *shall be deemed to be affected with notice* of the covenant as being an incumbrance on the land."

It seems implicit in the fact that the sub-section is concerned with the date when the notice is entered and not an earlier date (such as the date of creation of the covenant) that it is not possible to rectify retrospectively. This is also the case in section 48 (1) (as extended by section 49) concerned with notices of minor interests other than restrictive covenants, and in section 66 concerned with liens by deposit. The possibility of retrospective rectification would, indeed, breach what Walton J. refers to at page 616 as "the general scheme of the Act that one obtains priority according to the date of registration and one is subject or not subject to matters appearing on the register according to whether they were there before one took one's interest or after one took one's interest."

## *Indemnity*

The provisions for indemnity are supposedly intended to complement the provisions for rectification so that by section 83 a person who suffers loss by reason of: (1) rectification of the register; or (2) non-rectification of the register; or (3) destruction of documents in the Registry, inaccurate land certificates (39 Conv.(N.S.) 316-317), searches etc. can claim compensation. Unlike the position in some jurisdictions there is, quite sensibly, no need before seeking compensation for the claimant to bring or attempt to bring any proceedings against the person who caused the loss. However, the Registrar as insurer is subrogated to the rights of the claimant by section 83 (10).

Although where the register is rectified, the amount payable relates to the value (if there had been no rectification) of the estate, interest or charge immediately before the time of rectification, where the register is not rectified the amount payable cannot exceed the value of the estate interest or charge at the time when the error or omission which caused the loss was made (s. 83 (6)). The true owner, where some years have elapsed, will thus recover very much less than the present value of the land and will wonder what are the advantages of the registered system. He will also need to see if too many years have not elapsed for where the land has been registered with absolute title or good leasehold title he will usually only have six years from the date of registration of the title in dispute in which to bring his claim for an indemnity.[32] Thus the plaintiffs in *Epps* v. *Esso Petroleum* [1973] 1 W.L.R. 1071 could not claim any indemnity though suffering loss from non-rectification. The difference between this six year period and the ordinary 12 year limitation period for the recovery of land seems anomalous. If the indemnity claim does not arise in consequence of a registration with absolute or good leasehold title the six year period does not commence until the claimant knows, or but for his own default might have known, of the existence of his claim: section 83 (11).

It should be noted that the Registrar's power to determine questions as to right or to amount of any indemnity under section 83 (7) has ceased since section 2 of the 1971 Act came into operation in October 1971 and the court is, instead, to determine those questions, though nothing is to preclude the Registrar from settling by agreement claims for indemnity (s. 2 (5)). The practice is first to seek agreement with the Registrar and only if the claim is refused, either on merit or quantum, to look to the High Court.[33]

## No Indemnity

No indemnity is payable in many instances. In *Freer* v. *Unwins Ltd.* [1976] Ch.288 Walton J. opined that there would be no indemnity where a claimant successfully obtains rectification but still suffers loss, the loss not being occasioned by reason of any rectification of the register. However, Ruoff and Roper (4th ed.), p.794, note 93 coyly states, "Happily events did not turn out in that way" and in correspondence the Chief Land Registrar has refused to disclose his legal reasoning

for allowing Mr.Freer's claim for an indemnity. At least a
exible liberal approach to granting compensation is to be
welcomed: if a person innocently suffers under a state-imposed
registration system then the state should compensate him. It is
expressly provided that there is no indemnity on account of any
mines or minerals unless a note has been expressly entered on
the register showing that mines and minerals are included in
the registered title: section 83 (5) (*b*). There is no indemnity if
the limitation period is breached: section 83 (11). There is no
indemnity for costs incurred in taking or defending legal
proceedings without the consent of the Registrar, as insurer,
except there is nothing to prevent an applicant for an
indemnity from applying to the court without any such consent.
The costs of any such application or of any legal proceedings
arising out of it may be recovered: section 83 (5) (*c*), Land
Registration and Land Charges Act 1971, s. 2 (2).

More significantly there is no indemnity where the applicant
or a person from whom he derives title (otherwise than under a
disposition for value registered or protected on the register) has
caused or substantially contributed to the loss by fraud or lack
of proper care: section 83 (5) (*a*). It is an open question
whether lack of proper care is to be judged objectively or
subjectively and it remains to be seen how rigorous the
standard of proper care is to be.

For example, a registered proprietor, M, might transfer her
house to her 35-year-old son or nephew, S, living with her on
the express arrangement that she is to have a *life* interest, but
otherwise the facts are as in *Hodson* v. *Marks* [1971] Ch. 892,
S selling to T, who becomes registered as proprietor. T then
discovers M still residing there and claiming rectification by
entry of herself as registered proprietor, being Settled Land Act
tenant for life: *Bannister* v. *Bannister* [1948] 2 All E.R. 133,
*Binions* v. *Evans* [1972] Ch. 359, sections 86 (1), 87 (3). Since
T is not a proprietor in possession rectification is ordered under
section 82 (1) (*g*) for if the land were unregistered M and not
T would be the estate owner (S.L.A. 1925, s. 4 (1)). Thus T
seeks an indemnity.

Is he guilty of lack of proper care if he failed to make any
inquiry as to M's rights? Is his age, shyness, poor
understanding of English (being a foreigner) relevant? What if

his solicitors had asked S's solicitors whether any overriding interests existed and obtained the truthful reply that none existed so far as they knew (M having a minor interest only under section 86 (2)) so his solicitors then relied upon section 20 to obtain the legal estate free from minor interests not then protected on the register. Indeed, since T seems to be the Registrar's darling it is questionable whether M's prima facie claim to rectification under section 82 (1) (*g*) ought to have been allowed in the first place or if allowed whether it should then have been overcome by a further claim to rectification made by T under section 82 (1) (*a*). The question would then arise whether M's lack of proper care prevented an indemnity being payable to her.

It is most significant that where rectification is ordered to give effect to an overriding interest no indemnity is payable for no loss is suffered by reason of rectification, since the proprietor's title has in any event been subject to the overriding interest all the time under sections 5, 9, 20 or 23. Rectification merely formalises the existing situation: *Re Chowood's Registered Land* [1933] Ch. 574. It is thus vital to purchasers to check up on the rights of actual occupiers as was learnt the hard way in *Hodgson* v. *Marks* [1971] Ch. 892.

Exceptionally, where rectification is ordered to give effect to an overriding interest (or for any other reason) against "a proprietor of any registered land or charge claiming in good faith under a forged disposition" the proprietor is deemed to have suffered loss by reason of the rectification so as to be entitled to an indemnity—if not guilty of lack of proper care, of course: section 83 (4) circumventing *Att.-Gen.* v. *Odell* [1906] 2 Ch. 47. As to whether the right of a victim of forgery to claim rectification under section 82 (1) (*g*) amounts to a "right" of an occupier or receiver of rents under section 70 (1) (*g*) see p.95, *supra*.

## Haigh's Case

It is impossible to leave the topic without mentioning a practical and unforgettable instance of the payment of an indemnity. John Haigh, the acid-bath murderer, by means of a clever forgery had himself registered as proprietor in place of one of his victims and then sold the property to a purchaser for value, who upon registration thereof obtained a valid title. The victim's personal representative, upon discovering the whole horrible truth, sought and obtained a full indemnity from the insurance fund: he could not obtain rectification since there was an innocent proprietor in possession protected by section 82 (3)[34] By way of comparison, it should be noted that in unregistered conveyancing the personal representative would have no effective remedy against Haigh after he was hanged since Haigh had no assets to speak of, but he would have been able to recover the land from the innocent purchaser who would have had no defence, having taken under a forged and therefore void conveyance. The innocent purchaser would have lost out completely. Registered conveyancing thus has clear advantages though there is still plenty of scope for reform.

## Reform

It has already been suggested that the insurance funds should be held in a separate account and the scheme run on a proper actuarial insurance basis. Since the main purpose of the system of registration is to provide guaranteed titles to land[35] the rectification and indemnity provisions are fundamental to the system so that it is vital that they operate fully "in the interests of fair dealing and justice."[36] The principles of rectification and indemnity should thus be truly complementary and the amount of indemnity payable should relate to market value at the time immediately before rectification or refusal to rectify.[37] Indemnity should also be payable where loss is suffered by a claimant despite rectification in his favour as in *Freer* v. *Unwins Ltd.* [1976] Ch. 288. From this case it also emerges that there ought to be some provision made in the Land Registration Rules requiring notification of rectification applications to occupiers of the property to which the applications relate so as to have the opportunity to make submissions to the Register about the applications. It is astonishing that in *Freer* v. *Unwins Ltd.* it emerged that the Registrar had not served notice under rule 300 on the lessee of the claim for rectification.

It seems remarkable, at present, that the character of the

indemnity provisions is so "all or nothing," so that, for example, no indemnity is payable where the claimant caused or substantially contributed to the loss by lack of proper care (the new s. 83 (5) (*a*)). How can the system be fair if the law is so arbitrary and inflexible? Surely provisions similar to those in the Law Reform (Contributory Negligence) Act 1945 ought to apply: as in Land Registration (Scotland) Act 1979, s. 13 (4).

In fact, section 75 (4) though repealed by the 1971 Act, was in the van in this respect as it provided that where a squatter acquires a title by limitation and has himself registered then:

> "If in the opinion of the registrar, any purchaser or person deriving title under him whose title, being registered or protected on the register, is prejudicially affected by any entry [of the squatter] under this section, ought, in the special circumstances of the case, to be compensated, the registrar may award to him indemnity of such amount as he may consider just. . . . In determining whether or not an indemnity is to be awarded and in determining the amount of any such indemnity regard shall be had amongst the other considerations to the question whether or not the applicant and his predecessors have by negligence caused or contributed to the loss."

Under the general law a person who has lost his title by allowing another to acquire the title by limitation can have no recompense but section 75 (4) specifically provided for such a person to be compensated where the Registrar considered it just. There was only one such instance, where the facts have not been disclosed[38]; but it would seem that the discretion was of a sort which might well be exercised where the register is rectified to give effect to a squatter's title if the registered proprietor had wrongly assumed that his registered title *ipso facto* could not be divested. This would have been a small price to pay until the public became fully conversant with the mysteries of land registration.

In such a case within section 75 (4) compensation would have been awarded where rectification was to give effect to an overriding interest (within s. 70 (1) (*f*)) when, as we have seen, no indemnity is payable under the general rule enunciated in *Re Chowood's Registered Land* [1933] Ch. 574. In view of the uncertain width of overriding interests and the possibility of purchasers quite reasonably being unable to discover the existence of such interests, it would seem fairer if there were a discretion in the Registrar (subject to appeal to the High Court) to provide compensation where it would in all the circumstances be just and equitable (*e.g.* no compensation would normally be payable if a true owner were in actual occupation of part of the registered proprietor's land at the time the proprietor acquired the land and the true owner then had the register rectified though compensation might be payable if the occupation were not really apparent). This may savour of palm-tree justice but such justice is better than no justice at all. Moreover, where there are two innocent parties in a registered land matter, the state with its insurance system is ideally situated to prevent the unfortunate loser from suffering too much and so it should take on this role. The importance of discretionary compensation in these cases, however, would diminish most considerably if the reforms, earlier advocated, to define and refine overriding interests were to be adopted.

Correspondingly, it would be necessary to provide for discretionary compensation for those persons harshly affected by those reforms. After all, these reforms are all proposed in order to simplify and expedite conveyancing and so benefit the community and the state. In return it is only fair that the state insurance funds should be available to assist the minuscule number of persons cruelly sacrificed on the altar of conveyancing convenience as in the case of unregistered land where purchasers bound by land charges hidden behind the root of title are compensated under section 25 of the Law of Property Act 1969.[39] Since these cruel sacrifices are incapable of being exactly foreseen a discretion could be given to the Registrar (subject to appeal to the High Court) to award compensation where it would in all the circumstances be just and equitable, special regard being had to the claimant's circumstances and the reasons for the claimant's failure to protect his interest in any way. Persons like Mrs. Hodgson in *Hodgson* v. *Marks* [1971] Ch. 892 ought thus to receive some compensation if, under a reformed system, the law were changed to their detriment.

If it is felt that these provisions for discretionary

compensation may endanger the solvency of the insurance fund proposed in place of the present Consolidated Fund and lead to registry fees being increased, then, there could be written in a provision that discretionary compensation awards should not be payable till the end of the fund's financial year and, when paid, they should be scaled down proportionately where payment in full would absorb all the current income profit in that year (or 95 per cent. of such income if a reserve were being built up).[40]

Finally, should not some provision be made for cases where only both rectification and a cash indemnity can properly compensate the true owner e.g. where upon rectification the land is worth less than when formerly owned because of what has been done to it in the meantime as where growing timber has been cut down?[41]

## Notes

[1] T. B. F. Ruoff, *An Englishman Looks at the Torrens System,* p. 14.

[2] *Ibid.* p. 84, though no indemnity is payable if the applicant was guilty of lack of proper care: s. 83 (5) (*a*).

[3] Cretney and Dworkin (1968) 84 L.Q.R. 528, 549.

[4] *Chief Land Registrar's Reports* for 1977-78, 1978-79, 1979-80.

[5] *Ibid.* 1979-80 p.12.

[6] 84 L.Q.R. 548.

[7] *Ibid.* 556.

[8] The county court has jurisdiction here: *Watts* v. *Waller* [1973] Q.B. 153, 171; [1976] New L.J. 31. By *Lester* v. *Burgess,* 26 P. & C.R. 536 'decided' indicates a final and not an interlocutory decision.

[9] Strangely, the Court of Appeal in *Orakpo* v. *Manson Investments Limited* [1977] 1 W.L.R. 347 were prepared in *obiter dicta* to read unregistered land law into the statute to allow rectification under s. 82 (1) (*a*), though the registered proprietor on registered land principles should have taken free of the unprotected minor interest so that, strictly, the holder thereof had nothing on which to base a s. 82 (1) (*a*) claim. It is high time the courts became "registration minded" as pointed out by Professor D. C. Jackson in (1978) 94 L.Q.R. 239, 254.

[10] *Frazer* v. *Walker* [1967] A.C. 569, 585, *Jones* v. *Lipman* [1962] 1 W.L.R. 832. See pp. 19 and 135, *ante.*

[11] See *Assets Co.* v. *Mere Roihi* [1905] A.C. 176, 210.

[12] *Ibid.*

[13] See *ibid.* and *Wicks* v. *Bennett* [1921] 30 C.L.R. 81 In *Peffer* v. *Rigg* [1977] 1 W.L.R. 285 there seem to have been grounds for a claim under s. 82 (1) (*d*): see [1977] Camb L.J. 227 (D.J.H.). Further see *Efstratiou* v.

*Glantschnig* [1972] N.Z.L.R. 594, *Waimiha Sawmilling Co.* v. *Waione Timber Co.* [1926] A.C. 101, 106.

[14] *Re Leighton's Conveyance* [1936] 1 All E.R. 667.

[15] *Parkash* v. *Irani Finance Ltd.* [1970] Ch. 101, 109 (Plowman J.)

[16] Brickdale & Stewart-Wallace, p. 278.

[17] *Cf. Franzom* v. *Registrar of Titles* [1975] 50 A.L.J.R. 4, 7 A.L.R. 383.

[18] *Magee* v. *Pennine Insurance Co.* [1969] 2 Q.B. 507, *Laurence* v. *Lexcourt Holdings Ltd.* [1978] 1 W.L.R. 1128.

[19] But see Farrand (2nd ed.) pp. 211-212; Potter's *Land Law under the Land Registration Act 1925*, p. 91; (1968) 84 L.Q.R. 539-540.

[20] For similar Parliamentary blindness see Land Registration Act 1966, s.1 (4) criticised by Cretney & Dworkin (1968) 84 L.Q.R. 528 and remedied by Land Registration and Land Charges Act 1971, s.3 (1).

[21] *Chowood* v. *Lyall (No. 2)* (1930) 1 Ch. 426; *Re 139 High Street Deptford* (1951) Ch. 884; *Re Sea View Gardens* (1967) 1 W.L.R. 134.

[22] (1930) 1 Ch. 426, 435.

[23] (1967) 1 W.L.R. 134, 141.

[24] It is thus all the more significant that 12 per cent. of the plans on conveyances which are presented for first registration are *discovered* to be seriously defective: 84 L.Q.R. 534.

[25] *Epps* v. *Esso Petroleum* (1973) 1 W.L.R. 1071, 1079.

[26] *Chowood* v. *Lyall* [1930] 2 Ch. 156; *Hodges* v. *Jones* [1935] Ch. 657; *Re 139 High St., Deptford* [1951] Ch. 884; *Epps* v. *Esso Petroleum* [1973] 1 W.L.R. 1071; *Freer* v. *Unwins* [1976] Ch. 288.

[27] About four claims a year arise out of forged instruments:

[28] See Law Commission Working Paper No. 45, para. 81.

[29] See F. R. Crane (1967) 31 Conv. 332; *Ives* v. *High* [1967] 2 Q.B. 379; *Inwards* v. *Baker* [1965] 2 Q.B. 29; s. 82 (1) (*g*).

[30] See p. 58, *supra*; Palk (1974) 38 Conv. 236.

[31] Useful case notes: 92 L.Q.R. 338; [1976] New L.J. 523; [1976] C.L.J. 211.

[32] (1964) 108 S.J. 295: s. 83 (11).

[33] Ruoff and Roper, pp.802-803.

[34] Ruoff and Roper (3rd ed.), p.853.

[35] Ruoff, *An Englishman Looks at the Torrens System*, pp.86-87.

[36] Ruoff and Roper, p.786.

[37] 84 L.Q.R. 553, 555.

[38] Curtiss and Ruoff's *Registered Conveyancing* (2nd ed.), p. 743.

[39] Unless falling within the proviso to s. 25 (9).

[40] *Cf.* the original proviso to s. 75 (4) repealed by s. 3 (2) of the 1936 Act.

[41] For reform generally see Law Com. Published Working Paper No. 45.

# APPENDIX 1

## Notes of Cases

*Abigail* v. *Lapin* [1934]A.C. 491 (P.C.)

To secure a debt due to Mr. H the defendants gave title certificates and transfers expressed to be for money consideration in favour of Mrs. H who became registered as proprietor, but who was to retransfer on payment of debt and interest. Mrs. H then borrowed £5,500 by way of registrable mortgage from the plaintiff who lent without searching register (though nothing there). Plaintiff lodged caveat prior to delivering mortgage for registration but defendants lodged caveat before such delivery.

*Held*: Defendant's presumptive priority as first in time of two equitable interests displaced on estoppel priciples by their conduct in arming Mrs. H with power as seeming absolute owner to execute transfers or mortgages.

*Barclays Bank* v. *Taylor* [1974] Ch.137 (C.A.)

Proprietors deposited land certificate with bank June 1961 to secure overdraft and notice of deposit put on register. Memorandum of deposit under seal agreeing to execute legal mortgage if requested: September 1961. Mortgage in legal form executed August 1961 but not registered. Proprietors contracted to sell to defendants (sister and brother-in-law of proprietors) in February 1968 who paid over price by July 1968 and entered caution in August 1968. Bank sought registered charge to exercise remedies *qua* mortgagee. Defendants objected.

*Held*: Bank prevailed as first in time of two equitable interests, nothing in its conduct (sitting on land certificate with notice of deposit on register)to displace priority. While former section 106 (2) provides that a mortgage by deed in unregistered fashion may be protected by a special mortgage caution "and in no other way," section 106(4) provides until then for the mortgage to be equitable and capable of being overridden as a minor interest. However, only registered dispositions like transfers or registered charges override minor interests and de facto protection of retention of land certificate prevents transfers and charges being registered. [Query whether priority crystallised under section 66 in June 1961.]

*Re Beaney* [1978] 1 W.L.R.770 (Martin Nourse Q.C.)

Mrs. B. suffering from senile dementia, gave away her house, representing fourteen-fifteenths of the value of her estate, to a daughter, V. when Mrs. B. had insufficient understanding of what she was doing. She died intestate and her administrators claimed the transfer was void and sought an order that V.'s name be deleted from the register and replaced by their names.

*Held*: Transfer was void and the register should be rectified as sought (but no mention made of which paragraph of 82 (1) or (3) was applicable).

*Re Boyle's Claim* [1961] 1 W.L.R. 339 (Wilberforce J.)

B, proprietor with absolute title in boundary dispute with neighbour, N, who claimed rectification under section 82. Boundary redrawn so small triangle cut off B's land, part of N's garage being on this triangle. B claimed indemnity.

*Held*: No indemnity for garage part since N had overriding interest of actual occupier (s. 70 (1) (g)) subject to which B took his land at date of registration as proprietor (s. 5 (b)). Indemnity for rest of triangle.

*Bridges* v. *Mees* [1957] Ch. 475 (Harman J.)

1936, land sold to plaintiff under oral contract. No conveyance taken, no caution entered, but plaintiff took possession. 1955, defendant purchased same land and became registered proprietor and claimed possession from plaintiff who claimed rectification.

*Held*: Rectification be ordered since defendant took subject to overriding interests of plaintiff under section 70 (1) (f) (adverse possession) and section 70 (1) (*g*) estate contract of actual occupier.

*British Maritime Trust* v. *Upsons Ltd.* 171 L.T. 77 (Clauson
    J.)

Proprietor of leasehold mortgaged it by registered charge to plaintiffs and then let for over 40 years to U. Ltd. in breach of covenant with plaintiffs. Sub-lease two days later for 28 years by U. Ltd. to P. Possession claimed by plaintiffs on basis lease to U. Ltd. not registered in pursuance of section 123.

*Held*: The interests of U. Ltd. and P were only equitable, the legal interest being divested under section 123 after two months expired so plaintiffs with legal interest entitled to possession [*semble* s. 123 inapplicable, the lease and sub-lease being dispositions by a registered proprietor within s. 22 (2) and so equitable till registered]

*Butler* v. *Fairclough* (1917) 23 C.L.R. 78 (High Court
    Australia approved by P.C.)

Proprietor of lease (subject to registered charge with title certificate deposited at Registry) executed equitable mortgage by deed in plaintiff's favour on June 30 but on July 2 contracted to sell lease (subject to registered charge) to defendant. This sale completed same day after defendant had searched register where there was nothing to indicate plaintiff's interest. Purchase money handed over in return for registrable transfer. Plaintiff lodged caveat on July 7. Defendant delivered transfer for registration July 12. Plaintiff claimed priority. *Held*: Plaintiff's presumptive priority as first in time of two equitable interests displaced on estoppel principles since plaintiff's failure to enter caveat had induced defendant to part with purchase money believing after his search that he was purchasing subject only to registered charge.

*Cator* v. *Newton* [1940] 1 K.B.415 (C.A.)

Plaintiff transferred land to defendant who covenanted to contribute to maintenance of roads etc. on estate and who was registered as proprietor subject to covenant entry. Defendant then transferred to P. who entered into no covenant to indemnify defendant against defendant's covenant liability. Plaintiff successfully claimed contribution from defendant who claimed indemnity from P.

*Held*: P taking subject to entries on register under section 20 not subject to positive covenant whose burden could not run on basic land law priciples, so could not be liable to plaintiff, nor could section 20 render him liable to indemnify defendant.

*Chowood* v. *Lyall* [1930] 1 Ch.426 (C.A.)

C. took conveyance of land including strips of woodland to which his vendor had no title and C. became first registered proprietor. L by virtue of adverse possession had title to the woodland strips and was in possession of them.

*Held*: Rectification ordered in L.'s favour under section 82 (1)(*a*)(*g*)(*h*), the restriction on rectification against a proprietor in possession (s.82 (3)) being inapplicable since C. was not in possession, though Luxmoore J. in the court below had treated it as applicable but circumvented it on the basis that C. had caused or substantially contributed to the mistake (s.82 (3) (*a*)) by submitting a conveyance for registration which by itself was inoperative to pass title.

*Re Chowood's Registered Land* [1933] Ch.547.

Since rectification was ordered in *Chowood* v. *Lyall* C. claimed an indemnity.

*Held*: No indemnity since loss not suffered by rectification, for by section 5 (*b*) C. always held land subject to overriding interest of L. under section 70 (1)(*f*). Rectification merely regularised the position, the loss being suffered because C. bought land subject to an overriding interest.

*City P.B.S.* v. *Miller* [1952] Ch.840 (C.A.)

First defendant about to contract to purchase land agreed in writing to grant lease for three years and weekly thereafter to second defendant who paid three years' rent in advance but did not go into possession (so no common law periodic tenancy within s. 70 (1)(k) could arise). On January 11 following, first defendant became registered proprietor and plaintiff became registered chargee in respect of its moneys lent to the first

defendant on mortgage. On January 16 second defendant went
into possession. Plaintiff claimed possession to enforce remedies
*qua* mortgagee.

*Held*: Term of second defendant necessarily exceeded three
years by one week so to be legal needed to be created by deed
and it was only in writing. Section 70 (1)(k) only made
overriding interests of legal leases granted at a rent without
taking a fine for any term not exceeding 21 years, despite
section 3 (x) defining lease unless the context otherwise
requires as including an agreement for a lease, underlease, or
tenancy. Possession ordered.

*De Lusignan* v. *Johnson* (1973) 230 E.G. 499 (Brightman J.)

H in writing contracted to sell house to W. H's solicitor was
informed, though the contract was not protected on the register.
The land certificate was with H's solicitor thereby enabling
him to register a charge in his own favour for £1,000 owed him
by H. House then transferred for value to W who became
registered proprietor, later seeking a declaration that the charge
was void against her.

*Held*: W's action be dismissed since H's solicitor on
becoming registered chargee took the charge subject only to
overriding interests and minor interests then protected on
register. As W's minor interest not protected the chargee took
free of it despite his actual knowledge of it.

*Dovto Properties Ltd.* v. *Astell* (1964) 28 Conv. 270 (Judge
        Herbert, County Court)

Proprietor of flats and restaurant granted lease of flat to D
who covenanted to pay lessor £20 monthly towards running
restaurant in return for which entitled to meals to that value.
D assigned lease to defendant who took only because lessor
agreed for duration of lease to waive covenant rights if
defendant absent. Lessor's interest purchased by plaintiffs who
did not know of covenant waiver agreement, having made no
inquiries of defendant. Plaintiffs demanded payment but
defendant alleged plaintiffs bound by lessor's waiver.

*Held*: Lessor's waiver promise estopped lessor on *High Trees*
(1947] K.B. 130 equitable estoppel principles and was an

equitable right vested in defendant analogous to deserted wife's equity just held by C.A. in *N.P.B.* v. *Hastings* [1964] Ch. 665 to be within section 70 (1)(g) rights of actual occupiers. Thus plaintiffs bound by waiver promise. [C.A. reversed by H.L. in [1965] A.C. 1175 holding deserted wife only a personal right.]

*Elias* v. *Mitchell* [1972] Ch.652 (Pennycuick V.-C.)

Plaintiff and first defendant were partners in property owning business so property had to be held on trust for sale for them equally. House registered in name of first defendant only, who in October 1970 sold and executed a transfer of the house to the second defendant who had no notice of the trust for sale circumstances. The second defendant did not deliver the transfer for registration till March 1971, whilst the plaintiff had lodged a caution in December 1970. The second defendant moved for an order removing the caution, the plaintiff having no *locus standi* to lodge it.

*Held*: An interest in proceeds of sale is a minor interest in land (s.3 (xv)) so plaintiff could caution under section 54 as a "person interested . . . howsoever in any land."

*Epps* v. *Esso Petroleum* [1973]1 W.L.R. 1071 (Templeman J.)

House adjoined a petrol station. Conveyance of house included extra 11 foot strip on petrol station side of dividing wall. Purchaser covenanted for self and successors to demolish wall and put up new boundary, but never done. Petrol station in 1959 conveyed to B including the strip and B became first registered proprietor thereof. B sold to defendants who became registered proprietors. House sold to plaintiffs purporting to include strip but Registry only registered them as proprietors of house excluding strip. Plaintiffs sought rectification excluding strip from defendant's title and adding it to plaintiff's title.

*Held*: Plaintiffs had no overriding interest to justify rectification since the parking of a car (by plaintiff's predecessor when defendants became proprietors) on an unidentified part of disputed strip for undefined time was not actual occupation within section 70(1)(g). Since the defendants were in possession within section 82 (3) rectification was discretionary, and the plaintiffs could not show under section

82 (3)(c) that it would be unjust not to rectify the register against the defendants, even though on rectification the defendants would be entitled to an indemnity at current values (s. 83 (6) (b)) whereas on refusal the plaintiff would not be entitled to any indemnity, more than six years having elapsed since B's 1959 registration (s. 83 (11)). The plaintiffs should have made proper inquiries before purchasing.

*Re Evans' Contract* [1970] 1 W.L.R. 583 (Stamp J.)

V agreed to sell to P registered land and appurtenant rights of way and drainage granted by a London borough over its neighbouring unregistered land. P demanded that V procure registration of V as proprietor of these appurtenant easements. V sought declaration good title shown without such registration.

*Held*: Good title already shown since (a) if easements fell within section 3 (xxiv) definition of registered land V was registered in respect of them as appurtenant to land of which he was registered proprietor and (b) if easements not registered land then section 110 (5), requiring V to procure registration of self, did not apply since it was only concerned with dispositions of registered land.

*Faruqi v. English Real Estate Ltd.* [1979] 1 W.L.R. 963 (Walton J.)

Plaintiff contracted at auction to buy registered land expressly subject to the entries on the register of title. The charges register referred to restrictive covenants contained in 1883 deed. Plaintiff's requisitions were answered by reply that 1883 deed could not be found so covenants unascertainable. Plaintiff claimed recovery of his deposit.

*Held*: Although at law the defendant had discharged his contractual obligation to show title ("the purchaser is bound to take the property subject to the entries on the register, whatever they may be") the plaintiff was not bound in equity since defendant had not specifically drawn plaintiff's attention to title defect of which defendant aware. Equity would not specifically enforce the contract so plaintiff could recover deposit under L.P.A. s.49 (2).

*Freer* v. *Unwins Ltd.* [1976] Ch. 288 (Walton J.)

Unregistered land laid out as parade of shops. Conveyance of first shop in 1955 to plaintiff with benefit of restrictive covenant rest of shops not to be used for selling tabacco cigarettes or confectionery. Freehold title to second shop registered many years later but it somehow omitted notice of plaintiff's restrictive covenant which he had at outset registered at Land Charges Registry against his vendor's name. In 1969, a 21 year nonregistrable lease of second shop granted, which in 1974 was assigned with new registered proprietor's permission to the defendants who checked that no entries affected them and carried on an off-licence business selling tabacco cigarettes and confectionery. Plaintiff successfully sought rectification of the register so notice of the covenant entered as of April 28, 1975. Plaintiff then claimed injunction against defendants.

*Held*: After expressing very great surprise that rectification had been allowed, there would be no injunction since the 1969 lease took effect as a registered disposition (s. 19 (2)) subject to overriding interests and to minor interests then on the register (s. 20). The 1969 lessee thus took free of the notice as did his successors, the defendants. Unfortunately, the plaintiff would not be entitled to an indemnity since no loss occasioned by the rectification, and since rectification had taken place it could not be said that he had suffered loss by reason of non-rectification [Happily events did not turn out in that way according to Ruoff & Roper p.794 without giving any explanation]

*Grace Rymer Investments Ltd.* v. *Waite* [1958] Ch.831 (C.A.)

W orally agreed to lease flats to three defendants who paid three years' rent in advance for weekly tenancies receiving a receipt. W contracted to purchase the registered flats from V and let the three defendants go into occupation of the flats. On December 30, the purchase from V was completed and a charge executed in the plaintiff's favour. On January 9, W was registered as proprietor and the plaintiffs as chargees. Plaintiffs sought possession *qua* mortgages.

*Held*: Plaintiffs did not obtain legal charge on December 30 (despite s. 27 (3)) but only on January 9, a split second after W obtained the legal title (ss. 20, 69). W was bound by the defendant's equitable right to occupy the land for three years within section 70 (1) (*g*) and so were the plaintiffs who should have made inquiries of the defendants. [Query whether a tenancy by estoppel being fed by W's legal estate could have been an overriding periodic tenancy within s. 70 (1) (*k*).]

*Re* 139 *High Street, Deptford* [1951] Ch.884 (Wynn-Parry J.)

Shop sold and conveyed by description, "139 High Street, Deptford," apt to include an annexe which belong to British Transport Commission. No plan attached to conveyance. P submitted the conveyance to the Registry and became first registered proprietor of the shop and the annexe as revealed by the plan in the land certificate. P carried on business in the shop and the annexe but the B.T.C. claimed rectification.

*Held*: P had substantially contributed to the mistake within old section 82 (3) (a) merely by lodging, albeit innocently, a misleading description of the property so rectification ordered, the judge opining that otherwise section 82 (3) (c) was inapplicable. [P subsequently obtained an indemnity: Ruoff and Roper, p.838]

*Hodges* v. *Jones* [1935] 1 Ch. 657 (Luxmoore J.)

Plaintiffs were proprietors (of land forming part of estate) who had purchased from J the previous proprietor. A plan had been produced before the plaintiffs' purchase showing a strip designated for tennis courts. Plaintiffs alleged oral collateral agreement inducing purchase that strip only be used for courts. J sold rest of estate for value to J Ltd. which was registered as proprietor and erected three garages on the strip. Plaintiffs claimed rectification by entry of notice that strip bound by the agreement restricting user [assuming such a notice would bind the defendant but see *Freer* v. *Unwins Ltd.*].

*Held*: Plaintiffs had not proved collateral agreement but even if they had they could not obtain rectification as they had no overriding interest within section 70 (1) (*a*) and could not show it would be unjust not to rectify the register against the defendant, especially since under section 20 the defendant took free from minor interests not protected on the register and,

"Notice of the existence of a restriction which is not registered does not affect the property alleged to be subject to it" (p.671).

*Hodgson* v. *Marks* [1971] Ch.892 (C. A.)

Plaintiff transferred legal title to her lodger but oral agreement that beneficial ownership to remain in plaintiff. Lodger registered as proprietor, and plaintiff and he continued to live in the house as owner and lodger. Lodger sold house to first defendant who saw plaintiff twice casually and accidently, without being introduced, but believing her to be lodger's wife. First defendant charged house in favour of second defendant, a building society and first defendant registered as proprietor subject to second defendant's registered charge. Plaintiff who had been in occupation throughout sought order that house bound to to be transferred to her free from charge.

*Held*: Plaintiff succeeded, the full equitable interest remaining in her being a right of a person in actual occupation (s. 70 (1) (*g*)). "Actual occupation" is not "actual and apparent occupation" as trial judge held, though even then plaintiff's occupation was apparent. Actual occupation must depend on circumstances and plaintiff in actual occupation despite the fact that the vendor-lodger appeared also to be in actual occupation and her presence could have been consistent with that (restricting *Caunce* v. *Caunce* [1969] 1 W. L. R. 286 to its particular facts).

*Hughes* v. *Waite* [1957] 1 W. L. R. 713 (Harman J.)

W negotiating the purchase of a freehold being converted into three flats agreed to let M, C, and D have weekly tenancies, three years' "rent" to be paid in advance which was done. Without any preceding contract W, on October 26, completed the purchase subject to a charge in the vendor plaintiff's favour for the outstanding balance of the purchase moneys. On November 14, W became registered proprietor and the plaintiff registered chargee. C took possession on October 31, M on November 5, D on November 21. The plaintiff sought possession.

*Held*: Possession ordered since advance "rent" amounted to a fine so tenancies granted for a fine and so outside W's powers as mortgagor to grant under L. P. A., s.99 (6) if, indeed, W. was a mortgagor at time of granting tenancies since he then had no interest in the property. [No mention of s. 70 (1) (*k*) tenancy by estoppel or s. 70 (1) (*g*) rights as overriding interests on November 14, for C and M.]

*Jones* v. *Lipman* [1962] 1 W. L. R. 832 (Russell J.)

First defendant contracted to sell his registered land to plaintiff, but before completion transferred the land to the second defendant, a company that was wholly the creature of the first defendant and which became registered proprietor allegedly taking free of the plaintiff's unprotected minor interest: sections 20, 59. Plaintiff sought specific performance.

*Held*: Second defendant a device and a sham for first defendant, whose control of second defendant enabled plaintiff's contract to be completed if specific performance ordered - so ordered.

*Kitney* v. *M. E. P. C. Ltd.* [1977] 1 W. L. R. 981 (C. A.)

In 1933 a 42 year underlease of unregistered land was granted. It contained an option to renew for 21 years more but this option was not registered as a Class C (iv) land charge under L. C. A. 1925, s.10. The 99 year head lease was purchased in 1934 and then sold to the defendant in 1947. In 1969 defendant purchased the freehold and was made registered proprietor, the charges register making the title subject to the underlease (no mention being made of the option in the underlease).

In 1975 plaintiff claimed to exercise the option on basis that by s.5 defendant took freehold subject to underlease entered in register and so subject to option that was part and parcel of underlease.

*Held*: Option in 1934 had become void under L. C. A., s.13 for non-registration and L. R. A., s.5 should be restricted to entries referring to valid interests just as interests protected by notice under s.52 are only protected so far as otherwise valid. Thus plaintiff failed.

*Lee* v. *Barrey* [1957] Ch. 251 (C. A.)

Defendant purchased plot of registered land by reference to plan attached to transfer showing angled boundary. Land certificate plan issued showing straight boundary. Defendant erected house and laid out garden on assumption that boundary as on land certificate plan. In fact house encroached on plaintiff's plot so plaintiff claimed declaration boundary as shown on transfer plan, injunction, damages.

*Held*: On true construction of section 76 and rule 284 boundaries on land certificate plan not intended to be more than generally indicative and could not be set up to overturn result of defendant's bargain with his vendor as recorded in contract of sale and transfer plan. Relief granted to plaintiff. [Defendant obtained indemnity: Ruoff and Roper, p.62, Note 74.]


*Lee-Parker* v. *Izzet* [1971] 1 W. L. R. 1688 (Goff J.) [No. 2 on p. 202]

First defendant granted registered charge to plaintiffs on certain properties, one then occupied by second defendant as licensee who had paid deposit under contract of purchase from first defendant, and another then occupied by third and fourth defendants as tenants who had also contracted to purchase from first defendant and paid deposit. Plaintiffs sought declaration contracts unenforceable against them and possession against second defendant.

*Held*: Plaintiffs entitled to such relief, the contracts no longer subsisting for various reasons. Second defendant entitled to lien within section 70 (1) (*g*) for deposit and interest and for £50 monthly paid towards purchase price subject to fair occupation rent deduction. Third and fourth defendants entitled to lien within section 70 (1) (*g*) for deposit and interest, and to deduct from future rent cost of repairs (within landlord's repairing obligations that they had had to effect) so as not to be liable to be sued for such rent. [Second defendant initially claimed rectification of contract to reveal £1,000 deposit and not £600 but his counsel for some reason conceded that this equity could not bind the plaintiffs.]

*Lee-Parker* v. *Izzet (No. 2)* [1972] 1W.L.R. 775 (Goulding J.)

First defendant executed equitable mortgage in plaintiff's favour (supported by deposit of land certificate and entry of notice of deposit) when third defendant already in occupation under a contract of purchase "subject to the purchaser obtaining a satisfactory mortgage." Plaintiff sought possession.

*Held*: So ordered since contract void for uncertainty so it could give rise to no s.70 (1) (*g*) overriding interest which third defendant needed to prove to obtain priority under s.66 in absence of any entry protecting her interest before equitable mortgage created. In the circumstances she had no equitable proprietary interest arising out of her expenditure on the premises so as to fall within s.70 (1) (*g*). There was insufficient evidence of her claim to rectification of the contract to warrant deciding whether such a mere equity fell within s.70 (1) (*g*).[Query whether s.66 applied if equitable mortgage created by document and not by deposit of land certificate.]

*Re Leighton's Conveyance* [1936] 1 All E.R. 667 (Luxmoore J.)

Daughter fraudulently arranged for "sale" of registered land occupied by mother from mother to self. Had mother sign transfer without knowing real significance, being too prepared to sign business documents, etc., put before her by daughter. Daughter as registered proprietor created registered charges, the chargees giving full value without notice of the fraud. Mother sought rectification.

*Held*: Rectification by replacing daughter with mother as proprietor, but charges register to remain as it was. [Not argued that mother had overriding interest within section 70 (1)(*g*) so as to bind chargees, perhaps because it was assumed that her paragraph (*g*) rights were subordinated to chargees' on estoppel principles but did the chargees not have to make inquiry of her on *Hodgson* v. *Marks* principles she being entitled to rely on her overriding interest like Mrs. Hodgson? See also *London & Cheshire Insurance* v. *Laplagrene]*

*Lester* v. *Burgess* (1973) 26 P. & C.R. 536 (Goulding J.)

V agreed to sell to P. A dispute arose as to whether V had served an effective Notice to Complete enabling V to forfeit the deposit so P entered a caution against V's title. By interlocutory motion V sought vacation of the caution. P claimed the court had no jurisdiction.

*Held*: The Court could proceed under its general jurisdiction to make orders *in personam* against parties interested in property or under contracts (*e.g.* an order that the defendant take steps to remove his entry: *Rawlplug* v.*Kamvale Properties Ltd.*(1969) 20 P. & C.R. 32). An order for rectification under s.82. which has to be obeyed by the Registrar, could be made under s.82 (1) (*b*) but not under s.82 (1) (*a*) since "decided" means a final and not interlocutory decision nor under s.82 (1) (*h*) since V was not complaining of an error or omission or of an entry made under a mistake. [In *Price Bros.* v. *Kelly Homes* [1975] 1 W.L.R. the Court of Appeal vacated a caution under s.82 (1) (*b*)]

*London & Cheshire Insurance Co.* v. *Laplagrene* [1971] Ch. 499 (Brightman J.)

Vendors sold property to purchasers for £50.000. Receipt clause in transfer but no money actually paid. Statement, "Price paid £50.000" on proprietorship register of purchasers under rule 247. Purchasers leased property back to vendors for 21 years, vendors continuing in occupation. Purchasers then created £32,000 registered charge and chargee did not suspect £50,000 unpaid, though he made no inquiry of vendors in occupation. Vendors vacated property.

*Held*: Chargee bound by vendors' lien for unpaid purchase money under section 70 (1) (*g*) as of date of registered charge, subsequent giving up occupation immaterial (except where future purchasers concerned), and no estoppel operating aginst vendors since "price paid" merely denoted price payable, rule 247 being concerned with quantum and not receipt. Even if receipt had been recorded in register the prima facie sufficiency under L.P.A., s. 68 (1) would have been negatived by failure of chargee to inquire of occupying unpaid vendor within section 70 (1) (*g*).

*Marks* v. *Attallah* (1966) 110 S.J. 709 (Ungoed-Thomas J.)

Plaintiff (who was defendant in later case *Hodgson* v.
*Marks*) bought house from E, the sole proprietor, and became
registered proprietor. E was in occupation at time of sale as
was a Mrs.H whom plaintiff erroneously believed E's wife.
Plaintiff did not move in. E left. Mrs. H granted a lease to
defendant who moved in. Plaintiff brought summons for
possession and defendant's affidavit stated Mrs. H had
represented self as true owner and had referred to action
pending (*Hodgson* v. *Marks*) in which she claimed E held legal
estate as bare trustee for her.

*Held*: Since it was conceded by plaintiff that Mrs. H in
actual occupation and her equitable interest within section 70
(1) (*g*) and no inquiry had been made as to her rights they
bound plaintiff, who was therefore bound by defendant's lease
derived out of Mrs. H's interest.

*Murray* v. *Two Strokes Ltd.*[1973] 1 W.L.R. 823 (Goulding J.)

1960 proprietor granted defendant right of pre-emption and
defendant entered caution. Proprietor granted 99-year lease to
plaintiff who applied for registration as proprietor of lease with
absolute title. Defendant objected unless made subject to pre-
emption.

*Held*: Defendant's right not an interest in land, not a minor
interest, not capable of being protected by a caution so plaintiff
entitled to be registered free of it. [*Pritchard* v. *Briggs* [1980]
Ch. 338 now reveals can enter a caution or notice for although,
originally, pre-emption only personal it becomes proprietary as
soon as landowner decides to dispose of land so activating pre-
emption right, giving its holder proprietary option to purchase
before prospective disponee acquires any interest]

*National Provincial Bank* v. *Ainsworth* [1965] A.C. 1175
          (H.L.)

Husband, H, deserted wife, W, leaving her and children in
matrimonial home. Home conveyed by H to his company
which became registered proprietor and charged home to Bank
which made up no inquiries of W. Bank sought possession.

*Held*: W's rights to roof over her head, etc., were purely

personal so not capable of falling within section 70 (1) (*g*).
[Lords prepared to assume as was held by C.A. that deserted
wife in actual occupation within *(g)*]


*Parkash* v. *Irani Finance Ltd.* [1970] Ch. 101 (Plowman J.)

Irani obtained charging order against K's property and
entered caution on K's register of title. K contracted to sell to
plaintiff whose solicitors searched register, official search
certificate erroneously not mentioning caution. Plaintiff
completed contract lodging transfer and Building Society charge
for registration. Irani objected unless priority given to its
charge.

*Held*: Necessary implication from section 59 (6) is that
purchaser is to be affected by matters properly protected on the
register so Irani had priority. [In fact s. 59 (6) immaterial since
applies not to purchaser in course of acquiring title but only to
purchaser once he has become registered proprietor which, of
course, had not happened because of caution (*see Smith* v.
*Morrison*). However, as first in time and first protected Irani's
equitable interest would have priority.]


*Payne* v. *Adnams* [1971] Current Law Yearbook 6486
                    (Judge Duveen, County Court)

Proprietor granted right of way to plaintiff. Proprietor
contracted to sell to defendant who knew of grant, though just
before completion defendant discovered grant not noted on
charges register of property he was purchasing. Defendant
became new proprietor and obstructed plaintiff's right of way.

*Held*: Plaintiff's right of way not being noted against servient
title was equitable easement, amounting to section 70 (1) (*a*)
overriding interest binding defendant, since nothing in Act or
rules *requiring* equitable easement to be protected by notice
within last 13 exclusionary words of section 70 (1) (*a*) [Odd to
give no effect to 13 words of statute. Equitable easements
should not be overriding interests and defendant should not
have been bound in absence of equitable fraud: *cf. De Lusignan*
v. *Johnson, Jones* v. *Lipman, Peffer* v. *Rigg.]*

*Peffer* v. *Rigg and Rigg,* [1977], W.L.R. 285 (Graham J.)

P and R bought house in R's name as proprietor to provide home for Mrs. R's mother, P and R agreeing R to hold on trust for them as tenants in common equally. R and Mrs. R were divorced and R transferred whole beneficial ownership in house to Mrs. R for £1. Mrs. R knew of arrangement between P and R. P sued R and Mrs. R for breach of trust.

*Held*: R and Mrs. R liable for breach of trust. Mrs. R could not rely on section 20 to take free of P's unprotected minor interest as a transferee for value since she was not a bona fide transferee and where a transfereee in fact was a purchaser within section 59 (6) the transferee had to be bona fide just like a purchaser (s. 3 (*xxi*)). Alternatively, Mrs. R's conscience was personally affected, making her a constructive trustee. [Latter ground preferable in light of *De Lusignan* v. *Johnson, Jones* v. *Lipman,* s. 61 (6).]

*Re Sea View Gardens* [1967] 1 W.L.R. 134 (Pennycuick J.)

In 1934 company conveyed plot to H who in 1936 conveyed to M who conveyed to plaintiff before compulsory registration area arose. In 1964 company purported to convey plaintiff's plot together with other adjoining land to defendant who became first registered proprietor thereof. 1965 plaintiff discovered building work in progress on his plot, so sought rectificaion.

*Held*: Protection of defendant as proprietor in possession within section 82 (3) lost since he had substantially contributed to the mistake, albeit innocently, by lodging documents for registration. Rectification still discretionary but would be ordered unless after adjournment it transpired that plaintiff, knowing facts, had delayed in claiming rectification. [Plaintiff later withdrew claim and obtained indemnity: Ruoff and Roper, p. 841.]

*Smith* v. *Morrison* [1974] 1 W.L.R. 659 (Plowman J.)

September 1972 M agreed to sell farm to plaintiff. In November 1972 M contracted to sell to defendant. In early December 1972 defendant's solicitors informed of plaintiff's claim to contract but in view of what M told them they had honest doubts as to validity of plaintiff's claim. Meanwhile plaintiff trying to enter notice on register but requisitions were raised by Registry as to titles to various plots possibly subject to contractual claim. Defendant searched register and obtained clear search certificate so completed purchase, lodging transfer for registraion within priority period. Plaintiff issued writ against defendant and Chief Land Registrar claiming priority for entry of his notice on grounds that defendant not purchaser in good faith within Official Searches Rules and that defendant's application not "in order," the transfer being in common form and not company form, and defendant company's memorandum and articles not lodged.

*Held*: Defendant company acting in good faith since its solicitors had no ulterior motive and had honest doubt as to validity of plaintiff's claim, and "in order" meant "substantially in order" not "in perfect order" (now see Land Registration Official Searches Rules 1978, rule 5). Moreover, Registrar's discretion to accept applications in order as far as he was concerned was conclusive of sufficiency of application: rule 322

*Re Stone and Saville's Contract* [1963] 1 W.L.R. 163 (C.A.)

In 1961 under an open contract P agreed to buy from V a 40 per cent. share in Manor House and paid £3,000 deposit. Title had been registered in 1960 and an entry referred to a restrictive covenant that so long as W should be the owner of Corner Cottage the Manor House should not be used other than as a private dwellinghouse. In fact this covenant had been released in 1956 and W had sold Corner Cottage in 1957.

Since other user was intended P's solicitors raised a requisition on the covenant. V's solicitors ignored this and, when completion did not take place on the contractual date, served Notice to Complete. P's solicitors referred to the covenant and rescinded the contract. V's solicitors forfeited the deposit.

*Held*: P was entitled to the deposit having effectively rescinded the contract, V not having proved (as was the case) a good title.

*Strand Securities Ltd.* v. *Caswell* [1965] Ch. 958 (C.A.)

Proprietor of lease granted 39-year sub-lease to first defendant who later allowed his stepdaughter (and her children, having been deserted) to occupy the flat rent free. Lease transferred to plaintiffs in March 1962 having full knowledge of sub-lease. On April 5, first defendant applied to register sub-lease but refused by Registry for not being able to produce lease land certificate. On April 24, plaintiffs applied for registration of lease enclosing land certificate. Registrar treated land certificate as then available to register sub-lease. Plaintiff's sought declaration that sub-lease void against them since not protected by entry of notice on lease land certificate and sought possession—but failed.

*Held*: Section 64 (1) (*a*) only required production of land certificate when an entry to be made on title of existing registered interest and not when there was an application for first registration of interest having no land certificate of its own, so defendant's sub-lease was effectively registered as of April 5 (Russell L.J. pointing out, "The decision on the construction of the statute cannot, of couse, be affected by the fact that the plaintiffs knew all about the sub-lease" (p. 985)). Defendant's alternative claim to section 70 (1) (*g*) overriding interest binding plaintiffs failed, since he was not in receipt of rents and profits, and not he but his stepdaughter was in actual occupation and her rights were purely personal rights of a licensee incapable of binding the plaintiffs.

*Tiverton Estates Ltd.* v. *Wearwell* [1975] Ch. 146 (C.A.)

Oral agreement for sale of premises. Purchaser's solicitors wrote letter referring to details of agreement "subject to contract." Later they sent draft contract. Vendors decided not to proceed. Purchasers entered caution. Vendors moved for vacation of caution.

*Held*: Interlocutory motion for summary vacation of caution quite proper since caution casts dark shadow on property, paralysing dealings. Court can vacate under section 82 (1) (*a*) and (*b*) but if cautioner had substantial point in his favour would not be right to vacate before full trial of action. Court might say to cautioner, "You may keep the caution on the

register if you undertake to pay the owner any damages caused
by its presence if it is afterwards held that it was wrongly
entered, but if you are not ready to give such an undertaking
then the caution must be vacated." [Obviates difficulties of what
is "without resonable cause" in s. 56 (3) (also see *Clearbrook
Property Holdings Ltd.* v. *Verrier [1974] 1 W.L.R. 243)* and
should be available for notices as well as cautions.] Caution
vacated as agreement unenforceable under Law of Property
Act, s. 40.

*Watts* v. *Waller* [1973] Q.B. 153 (C.A.)

Proprietor, H agreed to sell to plaintiffs who obtained
search certificate of April 30, having priority period expiring
11 a.m. May 25. On May 10, H's wife applied for Class F
notice to be entered, H's land certificate being at Registry. On
May 24, H transferred house to plaintiffs but transfer, etc., not
delivered to Registry before 11 a.m. May 25.

*Held*: Plaintiffs' failure to deliver transfer, etc., to Registry
before priority period expired meant they took subject to wife's
Class F rights springing up on May 25.

*Webb* v. *Pollmount* [1966] Ch. 584 (Ungoed-Thomas J.)

Clause in seven-year lease gave plaintiff tenant option to
purchase freehold reversion, which was later conveyed to
defendant who became registered proprietor subject to lease.
Plaintiff exercised option. Defendant refused to sell. Plaintiff
sought specific performance.

*Held*: Specific performance ordered, defendant bound by
plaintiff's equitable right of an actual occupier within section
70 (1) (*g*) which not restricted to rights by virtue of which
person entitled to be in occupation and which not ousted by
section 59 requiring land charges to be protected by entry on
the register. [The lease itself was within s. 70 (1) (*k*) but no
derivative validity exists, it seems, for covenants not touching
and concerning the demised premises, *e.g.* a covenant to
purchase freehold reversion.]

*Re White Rose Cottage* [1965] Ch. 940 (C.A.)

Proprietor granted equitable mortgage to Bank created by
memorandum of deposit under seal supported by deposit of

land certificate and notice of deposit (having effect as a caution) entered on register. The memorandum conferred an irrevocable power of attorney on the Bank enabling it *qua* mortgagee to transfer the whole legal and equitable estate free from all rights of redemption. A judgment creditor with a charging order entered a caution. To realise its security the Bank as attorney for the proprietor executed a transfer (releasing its charge) in favour of a purchaser who executed a charge in favour of a Building Society. The transfer and the Building Society charge were sent for registration but the judgment creditor cautioner objected unless his charging order had priority.

*Held*: Bank's equitable interest as first in time and first protected had priority over judgment creditor and if Bank had sold as mortgagee under extensive overreaching powers conferred by memorandum of deposit coupled with Law of Property Act, ss. 101, 104, the purchaser and Building Society would have priority over the judgment creditor. Unfortunately, the transfer had to be construed as sale by proprietor with concurrence of Bank so purchaser and Building Society took same title as proprietor had subject to judgment creditor's cautioned interest (though free from concurring Bank's mortgage).

*Williams & Glyn's Bank* v. *Boland* [1980] 3 W.L.R. 138 (H.L.)

H was sole registered proprietor but H and W were equitable tenants in common of matrimonial home due to W's financial contribution. Later H mortgaged the house by legal charge to the bank which made no inquiries of W though she lived in the house. When H defaulted the bank *qua* legal mortgagee sought possession against H and W.

*Held*: Possession would not be ordered since bank's registered legal charge was subject to overriding interest of W under s. 70 (1) (*g*). Her physical presence meant she was "in actual occupation" and her right as an equitable tenant in common under a statutory trust for sale of the house bought to be lived in was a right subsisting in reference to land within s. 70 (1) (*g*). Overriding interests of spouses or others bind everyone irrespective of actual or constructive notice and irrespective of whether the interest, instead of being protected by actual occupation, could have been protected by entry of a notice, restriction, or caution. [Counsel did not argue that the Bank should have been treated as a donee, not being able to produce a valid receipt from a sole trustee for sale because of Trustee Act 1925, s. 14 nor that W had an equitable interest in land under a bare trust, no statutory trust for sale being imposed by Settled Land Act 1925, s. 36 (4) or any other statute despite *Bull* v. *Bull* [1955] 1 Q.B. 234)].

*Woolwich Equitable B.S.* v. *Marshall* [1952] Ch. 1
        (Danckwerts J.)

First defendant agreed to purchase unregistered house in compulsory area. On September 7, first defendant orally agreed to let second defendant have weekly tenancy of top floor flat. On September 11, second defendant went into occupation of flat. On September 13, house coveyed to first defendant executing legal charge in plaintiff's favour excluding defendant's powers of leasing. On September 28, first defendant and plaintiff registered as proprietor and chargee. Plaintiff claimed possession.

*Held*: At time first defendant and plaintiff obtained legal estate on registration (s. 19) they took subject to section 70 (1) (*g*) rights of second defendant who, having had tenancy by estoppel from the first defendant, had estoppel fed when first defendant became owner of legal estate split second before plaintiff became legal chargee. Second defendant's legal weekly tenancy (protected by Rent Restriction Acts) thus bound plaintiffs who made no inquiry of him at any time in September. [Legal estate passed forthwith as s. 123 shows, s. 19 only applying where transferred land already registered though this does not affect decision which approved by Court of Appeal in *Church of England B.S.* v. *Piskor* [1954] Ch. 553].

# APPENDIX 2

## Compulsory Registration Areas 1980

| County | Compulsory registration districts |
|---|---|
| AVON .. .. .. .. .. .. | Bath<br>Bristol<br>Kingswood |
| BEDFORDSHIRE .. .. .. .. | Luton<br>North Bedfordshire<br>South Bedfordshire |
| BERKSHIRE .. .. .. .. .. | wholly compulsory |
| BUCKINGHAMSHIRE .. .. | South Bucks |
| CAMBRIDGESHIRE .. .. .. | Cambridge<br>Peterborough |
| CHESHIRE .. .. .. .. .. | wholly compulsory |
| CLEVELAND .. .. .. .. | wholly compulsory |
| CUMBRIA .. .. .. .. .. | Barrow-in-Furness |
| DERBYSHIRE .. .. .. .. | Bolsover<br>Chesterfield<br>Derby<br>Erewash<br>South Derbyshire |
| DEVON .. .. .. .. .. .. | East Devon<br>Exeter<br>Plymouth<br>South Hams<br>Teignbridge<br>Torbay |

| County | Compulsory registration districts |
|---|---|
| DORSET .. .. .. .. .. .. | Bournemouth<br>Christchurch<br>Poole<br>Weymouth and Portland<br>Wimborne |
| DURHAM .. .. .. .. .. | Chester-le-Street<br>Darlington<br>Durham<br>Easington<br>Sedgefield |
| DYFED .. .. .. .. .. .. | Llanelli |
| EAST SUSSEX .. .. .. .. | wholly compulsory |
| ESSEX .. .. .. .. .. .. | Basildon<br>Brentwood<br>Epping Forest<br>Harlow<br>Southend-on-Sea<br>Thurrock |
| GLOUCESTERSHIRE .. .. .. | Gloucester |
| GREATER LONDON .. .. .. | Bexley<br>Bromley<br>Croydon<br>Greenwich<br>Kingston upon Thames<br>Lambeth<br>Lewisham<br>Merton<br>Richmond upon Thames<br>Southwark<br>Sutton<br>Wandsworth<br>Barnet<br>Brent<br>Camden<br>City of London<br>City of Westminster<br>Ealing<br>Enfield<br>Hackney<br>Hammersmith and<br>    Fulham<br>Haringey<br>Harrow |

| County | Compulsory registration districts |
| --- | --- |
| | Hillingdon |
| | Hounslow |
| | Inner Temple and the Middle Temple |
| | Islington |
| | Kensington and Chelsea |
| | Tower Hamlets |
| | Barking and Dagenham |
| | Havering |
| | Newham |
| | Redbridge |
| | Waltham Forest |
| GREATER MANCHESTER .. | wholly compulsory |
| GWENT .. .. .. .. .. .. | Islwyn<br>Newport |
| HAMPSHIRE .. .. .. .. | Eastleigh<br>Fareham<br>Gosport<br>Havant<br>New Forest<br>Portsmouth<br>Southampton |
| HEREFORD AND WORCESTER | Bromsgrove<br>Hereford<br>Worcester |
| HERTFORDSHIRE .. .. .. | wholly compulsory save for the districts of Dacorum and North Hertfordshire |
| HUMBERSIDE .. .. .. .. | Cleethorpes<br>Great Grimsby<br>Kingston upon Hull<br>North Wolds<br>Scunthorpe |
| KENT .. .. .. .. .. .. .. | wholly compulsory |
| LANCASHIRE .. .. .. .. | Blackburn<br>Blackpool<br>Burnley<br>Fylde<br>Preston<br>Rossendale |

| County | Compulsory registration districts |
|---|---|
| LEICESTER | Blaby<br>Charnwood<br>Hinckley and Bosworth<br>Leicester<br>North West Leicestershire<br>Oadby and Wigston |
| LINCOLNSHIRE | Lincoln |
| MERSEYSIDE | wholly compulsory |
| MID GLAMORGAN | Ogwr<br>Rhondda<br>Taff-Ely |
| NORFOLK | Norwich |
| NORTHAMPTONSHIRE | Kettering<br>Northampton |
| NORTHUMBERLAND | Blyth Valley<br>Wansbeck |
| NORTH YORKSHIRE | York |
| NOTTINGHAMSHIRE | wholly compulsory save for the districts of Bassetlaw and Newark |
| OXFORDSHIRE | Oxford<br>South Oxfordshire<br>Vale of White Horse |
| SOUTH GLAMORGAN | wholly compulsory |
| SOUTH YORKSHIRE | wholly compulsory |
| STAFFORDSHIRE | Cannock Chase<br>Lichfield<br>Newcastle-under-Lyme<br>Stoke-on-Trent<br>Tamworth |
| SUFFOLK | Ipswich |
| SURREY | wholly compulsory |

| County | Compulsory registration districts |
|---|---|
| TYNE and WEAR .. .. .. .. | wholly compulsory |
| WARWICKSHIRE .. .. .. | wholly compulsory save for the district of Stratford-on-Avon |
| WEST GLAMORGAN .. .. .. | wholly compulsory |
| WEST MIDLANDS .. .. .. | wholly compulsory |
| WEST SUSSEX .. .. .. .. | wholly compulsory save for the districts of Chichester and Horsham |
| WEST YORKSHIRE .. .. .. | wholly compulsory |

# INDEX

ABSOLUTE TITLE, 34-36
  effect of transfer, 36
  good holding title, registration as, 38, 164
  leaseholds, 35, 36
ADVERSE POSSESSION, 85, 187

CAUTION AGAINST DEALINGS, 25-28, 115, 124-125, 140
CAUTIONS,
  conversion, against, 39
  first registration, against, 25-26, 110-111
  minor interests, protection of, 25-28
  protection generally, 25-28, 78, 133, 135, 141-144, 145, 149, 150, 151-153
  registrar's discretion, 27, 28, 141
  warning off, 27, 28, 141, 142
CERTIFICATE OF SEARCH,
  protection, 28-29, 110, 146, 150-153
CHARGE CERTIFICATE, 22, 118, 120
CHARGES REGISTER, 30, 31
  contents, 63-65
  land certificate, production of, 51, 52
  lease, note of, 72
  overriding interests, entry of, 80
  subordinate interests, noting of, 51
CHARGING ORDER, 26, 124, 142, 151-153
COMPANIES,
  inquiries as to right of, 102
  See OCCUPIERS.
COMPLETION, 71, 81, 160
COMPULSORY REGISTRATION, 41
  date of registration, 52-53
  dealings before application, 53
  effect, 57-58
  failure to register, 53-55
  land charges, relief from registration, 56, 57
  sale, meaning of, 50

COMPULSORY REGISTRATION AREAS, 214-218
CONTRACTUAL LICENCES, 101, 115
CONVERSION OF TITLE, 39
  cautions against, 39
  indemnity, 39
  registrar's discretion, 39
CONVEYANCING COSTS, 74
COVENANTS FOR TITLE, 67-71, 82
CURTAIN PRINCIPLE, 18, 24, 164

DATE OF REGISTRATION,
  dealings, effect on, 54, 110, 136
  overriding interests, effect on, 81, 82, 104
  priorities, 131, 132, 134, 137-140
  rules, 53, 81
  See PRIORITIES.
DEALING, 136
DEEDS AND DOCUMENTS,
  off register, 23, 60, 61, 84
DESERTED WIFE,
  class F rights, 25, 26, 145-6, 148-150
  rights, 196, 205
DISPOSITIONS, 61, 131, 135, 143, 151, 159, 160
  registration, effect of, 2, 3
  void, 3, 57, 58, 177, 185
  See FORGERY; REGISTERED DISPOSITIONS.

EASEMENTS AND PROFITS,
  noting on register, 21, 25, 80, 83, 84, 136
  overriding interests, as, 83-84, 137
EQUITABLE INTERESTS,
  effect of 1925 legislation, 15-18, 111
  overreachable interests, 16, 17
  priorities, 140-157
  registrable land charges, 17
  See MINOR INTERESTS.
ESTATE CONTRACT,
  protection, 17, 25, 26, 96, 138-139, 145-155, 160, 161

ESTOPPEL, 75, 142, 145, 146, 149, 152-154
  equitable interests 20, 96, 101, 162
  tenancy by estoppel, 125-128

FAILURE TO REGISTER, 53-56, 84, 143, 145, 148, 149, 152-154
FIRST REGISTRATION,
  effect, 57-58
FORGERY, 177, 185-186
FORMS, 60-61, 69-71, 132, 134, 135, 142, 167, 168-169, 177
FRAUD, 19, 20, 138

GOOD LEASEHOLD TITLES, 36-37
  absolute title, compared, 37

IMPLIED COVENANTS,
  title for, 68-71, 82
INDEX MAP AND PARCELS INDEX,
  inspection, 33, 34
INSPECTION OF REGISTER, 31-33

LAND CERTIFICATE,
  deposit at registry, 121-123
  evidence of title, as, 20-21, 31
  lessor's, production of, 51, 52
  notice of deposit, 122, 123, 136
  overriding interests, 80
  production at registry, 22, 25, 51, 52, 111, 157
  protection of, 121-123, 136
  retained at registry, 21, 31
  substantive registration, 20
LAND CHARGES,
  lease or sub-lease, in, 95-97, 101-104
  non-registration, effect of, 16, 23, 29, 112-115, 132-133, 161
  overriding interests, as, 111, 112, 115
  protection of, 29, 36, 161
  registered charges, as, 41, 123
  relief from registration, 56-57
LAND REGISTRATION ACT 1925,
  registered land, classification of interests, 19, 20
LAND REGISTRY,
  practice, 4, 5, 27, 51-52, 120, 183
LEASES, 43-49, 137
  agreement for, 44, 45, 111-115
  inalienable leases, 44, 49

LEASES—*cont.*
  incapable of registration, 44
  length of, reform, 46, 47
  minor interests, as, 45, 46
  overriding interests, as, 45, 91, 109
  registrable interests, as, 44, 45
  registration, form of, 72, 73
  reversionary, 47, 48
  tenancy by estoppel, 125-128
LICENCES, 100, 101, 115
LIENS,
  overriding interests, as, 78, 96, 111, 112, 115
  protection on register, 112, 115, 161
  purchaser, of, 96, 111, 112
  vendor, of, 96, 111, 112
LOCAL LAND CHARGES,
  overriding interests, as, 12, 79
  registration, 12

MERGER, 71, 130
MINES AND MINERALS, 20, 184
MINOR INTERESTS, 19, 23-30
  index, 131
  land charges, 23, 25
  leases, 45
  mortgages, 122-123
  off-register dealings, 23, 84
  overriding interests, as, 111-115
  protection, 23, 25, 140-154
    caution, by, 26-28, 111
    inhibition, by, 28
    notice, by, 25, 26, 111
    restriction, by, 23, 111
    retention of land certificate, by, 122-123, 153
    search certificate, by, 28, 29
  *See* CAUTIONS, OVERRIDING INTERESTS, PRIORITIES.
MORTGAGES, 118-130
  caution, protection by, 122, 126, 127
  criticisms, 119-120, 158-159
  deed, registration of, 121
  discharge, 130
  equitable, 121-123, 153-154
  land certificate deposit, 120, 122-123, 153
  legal, 121
  lien, 123, 143, 161
  notice on register, by, 122-123

MORTGAGES—*cont.*
overriding interests, subject to, 104, 124-128
powers of mortgagee, 123-125
priorities, 104, 127, 129, 136, 138, 143, 152, 156, 157
protection, 97, 121-124, 152
registered charges, as, 121, 124-125, 144
registered land on, 121-125
registration, need for, 121-122
subsequent charges, 120, 121
tenancy by estoppel, 125-128
unregistered land on, 118
*See* PRIORITIES.

NOTICE,
protection,
by entry of, 24, 25, 26, 115, 140
by equitable doctrine of notice, 17, 19, 86, 87, 116, 131-135
NOTICE OF DEPOSIT, 74, 122, 136, 142
NOTING OF INTERESTS, 21, 25, 51, 52, 72, 80

OCCUPATION,
actual, 87-91
inquiries as to rights of, 101-107
licensees, 101, 115
mortgagee, rights against, 88, 95, 104, 125-128
rectification against proprietor, in possession, 171-174
right, reform of system, 108-117
rights of, as overriding interests, 93-101, 111, 112
squatters, 85, 187
*See* OVERRIDING INTERESTS.
OVERRIDING INTERESTS, 76-117
adverse possession, 85
bare trusts, 78, 97
caution, entry of, 78
definition, 22, 23, 79, 80, 97
disposition of registered land, effect on, 81-82, 125-128
easements and profits, 83-84
entry on register, 80-81
equities, 94-95
generally, 76-79
implied covenants for title, 68-71, 82

OVERRIDING INTERESTS—*cont.*
inquiries as to, need for, 101-107
leases, 45, 91, 109
legal interests, analogy to, 22, 23, 137
licences, 101, 115
liens, 112, 114, 115
local land charges, 12, 79
minor interests, 111, 112
notice of, 22, 23, 69-70, 85-91
occupiers' rights, 93-101, 111, 112
against mortgagee, 88, 95, 104, 125-128
beneficiaries', 93-101
inquiries as to, 101-107
lessees, 45, 85-86, 91-93, 125-128
licensees, 101, 115
reform, 108-115
squatters, 85, 187
priorities, 134, 137-140
receiver of rents and profits, 85-86, 91-93
rectification and indemnity, 77, 171-174, 185
registrable interests, 109-111
trusts for sale, 97-100
undisclosed interests, 75, 101-105

POSSESSION, 47-49, 50, 171-173
POSSESSORY TITLE, 37-38
PRIORITIES,
circular, 153-154
crystallisation, 82, 137, 191
minor interests, 131, 140-154
mortgage by deposit, 123, 143, 161
official searches protection, 28, 29, 146, 150-154
overriding interests, 125-128, 137-140
reforms, 154-160
registered charges, 129
registered disposition, 131-136
tenancy by estoppel, 125-128
PRIORITY CAUTIONS, 131
PRIORITY INHIBITIONS, 131
PRIORITY NOTICES, 26, 110
PRIORITY PERIODS, 28, 29, 30
PROPERTY REGISTER, 30-31
contents, 61, 62, 72-73, 75
freedom from overriding interests, notice of, 81

PROPRIETORS,
in possession, meaning of, 171-173
PROPRIETORSHIP REGISTER, 31, 62-63, 73
PURCHASER, 133, 151

QUALIFIED TITLE, 38

RECTIFICATION AND INDEMNITY, 40, 163-190
discretion to rectify, 177-179
discretionary awards, 186-189
forgery, 177, 185, 186
generally, 40, 163-166
indemnity, 182-186
insurance fund abolition, 164
jurisdiction to rectify, 166-171
mines and minerals, 184
possession of proprietor, 171-172
reform, 186-190
restrictions on, 171-177, 183-185
contribution to mistake, 174, 184
court order, 173-174
limitation period, 183
overriding interests, 174, 185
unjust not to rectify, 176-177
void disposition, 177
state as insurer, 1, 18, 163-166
REGISTER,
charges register, 31
contents, 63-65
inspection, of, 31-33
meaning of, 31
new edition, 72, 179
property register, 30-32, 61-62
proprietorship register, 32, 62-63
REGISTERED CHARGES. *See* MORT-GAGES.
REGISTERED DISPOSITIONS, 131-136, 159, 160
REGISTERED LAND,
classification of interests, 19, 20

REGISTRABLE INTERESTS, 20, 21
REGISTRAR,
discretionary powers, 4, 5, 6, 27, 28, 39, 81, 141, 176, 183, 188
REGISTRATION OF LAND CHARGES, 10-12, 54, 56, 57
RENTS AND PROFITS,
rights of receiver, 91-93, 108, 109
RESTRICTIONS, 24, 25, 71
RESTRICTIVE COVENANTS, 30, 56, 64, 65, 136, 143, 160, 163

SEARCH CERTIFICATE, 28, 29
omission, effect of, 152-153
priority obtained by, 28, 29, 153, 154
SETTLED LAND, 41, 97, 112, 170, 184-185
SOLICITOR,
investigation of title duties, 106-108
negligence, action for, 106, 107
protecting minor interests, 144
SQUATTERS, 85, 187

TENANCY BY ESTOPPEL, 125-128
TRANSFER,
on sale, 66-67
registration of, 71
*See* IMPLIED COVENANTS.
TRANSFEREE, 133
TRUSTS FOR SALE,
beneficiaries' rights, 97-100, 104-105
minor interests, 19, 23-24, 97
overriding interests, 97-100

UNREGISTERED LAND,
classification of interests, 15-18
mortgages, 118

VOLUNTARY REGISTRATION, 40